UNLEASHING PRODUCTIVITY!
Your Guide to Unlocking the Secrets of Super Performance

Richard Ott

with *Martin Snead*

IRWIN
Professional Publishing

Burr Ridge, Illinois
New York, New York

This publication is designed to provide accurate and
authoritative information in regard to the subject matter
covered. It is sold with the understanding that neither the
author or the publisher is engaged in rendering legal, accounting,
or other professional service. If legal advice or other expert
assistance is required, the services of a competent professional
person should be sought.

*From a Declaration of Principles jointly adopted by a Committee
of the American Bar Association and a Committee of Publishers.*

Sponsoring editor: Cynthia A. Zigmund
Project editor: Amy E. Lund
Production manager: Laurie Kersch
Designer: Jeanne M. Rivera
Cover designer: Tim Kaage
Compositor: Precision Typographers
Typeface: 11/13 Palatino
Printer: Book Press, Inc.

Library of Congress Cataloging-in-Publication Data

Ott, Richard (Richard Alan)
    Unleashing productivity! : your guide to unlocking the secrets of
super performance / Richard Ott, with Martin Snead.
        p.   cm.
    Includes bibliographical references and index.
    ISBN 1-55623-931-9 (alk. paper)
    1. Labor productivity. 2. Performance. I. Snead, Martin.
II. Title.
HD57.O83 1994
658.3´14—dc20   93-11585

Printed in the United States of America
1 2 3 4 5 6 7 8 9 0 BP 0 9 8 7 6 5 4 3

Preface

This book is about you. Specifically, it's about how you can become a more highly productive human being. Improving your own productivity is important not only to you (I'm assuming you're interested in doing so, or you wouldn't be reading this now) but to the rest of us as well. This is true for three main reasons:

WE'RE ALL DEPENDING ON YOU

First, your family depends on your productivity. Your spouse, children, parents, or other family members may depend on you for their continued support, or they may depend on you to support yourself so the burden doesn't fall on them. Either way, it means you've got to be productive to earn the necessary money.

The company you work for depends on you. It needs you and its other employees to turn in good work day after day, lest the firm fail to compete and get into trouble.

And people you don't even know are depending on your productivity. I, for example, depend on others—including you, directly or indirectly—to produce many of the things I need in my life. I depend on people at the grocery store to have good food available when I shop. I depend on people to fix my cars, to supply my house with electricity, and to write the computer programs I use. And I'm just one guy. Make no mistake about it, there are many people out there depending on you to produce every single day. And, of course, you depend on others in the same manner.

The second reason your personal productivity is so important is the country depends on you. American companies trade goods and services internationally, competing against foreign companies for what we collectively call a "favorable balance of trade" for the nation—it's favorable to nations that sell more than they buy. The problem is, the United States has an *unfavorable* balance of trade.

We have a trade deficit, meaning our money is going out faster than it's coming in. (The deficit was over $67 billion in 1992. We haven't had a trade surplus since Gerald Ford was president.)

No wonder it now takes two income earners per household to maintain the same standard of living that one could earn a generation ago. Foreign workers have become increasingly productive, and they're earning financial rewards that historically went to American workers. Other countries are getting wealthier, and we're getting poorer. That means the citizens of the United States— including you and everyone you know—are working harder and getting less for it. (In our global economy of the 90s, money goes to the most productive, regardless of nationality. Take the manufacture of automobiles, for example. So-called American autos actually contain a plethora of foreign-made parts and are often assembled by foreigners. And so-called foreign autos contain many American-made parts and are often assembled by Americans.)

Our government has recognized the problem. The day after Bill Clinton was elected president in 1992, he summarized the situation quite succinctly when he told Ted Koppel on a "Nightline" special, "The problem that has gone on now for nearly 20 years is steadily declining American productivity. We're not generating wealth at the same rate as many of our competitors. For over a decade now, based on the census figures, people are working harder for lower wages than they were making over 20 years ago."

How has that come to be? It all boils down to one thing: the productivity of individuals. People no different than you and me, except that they're citizens of other countries, are more productive than we are. Don't get me wrong, I'm not chiding American workers as a whole. I'm merely pointing out that the prosperity of a nation rises and falls in direct relation to the productivity of its people—individual people like you and me.

The third reason your personal productivity is so important is your own happiness and well-being depend on it. You can look to your own productivity as one of the main sources of achieving a happy, fulfilled life, which I'm assuming you want to do.

Highly productive people, after all, seem to get the lion's share of reward. Recognition and admiration, advancements and promotions, love and companionship, money—you name it, and productive people are earning it. If you're ready to become one of them, to get your share of life's finest rewards, you're in the right place. You'll be well on your way before you get even halfway through this book.

WHO MAKES YOU MORE PRODUCTIVE?

Other people don't make you more productive. Others, including your supervisors and your company's top brass, can create an enriching environment that nurtures personal productivity, but they can't help you beyond that. Even the best coaches can only instruct and inspire. It's up to each individual player to distinguish herself to make it happen, with self-generated productivity.

The government doesn't make you more productive. It can create tax incentives and special programs that foster research and development, education, and training. But all of that can go for naught unless you add your productive ability to it and turn it into something.

This book won't make you more productive. It will give you all the information you need to increase your personal productivity immensely, but simply reading it won't change anything. You have to put forth effort and implement the techniques to get results.

You and only you can make yourself more productive. The brain is the engine that drives productivity, and how you use your brain—how you think and act—is the key to raising your personal productivity. You don't need a superior mind or unlimited talent to do it. Even people of limited intelligence or abilities can increase their personal productivity simply by using their brain a little differently.

WHAT THIS BOOK WILL DO FOR YOU

When you implement the techniques we discuss, you'll enjoy immediate and ever-increasing improvement in your level of productivity, or what you are able to accomplish. You'll see marked results in two areas:

First, you'll boost your productivity in short-run tasks. The things you do every day, on the job and at home, will get done quicker and with greater ease. You'll get more done in less time.

Second, you'll boost your productivity in long-term endeavors. The things you want to accomplish over the years, relating to your career and personal life-style, will happen with ever-increasing frequency. If the notion of turning your dreams into reality seemed like nothing more than silly wishful thinking in the past, it will seem entirely possible as you learn the secrets of super productivity.

A FUN, EXCITING JOURNEY

As your personal tour guide through the world of productivity improvement, I feel obligated to get you through quickly, easily, and profitably. To do that, I've vowed to:

- **Keep it simple.** Although the material in this book is based on complex psychological principles, I've simplified and codified it all for you. I'll spare you all the background research and underlying theories—the boring stuff you don't want to deal with anyway. Instead, I'll present you with the only the powerful, bottom-line information that produces big results quickly.
  (Don't be fooled by the simplicity you encounter. The simple procedures and techniques we discuss actually contain strong, potent forces capable of producing major changes in the way your mind operates and the results you get. In fact, the first step in solving problems and bettering yourself is to denounce the "life is overwhelmingly complex" notion and embrace simplicity. That puts you ahead of the game even before you start.)

- **Make it accessible, usable, and practical.** You will be able to understand and use this material no matter who you are. Everyone, including corporate CEOs, governmental leaders, entrepreneurs, laborers, managers, students, professionals, and anyone else who can read will find a cornucopia of meaty, usable information here. And unlike a lot of guidebooks that leave you wondering what it is you're supposed to do, *Unleashing Productivity!* provides practical, step-by-step implementation procedures. As you finish each chapter, you'll know exactly how to put the techniques we discuss into practice immediately. You'll start to experience real results quickly.

- **Make it fun to read and experience.** What good is it if it isn't any fun? You'd most likely bail out halfway through the first chapter and wouldn't take advantage of what's here. To prevent that, I'll do my part by keeping the discussion interesting and moving along at a good clip. You do your part by answering the questions and implementing the techniques. Together we'll have a great time.

You'll also encounter some interesting assertions as you read. You'll come across a total of 50 boxed Realizations sprinkled throughout the text. Here's the first of them:

Realization 1

Your brain is the engine that drives your productivity.
The ways in which you think and act determine your level of productivity.

Many of the Realizations will be familiar to you, as I'm sure you already know, either intellectually or intuitively, what I'm stating. Quite often, however, we can benefit by seeing things placed before our eyes in black and white and discussed in terms that make them strikingly illuminating.

YOUR PRODUCTIVITY IS ABOUT TO BE UNLEASHED

Sit back, relax, and enjoy the journey. Let your productive abilities naturally flourish, as they become liberated with each chapter you read and apply. Long before you finish the book, you'll be on your way to becoming the highly productive person you were destined to be.

Richard Ott

Acknowlegments

Martin Snead contributed greatly to the creation of this book. He collaborated with me on the development of the material and also edited the manuscript, which came together in coherent form under his expert direction.

I want to thank Cindy Zigmund, Jeff Krames, and the entire Irwin Professional Publishing staff for their guidance and support throughout the writing and publishing process.

The following people also deserve mention for various contributions: Stephanie Bowers, Tammy Kirby, Nita Hayden, and Kevin Hayden.

Contents

Understanding that your overconcern with when you will accomplish your objectives and receive your just rewards slows productivity. How to cure When Disease and allow your productivity to gush forth.

Tension and stress: the two opposing forces that prevent you from being more patient and relaxed while you perform. How to invite patience and relaxation into your mind and body.

Why operating in anything-can-happen mode hampers productivity. How to enter highly-concentrated-attention mode.

Being both a detail person and a concept person. Knowing when to concentrate on the details and when to step back and see the big picture to increase your productivity.

Why visualization *doesn't* work most of the time. How to get visualization to work for you. The right visualization techniques for optimum results.

Chapter One

Your Map To Super Productivity

W hat exactly is a productive person? Simply put, productive people get things done. They accomplish. They produce impressive results. And they do so on a regular basis. They accomplish small things in small increments of time—hours and days. And they accomplish larger things over larger time intervals—months, years, and even decades. Over the course of their careers or lives, highly productive people can accomplish even beyond their wildest dreams.

How do they do it? What makes them so special? First, productive people have learned how personal productivity works; they know precisely what to do to realize their productivity potential. Second, they take that knowledge and spread it around to others. They teach and inspire others to be highly productive. By doing so they get *productivity leverage* going. If you inspire numerous other people to increase their personal productivity, your own productivity can burst through the roof, especially if you're an entrepreneur or manager. (You don't think Ted Turner, Ross Perot, Richard Branson, and others built billion-dollar companies all on their own do you? Inspiring productivity in others is a common trait among all great leaders.)

IS "WORKING SMARTER" THE ANSWER?

How are you supposed to go about increasing your personal productivity? Some people say the answer is very simple: "Work smarter, not harder." It's become a cliché. Work smarter, not harder. Wonderful concept. But is it valid? Are the people who advocate it correct?

Is "working smarter, not harder" the secret to increasing your productivity? After a good deal of thought and analysis, I've concluded that the "work smarter, not harder" strategy is valid. It makes sense, and I'm certainly not going to argue against it.

But there is a problem. The "work smarter, not harder" strategy, as unarguable as it may be, is just not definitive enough to be applicable. What exactly does "work smarter" mean anyway? It's not like we're all going into work every day now and working dumb. It's not like we work dumb all week long and then say, "Hey, I've got an idea! Next Thursday, at 2:30 in the afternoon, I'll go ahead and work smarter for an hour and-a-half! I'll really shoot my productivity up. I'll dazzle the office. I'll be the talk of the building! Then I'll go back to working dumb like I normally do."

The real question is: What is the difference between "working smarter" and what you're doing now?

Two Underlying Postulates

In an effort to find the answer to increasing personal productivity, to find out specifically how to "work smarter," Martin Snead (who collaborated with me on the creation of this material) and I discovered to two underlying postulates:

- **Postulate 1: Productivity is a trait we're born with, it's not an acquired skill.** Don't slump in your chair thinking you'll never get it. The truth is, you already have it. We humans are created with productivity potential built in. You have it, I have it, we all have it. Even people with disabilities have the potential to be highly productive.

  A few years ago, "60 Minutes" ran a story that illustrates this point quite well. They profiled a guy named Leslie Lemke. Leslie was born mentally retarded, blind, and with cerebral palsy—not one, not two, but three heavy-duty disadvantages. As you might imagine, Leslie was not very productive. He didn't walk until he was 10 years old, and he didn't talk until he was well into his twenties (he was 31 when this story aired). He just lay around, totally unproductive.

  But Leslie's foster parents, May and Joe Lemke, believed he was capable of doing something productively. It was just a matter of finding that one special something, whatever it might be, that would spark his interest. Then, Leslie would realize his productivity potential.

So they exposed him to a variety of things, but nothing seemed to inspire him. One of the things they exposed him to was a piano, which they rolled into his bedroom. May played a few tunes herself along with some piano recordings, hoping to pique Leslie's interest. Still nothing happened.

Then, one night about a week later, May and Joe were awaken in the middle of the night by piano music. Incredibly beautiful piano music was coming from downstairs. They got up, went downstairs, and followed the music into Leslie's room. To their utter astonishment, they found their son playing the piano like Horowitz! And he hadn't taken any lessons or even practiced before that night!

It turns out Leslie has the incredible talent of hearing a piano piece once—it can be a complex piece from one of the masters—and duplicating it perfectly without practicing. How does he do that? The psychologists who work with Leslie have no idea. (The condition is called *savant syndrome,* but there is no medical or scientific explanation for it.) Leslie himself doesn't know how he does it. He just listens and plays.

Leslie is now a concert pianist by profession. He's toured Japan and Europe. He's turned himself into a celebrity. He's admired and respected all over the world. And he's making money. He's a productive guy.

All of us, even those of us with severe disabilities, have the potential to be highly productive in some way. You have at least one talent you can use to be highly productive, no matter what your situation is. You probably have more than one talent—some you don't even know you have. Think about that tonight as you prepare to sleep. What is your main talent? What other talents do you have that may be hiding beneath the surface? Are you using at least one of your talents every day?

The news gets better. The real truth is, it doesn't even take any special talent or ability to be highly productive. Normal, everyday activity can produce major results. Normal, everyday activity can lead to incredible accomplishment. Normal, everyday activity is all you need to be highly productive.

But—you knew there was a major "but" forthcoming—normal, everyday activity usually doesn't lead to high productivity, does it? It *can,* but it usually *doesn't*. Simple observation tells us that normal, everyday activity leads to mediocre productivity at best. Normal, everyday activity leads to no more than mere survival for many, it turns out.

Why is that? If normal, everyday activity can be highly productive, why isn't it most of the time? The answer to that brings us to the second key postulate.

- **Postulate 2: There exist certain *productivity barriers* that impede or hamper our ability to produce.** These productivity barriers are a natural phenomenon. They exist like gravity or oxygen. There's nothing you can do to get rid of them. They affect us all every day. That's why our normal, everyday activity, which can result in tremendous productivity, usually doesn't. The productivity barriers are dampening our efforts, holding us back. It's like running with a sack of potatoes on your back. Those darn productivity barriers can be formidable foes.

Although you can't get rid of the barriers or inoculate yourself against them, you can (1) learn what they are, (2) find out how they're affecting you now, and (3) take specific measures to circumvent them. By doing so, you are able to neutralize the barriers as they pop up and unleash the tremendous productivity you inherently possess.

By successfully hurdling the productivity barriers, your normal, everyday activities become many times more powerful than before. Without the productivity barriers negating your efforts, your productivity can gush forward, like a powerful river bursting through a dam.

There are five productivity barriers. You are probably being affected by one or more in your life at the present time. Let's assume, for the moment, that your productivity is being hampered equally by all five at present. What would happen if you conquered just one of the barriers? Your productivity would rise 20 percent. Learn to clear a second barrier, and you're operating with a 40 percent improvement. Clear all five barriers, and you have a 100 percent rise in your level of productivity! Suddenly, you're accomplishing twice as much in the same amount of time every day, week, month, and year. And here's the real beauty of it: Your productivity rises without your working longer or harder. It will take effort to conquer each barrier and to maintain your barrier-free state over time, but that's the fun part. You may not even think of it as effort at all once you see the results.

Conquering the five productivity barriers is precisely how you work smarter, not harder.

THE FIVE PRODUCTIVITY BARRIERS

Chapters 2 through 6 each deal with one of the productivity barriers in detail. Let me give you an overview of what is to come by identifying the barriers.

The first barrier that impedes your productivity is *worry*. When you worry, you're using a lot of brainpower that could be better spent on productive endeavor. Worry diverts your brainpower away from productive thinking and contributes absolutely nothing to your well-being in return. In fact, worry even negates your ability to solve the very problems you're worried about! In Chapter 2, you'll learn why your brain produces worry in the first place, and you'll learn a powerful six-step procedure for vaporizing worry every time it rears its ugly head.

Productivity barrier number two is the *erosion of energy and enthusiasm*. It happens to the best of us. No matter how much we love what we're doing, there comes a time when we realize our energy and enthusiasm for doing it has eroded considerably. The erosion itself can happen quickly or gradually. In the latter case, the erosion often goes unnoticed during most of its decline. Then one day, we wake up and realize our energy and enthusiasm is virtually nonexistent.

So how do we get our energy and enthusiasm back? Or better yet, how do we keep it from eroding in the first place? You'll learn how to revive your energy and enthusiasm and keep it pumping hard in Chapter 3.

Negative emotions comprise the third productivity barrier. Anger, frustration, jealousy, depression, disappointment, loneliness, fright, and others all poison your productivity. Trying to be productive while experiencing a negative emotion is like baking a cake using contaminated ingredients. No matter how hard you work, even one small dose of contamination will spoil the whole thing.

We tend to experience negative emotions much more often and in much greater doses than we should. "Maybe so," you argue. "But I don't control my emotions. They just appear on their own." So it seems. In Chapter 4, you'll learn how your negative emotions are created and what you can do to keep those emotions under control.

The fourth productivity barrier is *action avoidance*. We may have the best of intentions and aspirations yet be quite unproductive. Somehow, we just never get around to taking the actions necessary to get our productivity going. In Chapter 5, you'll learn why you avoid taking action (others will tell you it's fear, but the word *fear* never appears in Chapter 5), and how you can get yourself into action now.

The fifth and last productivity barrier is *When Disease*. If you're like most people, you're constantly asking yourself "when" questions. When will this or that happen? When will he or she do what I want them to do? When will I get rewarded for my accomplishment? When, when, when?

As logical as it seems to wonder about when something is going to happen, it's a major deterrent to productivity. Why is that? And why do we have so much interest in "when" if it's dysfunctional? Chapter 6 answers those questions and tells you how to cure any amount of When Disease you may be suffering from.

THE FIVE PRODUCTIVITY THRUSTERS

Conquering the five productivity barriers unleashes the inherent productivity hiding inside of you, which can dramatically raise your level of accomplishment and reward. But there's more. Once you've released your productivity by clearing the barriers, you'll be ready to step into a frontier beyond which your productivity can shoot to levels you wouldn't have believed possible.

There exist five *productivity thrusters*—the techniques used by the world's most productive people to experience larger-than-life accomplishments. Any one of these five thrusters can propel your productivity into the stratosphere; master all five, and you'll be in the top 3 percent of all people. If you've ever wished you could "go for your dreams" but didn't know how to go about it, you will wonder no more when we discuss the five productivity thrusters in Chapters 7 through 11.

Here's a preview of the productivity thrusters and how they work:

The first productivity thruster is *patience and relaxation*. Few people seem to realize that they're supposed to be patient and relaxed while they perform. Even fewer people know how to become patient and relaxed while performing. That's why most people are huffin', puffin', scratchin', and clawin' yet achieving average results. Meanwhile, highly productive people appear to be calmly cruising to victory time and time again. You'll be in the latter group once you implement the techniques we discuss in Chapter 7.

Thruster number two is *highly concentrated attention (HCA)*. The ability to concentrate your mental focus, even for short periods of time, will do wonders for your productivity. Chapter 8 tells why it's often very difficult to concentrate, and gives you the techniques you need to put yourself into HCA mode on demand.

Micro-macro vision is the third productivity thruster. It has to do with the way you view things—whether you're detail oriented or concept oriented. Most people are one or the other, like being left-handed or right-handed. But the world's most productive people are *both* detail oriented *and* concept oriented. They are able to focus on the details with precision, and they're able to step back and assess the big picture. And they know when to do each. Chapter 9 will tell you how to develop micro-macro vision.

You've read about it. You've tried it. And you're not sure whether it's for real or not. It's *visualization*. And it is productivity thruster number four, which tips you off that it is for real, despite the fact that most people can't seem to get it to work for them. We'll talk about why visualization, the process of imagining something in your mind as a means of making it happen in reality later, doesn't work most of the time. Others advocate visualization, but they don't tell you how it really works, how to get it to work for you, and how it can improve your performance immediately. In Chapter 10, you'll get the real story.

The last productivity thruster is *creative thinking*. You are a much more creative person than you think. In Chapter 11, you'll learn two different methods of creating ideas and solutions. Then, you'll find out how to take an idea and create the ways and means of putting it into effect or making it happen. Life's finest rewards are reserved for the people who execute ideas. You will not only create ideas and solutions, but you'll create the methods of executing them as well.

To make these productivity-boosting techniques really work for you, you have to install them in your subconscious mind. It's your subconscious that activates the techniques and makes them come alive. Chapter 12 is a bonus chapter designed to help you understand how your subconscious accepts new information. It will aid you in programming all the techniques you've learned into your subconscious, which is crucial to obtaining top-notch results.

BREAKING THROUGH THE FIVE PRODUCTIVITY BARRIERS

Chapter Two

Vaporize Worry

W orry drains brainpower. It burns an incredible amount of mental fuel, thereby negating our ability to devote attention to productive endeavors. Worry uses up so much mental energy it negates our ability to think clearly and creatively. In fact, worry keeps us from solving the very problems we're worried about! How's that for a major barrier to your personal productivity?

It gets worse. Have you ever been so consumed with worry you couldn't do much of anything? You couldn't perform your job properly? You couldn't interact with others at work or at home? You couldn't eat, sleep, think, or act? Worry can be debilitating. It can not only prevent you from functioning, it can actually cause even greater problems. Some people worry so much they develop physical ailments—tension, stress, ulcers, heart attacks, diseases, you name it. *Worry*, which is productivity barrier number one, is a powerful, destructive force.

Worrying about a particular task or endeavor can impede your productivity in that same area. You may worry that your supervisor won't like the report you're writing, and your worry lowers your confidence and makes writing it all the more difficult. You may worry about whether you're going to get the report done in time, and your worry eats up some of the precious time you could have spent writing. I know one guy who says he's a hopeless insomniac. He says he can't sleep because he worries all night long. When I asked him what he's so worried about, he said "about not getting the proper amount of rest." No kidding.

Worry in one area can affect your performance in a completely unrelated area also. Have you ever worried so much about a personal problem, a relationship let's say, that your on-the-job productivity suffered as a result? One of the biggest causes of poor on-the-job productivity is personal problem–related worry. It's virtually impossible to keep your mind sharp and focused on your job when you're consumed with personal worries. Or perhaps you can recall a time when your job-related worry adversely affected your personal life. Regardless of what we're worried about, worry greatly reduces our productivity in many areas.

"All this is true," you may say. "But isn't worry just a natural, normal part of life?" Worry can sometimes seem normal. But that's because we spend so much time doing it, it takes on feelings of normality. In reality, worry is not a natural, normal part of life. Worry is actually an *abnormal function the brain resorts to in an attempt to produce a desirable outcome.* The outcomes the brain craves, such as feelings of sympathy or love, pain avoidance, and guilt aversion, are normal human desires. And the brain thinks that worry is a shortcut to those desirable outcomes.

THE FIVE REASONS WHY WE WORRY

Why do we worry so much? "Because we have a lot of problems," you point out. Not exactly. Problems are not really causes of worry, though they are the subject of worry. What causes worry—why our brain jumps into worry mode—is, once again, to bring about some desirable outcome.

Let's look at the five outcomes the brain tries to produce through worry. Our purpose in examining these outcomes is so you can conclude that worry is silly and you needn't spend your time doing it.

1. **We worry to stimulate our emotions.** Humans crave emotional stimulation. We have an innate desire to experience emotional feelings. Positive emotions, such as love, excitement, laughter, sexual attraction, and others, are pleasurable to experience, so the brain instinctively seeks them—or seeks the things it believes will produce them.

    But in a funny way, our brain can interpret negative emotions, such as fright, sadness, loneliness, and anger, as pleasurable. It sounds strange, but why else do we watch horror movies or take our kids to haunted houses on Halloween? To experience the fright emotion. Why do we listen to sad songs and watch tear-jerking movies? To experience the sadness emotion. Even though fright and sadness are negative emotions, and you wouldn't think we humans would want to experience them, the brain often interprets them as pleasurable. Because the brain craves emotional stimulation, any emotion, negative or positive, can be interpreted as pleasurable. (To learn how this psychological phenomenon is used in the world of marketing and advertising, read my first book, *Creating Demand.*)

When we worry, we are running a negative scenario in our brain. We're thinking of something bad that might happen, is happening, or has happened. Many times we run those negative scenarios in order to stimulate negative emotions, which our brain interprets as pleasurable. Why is it that someone you know—your supervisor, co-worker, friend, or significant other—will sometimes start an argument strictly for the sake of arguing? (Something you would never do, of course.) Could it be because negative emotion is better than no emotion? When we're emotionally hungry, we stir up emotions, even negative ones, to satisfy our craving. And worrying—running a negative scenario in our mind—is an effective way of doing just that.

2. **We worry as a substitute for action.** We feel compelled to do something about a problem, but for whatever reason, we do not take action. Instead, we worry. It's as though worry is the action we're taking. How many times have you seen people at work worrying about a problem, when it seems obvious to you they should be doing something about it instead? Have you ever felt obligated to do something about a problem yet found yourself only worrying instead of acting?

Here's an analogy. Do you know people who habitually commit to something yet fail to follow through and do what they said they'd do? These people feel an obligation to do certain things, so they verbally commit themselves. Then they rationalize that they've met their obligation by verbally committing and that they needn't actually act accordingly, which they really don't want to do. Twisted logic? Of course. But these people view their verbal commitment as sufficient because it's a lot easier to commit than it is to act. Committing is acting, they rationalize.

Likewise, worrying about a problem can be a lot easier than actually doing something about the problem. Especially when the doing might entail a difficult decision or tough action. So we avoid the tough, difficult actions and worry instead, thereby fulfilling our obligation to "do something" about the problem.

3. **We worry to gain sympathy, love, or acceptance.** This occurs when people verbalize their worry. For example, someone may say to you, "I'm worried about my car that's in the shop." Why do people tell you such things? To gain sympathy. They're hoping to elicit some sympathetic response out of you, like "You poor thing, tell me all about it." Even if you don't respond sympathetically, just telling you of their worry can be cathartic.

What is the motive when people say they are worried about you? Love. They not only want to express it, but they want to receive it—from you, right now. They want you to reciprocate in some way. They want you to tell them or show them how much you love or accept them. Worry can be a rather selfish thing at times. We do it to gain something from others, usually expressions of love or acceptance.

Tomorrow, when you're at work, listen for the word *worry* to pop up in conversation. When you hear someone say they're worried about something, watch what happens next. After someone verbally expresses worry, they will usually pause, awaiting someone else to offer some expression of sympathy, love, or acceptance. Even though the conversation may be about some business-related topic, look for a sympathetic, loving, or accepting comment from someone else. Once the worrier hears what he wants, he'll usually stop expressing worry and change the subject.

Tammy, a friend of mine with a delightful knack for expressing herself ever so succinctly, spent a few days in the hospital recently undergoing tests. On the second day, her mother visited and said, "Oh Tammy, I can't eat or sleep . . . I'm so worried about you!" To which Tammy replied "Thank you so much. Your worry has benefited me greatly." Seeing her mother taken aback by the heavy dose of sarcasm, Tammy offered further explanation. "I appreciate that you care, mom. But your worry doesn't do me any good, and it hurts you. Please stop worrying."

Oftentimes we use worry as a way of manufacturing expressions of love. The love may be genuine, but the expressions of it are usually forced or contrived when we express worry about another. (Expressions of care or concern are another matter. We'll discuss the differences between worry and caring and concern shortly.)

4. **We worry to brace ourselves for pain.** Oftentimes we worry about future occurrences that we think may harm us, so as to brace for expected pain. Like tightening the muscles of your stomach if you believe someone is about to punch you there, it's a defense mechanism.

   Have you been worrying about some aspect of your job lately? Could it be you're worrying about a problem that really doesn't exist? Could you be worrying now about a problem you think might arise later? Is it possible the problem you expect to occur may never actually occur? Worrying in advance of an expected problem is quite common. You're doing it to brace yourself for something you think is going to cause you harm.

   Take a husband and wife, for example. The wife is late getting home, and the husband is at home waiting. (It doesn't matter which is which—whether the husband or the wife is the one running late. I've seen it happen equally either way.) It doesn't take long for the person at home to begin worrying, even when the other is only 15 or 20 minutes late. After an hour, the worry can get very intense, with thoughts of bad things happening. "Oh no, there's been an accident," the worrier says to himself. He may actually "see" an accident scene in his mind, and play out a scenario in which his spouse is rushed to a hospital in near-death condition. The worrier may actually feel the anguish and despair; he may experience the hurt and pain of such a situation.

   Or perhaps the worrier feels a completely different set of emotions. "She's having an affair at the office!" he might conclude. Imagining the spouse engaged in some amorous interlude, the worrier has feelings of despondence or anger. As the scenario plays out in his mind, the more intense his emotions become. The late wife may have simply been caught in a harmless traffic jam and expected her waiting spouse to greet her with joy when she finally walked in the door. Instead, she was greeted by a red-hot, fire-breathing dragon threatening divorce.

   When you worry, you are running a negative scenario in your brain. You are imagining something bad happening. And you're doing this to help brace yourself for something you believe will harm you. By worrying in advance of an actual problem, you're creating the pain in advance. Your brain believes that by creating the pain in advance, you'll suffer less pain than if the problem were to hit you unexpectedly out of left field.

Imagining problems and worrying about them in advance of their actual arrival is one of the worst things you can do. First, it causes you to experience a lot of painful emotions that you really do not need or deserve. Second, you alienate others. You may even destroy precious relationships through your worry. Worrying about phantom problems causes you to experience unnecessary and inappropriate emotions. When you express those emotions, others are surprised, confused, or even aggravated. The late wife did not deserve to have her head bitten off by the waiting, angry husband, right?

When you worry about a problem in advance, you're a *problem creator*. Hey, life will throw enough real problems at you without your having to create them. The last thing you want to do is create problems by worrying in the name of self-defense.

5. **We worry because we believe worry is our duty.** We sometimes mistakenly believe that we are obligated to worry. And we feel guilty if we don't. Beliefs like "I've got this problem, so I've got to worry about it," "Since it's my responsibility, I worry," or "I worry because I care" are common. If you have these or similar beliefs, you are needlessly setting yourself up for pain and sabotaging your productivity.

Realization 2

The quickest way to solve a problem is to first stop worrying about it.

Remember what I said at the beginning of this chapter. Worry negates your ability to think clearly and creatively. It will choke your brainpower and keep you from solving the very problems you're worried about.

To solve a problem as quickly as possible, you've got to be thinking clearly, creatively, and powerfully. You can't afford to have your problem-solving brainpower usurped by worry. It will leave little brainpower left for problem solving. You've got to stop thinking that because you have a problem, you're obligated to worry about it. Worrying about your problems only makes them more severe and longer lasting.

Responsibility and worry have nothing to do with one another. You can, and should, be a responsible person. That doesn't mean you need to worry about your responsibilities. Also, the absence of worry does not equal an absence of responsibility.

Realization 3

Responsibility does not entail worry.

I once knew a guy who truly didn't worry about a thing. He believed life was meant to be worry-free, and he lived that way. But he mistakenly believed that worry and responsibility are mutually exclusive. So to maintain his worry-free state, he took on no responsibilities. No job. No bank account. No wife or kids. No possessions except the clothes on his back. No anything to worry about. He lived with various friends and constantly moved when his welcome ran out. He'd perform odd jobs or play darts in the local saloon to eat. This guy was a real piece of work, although work was not a piece of him. He never understood that you can lead a highly responsible and worry-free life simultaneously.

Realization 4

Worry does not equal caring.

Worry and caring have nothing do with one another. This comes as a shock to some people who have always assumed worry is an expression of care. What they don't realize is that the person they're worrying about, from whom they want some expression of love, has no appreciation for their worry.

IF WORRY IS SO BAD, WHY DO WE KEEP DOING IT?

There is, of course, nothing wrong with wanting to stimulate your emotions, to solve your problems, to express love and feel accepted, to prepare for trouble, or to relieve feelings of guilt. They're all normal human desires. What is abnormal, however, is using worry as a shortcut to those outcomes.

Realization 5

Worry generates artificial, short-lived feelings of emotional pleasure, solution, love, and protection. Only with an absence of worry can you attain genuine, lasting emotional pleasure, solutions, love, and protection.

If you want your emotions stimulated, a solution to a problem, a feeling of being loved or protected against harm, and less guilt (you do want these things, even if you've never consciously realized it before), you must first stop worrying. Only with an absence of worry can you bring about the real desirable outcomes. And only then can you devote your attention to productive endeavors, both on and off the job.

So why do you keep worrying? Your brain will continue to fall into the worry mode throughout your life as long it views worry as a shortcut to the outcomes it craves. Remember, your brain will naturally seek the quickest route or method to produce the desirable outcomes, much like some peoples' brains believe alcohol or drugs are shortcuts to happiness. The artificial happiness created by the shortcut, however, is both short-lived and in the long run, harmful.

HOW TO VAPORIZE WORRY EVERY TIME IT POPS UP

Worry will appear from time to time, as your brain tries to bring about desirable outcomes as soon as possible. Luckily, there are ways to vaporize worry instantly whenever it rears its ugly head. Thus, you greatly reduce your vulnerability to worry, even though it looms about. By so doing, your personal productivity, on the job and at home, will rise automatically.

Here is the six-step procedure that will vaporize worry whenever your brain produces it:

- **Step 1: Catch yourself worrying.** For most people, this is not too difficult. The telltale sign of worry is that you're running a negative scenario in your mind. You're thinking of something bad that is happening or that may happen. When you find yourself running a negative scenario, say "Ah ha! I'm worrying!" Then go to Step 2.

  People who worry excessively have a more difficult time catching themselves worrying. Because they worry so much, they mistake their worried state as normal. They don't even realize they're worrying, because to them worry is not an abnormal function but a normal way of life. If that describes you, it's time to begin acknowledging all those negative scenarios you're running as worry. Admit your worry is abnormal and harmful.

- **Step 2: Identify the underlying problem.** Ask yourself "What is it that I'm worried about?" The underlying problem may not be readily obvious. Keep asking this question until you've come up with a plausible answer.

Realization 6

Nine out of 10 problems you worry about are phantom problems that will never affect you.

Ninety percent of all problems are not real problems. They are projected or phantom problems. They are things we believe will adversely affect us in the future, only we're worrying about them now in advance.

The best definition of problems I ever heard is an old one, and I'm not sure who originally came up with it. But someone once described problems as "10 cars barreling down the road toward me. I look down the road, see them heading right for me, and I worry about them. But one by one, the cars turn off on side roads. Nine out of 10 of them never reach me. They never affect me. They're never anything I have to deal with. Yet before they turn away, I see all 10 heading straight for me, and I worry about them all." In other words, we worry about potential problems that never become real problems.

What is it exactly that you're worried about? It's important that you identify the specific problem, then run it through the following qualifying question. Ask yourself, "Is this problem really something that demands my attention at this time?" With 9 out of 10 problems, you'll answer no. Then you know you've got a phantom problem on your hands. To negate a phantom problem instantly, go to Step 3.

- **Step 3: Pop the tape.** Remember, when you worry, you're running a negative scenario in your mind. You're thinking of something bad happening; you're playing out a bad-for-me scenario in your imagination, much like watching a movie on your VCR. (Movies are similar to your imagination in that they are really fabricated scenes; just actors acting out a fictitious story.) Now, what happens to the movie when you push the eject button? The movie immediately stops running, and the tape pops out.

That's exactly how you stop your worry dead in its tracks. Pop the tape. Picture yourself pushing an eject button and a videotape popping out of your brain. Actually see this happening in your imagination. See the negative, worry scenario you were running go blank. See yourself throwing the tape into a trash can.

It only takes a few such "ejections" to retrain your mind to stop worrying when you "pop the tape." Your logical mind will quickly accept the reasoning that it can't run a scenario when the tape has been ejected. You may start worrying again soon, however. That tape you threw in the trash—the one containing the bad-for-you scenario—may sneak back into your mind at any time. To prevent this from happening, execute Step 4 immediately after you pop the tape.

- **Step 4: Replace the tape.** A VCR can play only one tape at a time. Your conscious mind works the same way. To prevent your ejected tape from sneaking back in, put a replacement tape in your mind as soon as you pop the negative scenario tape.

Run A Positive-Angle Scenario

There are two types of replacement tapes or scenarios you can run in your mind's imagination. The first is a *positive-angle scenario.* Instead of running a worry scenario of a job not getting completed on time, run a scenario of the job getting completed ahead of time. Instead of a worry scenario in which a co-worker tries to undermine you, run a positive-angle scenario in which the co-worker helps you. Simply choose a positive angle of the situation and run it in your mind instead of a negative, worry-inducing angle.

Remember the story in which the waiting husband went into worry mode and created an auto accident scenario in his mind? A much better scenario for him to run would have been one with a positive angle, such as the late wife getting caught in a harmless traffic jam. He could reinforce that scenario by believing that the extra time the wife spends in the car will benefit her. Perhaps she'll hear a key piece of information on the radio or avoid a real accident because of the delay.

You can run any number of positive-angle scenarios. Perhaps the replacement tape you put into your mind shows your late spouse stopping off at the grocery store, dry cleaner, or video store and running into an old friend, and that chance occurrence will prove beneficial down the road. Or perhaps your spouse was called into an impromptu meeting at the office or plant, a meeting that will prove beneficial to him or her in some way. The idea is to see yourself putting a replacement tape into your mind's VCR and running that positive-angle scenario.

Realization 7

Ninety-nine percent of the time, good things happen.

Now don't tell me that a positive angle is not realistic. Don't argue that it's more likely the co-worker is going to successfully undermine you, or your spouse was involved in an accident, or the like. That kind of thinking is only realistic for an insecure mind, which isn't you.

Insecure people have the percentages reversed. They believe bad things happen 99 percent of the time, and good things only 1 percent. The truth is, good things happen to you 99 percent of the time, so run good-thing scenarios. The odds are greatly in your favor.

Run a Change-the-Subject Scenario

Another type of replacement scenario you can plug into your mind is the *change-the-subject scenario*. Instead of retaining the same subject only running a positive angle of it, you can totally change the subject. An example is a pleasurable vacation scenario. I keep a number of these replacement tapes on a "shelf" in my mind, and I grab them whenever needed.

When you have trouble falling asleep, you can bet it's because your brain is running some negative scenario, perhaps replaying what happened that day or what is going to happen tomorrow, instead of relaxing. Go ahead and pop that tape, and replace it with a change-the-subject scenario. Remember Realization 2: The quickest way to solve a problem is to first stop worrying about it. Don't feel guilty directing your mind away from worry. Feel good about it!

Perhaps your change-the-subject scenario has you lying on the beach in some exotic location, or playing tennis against the current world champion, or playing a practical joke on a friend. Go ahead and smile, laugh! This is supposed to make you happy. And believe me, it will keep worry away. Think about some fantasy experiences or places you want to be. Replay that vacation you took last year or one you'd like to take. Put your favorite people in them. Create a number of change-the-subject scenarios in advance, and use them as needed. Or create new scenarios as you run them.

You can vaporize 90 percent of your worry—that which is based on phantom problems—by executing Steps 1 through 4. But what about worry based on a real problem? What about that 1 car out of 10 that really does affect you? Life is full of real problems after all. Not all problems are phantom. In fact, if you don't have a real problem in your life right now, you can bet the next phone call is for you. To vaporize worry about a real problem, go to Step 5.

- **Step 5: Convert worry into concern through action.** Worry and concern are two different things; one bad, the other good. Worry is an endless loop of churning and burning brainpower that produces nothing of value and negates your productivity. Concern, on the other hand, is a *steady but dormant force that periodically requires action.*

Let me demonstrate the difference between worry and concern. Right now, as you read these words, are you worrying about your house or apartment burning down? My guess is that you are not. But you are concerned about your house or apartment, recognizing that it could possibly burn down, aren't you? Of course you're concerned about your home. Who wouldn't be? So why are you not actively worrying right now about your house burning down? Why is that a concern and not a worry?

Because at some time in the past, you took one or more specific actions, thereby converting worry into concern. You bought fire insurance. You put a smoke detector in the hallway. You taught the kids to not play with matches. You made sure the stove was off when you left the house. And what would happen if you were driving away one day and thought you may have left the stove on? What does your brain do? It drops into worry mode, that's what. And it keeps the worry churning and burning until you do what? Until you take an action. So you turn the car around and check on the stove. That action converts worry into concern, thereby rendering it dormant and harmless.

Realization 8

Action turns destructive worry into harmless concern.

You may need to take more than one simple action. Sometimes a series of actions, over a period of time, is required to fully negate worry. But each small action you take converts worry further into concern, rendering it more and more dormant.

What happens if you don't know what actions to take? The answers to complex problems are not always obvious, not always apparent. What then? Go to the sixth and final step.

- **Step 6: Help someone else with her problem.** How can helping someone else with her problem benefit you? You'll see as I explain.

I discovered the worry-negating power of helping others quite by accident. A couple years ago, I found myself neck-deep in a rather severe business problem. I was working late on a Friday evening, trying to determine what action to take. I was trying to convert worry into concern through action, but since none of the alternatives seemed good, I wasn't acting. Instead I was worrying.

The phone rang. It was a near and dear friend who was crying. It seems her boyfriend was seeing another woman, and she thought their relationship was headed for the skids. She wanted me to come over and console her.

Well, I came so close to saying "Don't burden me with your problems. I've got my own to deal with right now." The words were halfway out of my mouth, then I stopped and thought for a few seconds. I've always thought it good to help others, especially a good friend, when the need arises. Besides, I thought it might do me some good to get away from the office. So I said, "Okay, I'll be right over."

For the next three hours, I listened to her emotional story, offering comment when appropriate. And after three hours, she was feeling much better under the circumstances. It was definitely time well spent.

Then, as I was driving home, I discovered something else. My business problem, which seemed so severe three hours earlier, didn't seem to be nearly so severe now. And guess what? A good idea suddenly came to mind, right there on the road—a viable idea, an action to take to solve the problem!

Is there someone at work right now who would appreciate a little help? You don't have to walk around soliciting problems from people or become a full-time do-gooder, butting into everyone else's business. Just keep your eyes and ears open. Every hour of every day there's someone in your proximity who could use a little help with something. A little help goes a long way, let me tell you.

Helping someone else is always of value, even if there's nothing in it for you. But remarkably, when you help others with their problems, there is almost always something in it for you. By helping others, you're doing two important things for yourself.

First, you're taking your mind off of your own problems. When your mind is preoccupied with something different, something pressing, you're allowing it to clear and unclog. You're allowing your mind—both conscious and subconscious—to think on its own, to produce viable alternatives to your own problem.

Realization 9

When you help others, help comes to you.

Second, you get the law of reciprocation working for you, which states that when you help others, help comes to you. It never fails. Help others, and help comes to you. It usually doesn't come from the very person you're helping, nor is it guaranteed to come instantly. But help does come to you in due time. It's the way the universe works, and it's yours to tap into whenever you like.

IMPLEMENTATION HINTS FOR DIFFICULT CASES

The above six steps will work. They will help you negate the ravages of worry and unleash your productivity. But you will find that it takes a good amount of effort on your part. I never said it would always be easy.

Worry is a very strong force, not easily overpowered. Some people have a difficult time conquering worry, even with the six-step weaponry described above. ''I just can't help worrying,'' some people say discouragingly. Yes, there will be times when you execute the six steps as best you're able, and worry still proliferates. When you find that happening, try augmenting your worry-conquering arsenal with these three auxiliary steps:

- **Auxiliary Step 1: Identify the desirable outcome your brain is craving.** Remember the five desirable outcomes we talked about, the reasons why your brain goes into worry mode? We worry to stimulate our emotions, as a substitute for action, to gain sympathy or love, to brace ourselves for pain, and because we believe worry is our duty.

  After you've identified the underlying problem you're currently worrying about (Step 2), take the identification process one step further. Identify the specific desirable outcome your brain is trying to produce. It will be one of the five outcomes listed above. For example, say to yourself, ''I'm worrying about this problem to brace myself for pain. I'm creating the pain in advance to protect myself for what is coming.'' Or, ''I'm worrying about this problem to stimulate my emotions. By running this bad-for-me scenario over and over in my mind, I feel the hurt and despair. It's these emotions my brain wants to experience.''

- **Auxiliary Step 2: Use a substitute means of achieving the desirable outcome.** The outcome(s) you crave are normal, but using worry to attain them is not. Let's find substitutes for worry that will bring about the same desirable outcomes.

  Substitutes for stimulating your emotions. This is an easy one. There's a world full of emotion stimulators available to you at any time. Go see a movie or a sporting event. Listen to music. Read a good book. Go golfing, bowling, or whatevering. Let the substitute stimulator do what it's designed to do, stimulate your emotions, and let worry take a rest. You do this by concentrating on the substitute stimulator.

  Incidentally, your substitute stimulator should stimulate a different emotion than the one your worry is stimulating. If, for example, your worry is making you feel sad or depressed, don't put on a sad song or see a tear-jerking movie. Put on a party song or see a comedy. At first the substitute stimulator may seem out of place; it seems to be stimulating the "wrong" emotions. But after a few minutes it will overpower the previous, worry-induced emotion, provided you're open to it.

Substitutes for using worry in place of action. If you're worrying as a substitute for action, then it only makes sense that action is your primary substitute for worry. Taking an action also turns worry into concern, you'll recall. Believe me, you will feel much better taking a real action than using worry as though it were an action. It's like finally seeing the dentist instead of living with the toothache. Do it.

Substitutes for gaining sympathy, love, or acceptance. Your brain wants to experience feelings of sympathy, love, or acceptance. So you tell someone how worried you are, hoping to receive a dose of sympathy, love, or acceptance in return. Is there a better way of generating expressions of sympathy or love from that person than through expressions of worry?

There is one surefire way of gaining sympathy, love, or acceptance from another: Giving them plenty of sympathy, love, or acceptance yourself. The other person will respond, though most likely not immediately. And he may not respond in a like manner. You might love someone romantically, and he might love you back in a nonromantic way. Or you might express love verbally, and he might express it back by giving you something. But in one form or another, at one time or another, it always comes back.

Substitutes for bracing for pain. Instead of creating pain in advance through worry, and thus bracing yourself for what you think is going to hurt you, try these two ideas:

A tried-and-true pain-bracer is to ask yourself, "What's the worst that can happen?" When you think in terms of the worst, it ironically seems not so bad—or at least not worth grieving over. By recognizing the worst, you prepare yourself for it. You have braced yourself for pain and relieved yourself of much worry at the same time.

You may also wish to make contingency plans that would insulate you or rescue you if the bad thing actually happens. Devising a contingency plan can be comforting, even if you never have to execute it.

Substitutes for worry duty.   Relieve yourself of the worry assignment. Say "(your name here), you are hereby relieved of worry duty. You're being reassigned. From now on, worry will be handled by others." You may reaffirm your responsibility and reaffirm your care. Just be sure to remind yourself that responsibility does not entail worry and that caring does not equal worry. Keep reminding yourself until you believe it.

- **Auxiliary Step 3: Repeat the first six steps while in a more positive emotional state.** Your substitute stimulator may do the job, but it may be temporary. When the party music is over, your worry may reappear. To keep worry at bay for longer periods, repeat any of the first six steps while your different, positive emotions are activated. After the party music has been blasting for a while, and your sadness emotion is in remission, implement the steps. It is when you're in a different, positive emotional state that you can best overcome worry and the negative emotion it's trying to create.

Chapter Three

Stop the Erosion of Energy and Enthusiasm

Y ou need a healthy supply of energy and enthusiasm to
be productive. Yet there are times—perhaps most of the
time—when little energy and enthusiasm abounds. Why isn't
it around all the time? Because energy and enthusiasm tend
to naturally erode, like water tends to evaporate. And when
it goes, so does your personal productivity.

The *erosion of energy and enthusiasm* is productivity barrier
number two. To conquer the barrier, you must prevent your
energy and enthusiasm from eroding, or regain it if it's already
gone. You will accomplish that, and unleash another portion of
your incredible productivity, as you implement the techniques
outlined in this chapter.

Energy and enthusiasm are flip sides of the same coin.
Energy is the physical side, enthusiasm the mental. Have you
ever noticed that when you're enthused, you have a lot of
energy? Your supply of energy seems to rise in tandem with
your level of enthusiasm. Conversely, when you lack enthusiasm, you also lack energy. It's as though your supply of energy
rises and falls so as to meet the needs dictated by your level of
enthusiasm. When you think about it, you see that enthusiasm
really produces energy rather than the other way around.
Therefore, we're going to concentrate on raising your enthusiasm in this chapter and assume that your energy level will
automatically keep pace. Since energy and enthusiasm rise and
fall together, we'll treat them as one entity for purposes of this
discussion.

ENERGY AND ENTHUSIASM NATURALLY ERODE

Isn't it interesting. When we're young, fresh out of high school or college, and land our first job in our chosen profession, we're full of energy and enthusiasm (and, perhaps, a good measure of idealism). Yet we wish we could somehow leap ahead in time 5 or 10 years and have the same high level of experience and expertise as the veterans. It's the seasoned veterans, we notice, who have the experience and expertise necessary to be productive on grand scales. It's the veterans who seem to affect the most people; they're in power. It's the veterans who are able to really make things happen; they're in position. And it's the veterans who make all the money, a point that never escapes the young.

Well, time goes by. Here we are, 5, 10, 15, 20, or more years down the road. We've got all that experience and expertise we once coveted, but guess what? We're bored with it all!

"I've been doing this same ol' job for 17 years," goes a typical drone. "I crawl out of bed each day, make my way to work, plop down in my chair, and plod to the highlight of my day, lunch. Then I grind through the afternoon, finally making it to five o'clock. I get home, eat, and get my daily exercise working the TV remote. It's the same-old, same-old, day in and day out." The thrill is gone, all right. And so is any semblance of the energy and enthusiasm you brandished oh so very long ago. This may sound a bit extreme. But even a slight loss of energy and enthusiasm can be quite detrimental to your productivity.

Can you remember a time when you were really excited, when your energy and enthusiasm effortlessly gushed forth? For some people, it's been so long ago they can't even remember what it feels like. Even if you're not quite that drained, you probably display a lot less energy and enthusiasm than you have at times in the past.

If you find your energy and enthusiasm waning, don't feel alone or abnormal. It's a common affliction. Energy and enthusiasm naturally erode over time. They must be replenished regularly, and that takes effort. But the effort it takes to conquer the erosion of energy and enthusiasm barrier is less than the effort it takes to fight the barrier, as happens when you try to be productive without energy and enthusiasm. Conquering this barrier and maintaining lots of energy and enthusiasm makes life easier, more fun, and considerably more productive.

HAVE YOU HIT THRILL IMMUNITY?

I started out as a disc jockey years ago. At one station, I noticed the jock whose shift preceded mine doing a curious thing. He would spend a great deal of his time reading books during his air shift. The music would be pumping, the phones buzzing, thousands of people all over town tuned in—and he'd be so bored, he took to reading books to pass the time! Eventually he began bringing a television set into the studio so he could watch basketball games during his air shift. "An awful lot of people would give almost anything to have his job," I thought. "And he's taking it for granted—bored with it all. What a shame, what a shame."

A year or so later, I found myself bringing a magazine into work with me to read during my air shift. One day, I actually considered bringing a television set into work. Luckily, the thought of me watching some television program while I was on the air snapped me to attention. "What am I doing?" I exclaimed. "I'm getting to be just like that guy!"

The realization that my energy and enthusiasm had, over time, eroded was a shock at first. But from my newly awakened viewpoint, it became clear that for some time I had been performing my job without the benefit of much energy and enthusiasm. It's as though I had become *immune to the thrill* of being on the air.

Realization 10

You will become immune to the thrill of whatever you spend
a lot of time with.

When you find your level of energy and enthusiasm fading, you've hit what I call "thrill immunity." The rule states that you will become immune to the thrill of whatever you spend a lot of time with.

You spend 40 or more hours a week on the job, week after week, month after month, year after year. That's a big chunk of your life. No wonder the thrill is gone. What about your husband or wife? How long after marriage does it take for thrill immunity to set in? For some people, not long. The person that once thrilled you to the max is now a big yawn. That's because you live with him or her; you spend a lot of time together.

Why is it that when one person leaves a job, disinterested and bored, there's always another person ready to step into that job with interest and desire? Why is it that one person is totally bored with his spouse, when other people find the spouse totally captivating? The same qualities of your job, spouse, or lifestyle that once thrilled you are still there, it's just that you've developed an immunity to them. And unless you take deliberate action to counter your immunity, you're going to go through life inordinately underwhelmed and shamefully underproductive.

Check Your Thrill Immunity Level

Check your present level of thrill immunity for any particular endeavor or situation. It may help to think back to a time when you weren't immune, when the thrill was alive and vibrant, and compare that feeling to now.

Back to the disc jockey story. Once I realized my energy and enthusiasm had eroded, I began to recall the many times in the past when I was excited about being on the air. I recalled feeling the anticipation that built hours before I'd go on, then the moment I would enter the studio, take the controls, open the mike, and speak to the world. My air shift would feel like a four-hour emotional extravaganza. I would get off the air mentally drained from the exhilaration of the music, the callers on the hit line, the pace, and the fun and excitement.

I compared the two me's—the excited me of years past and the mundane me of present. What was different? What caused me to be excited then that isn't causing the same feeling now? The more I pondered, the clearer the answer became: the difference was not the actual event, it was the *perspective* from which I viewed or experienced the event. For example, in the past, when my level of energy and enthusiasm for air work was high, I thought a lot about the people listening to the radio while I was on. I actually pictured them in my mind listening as I spoke and reacting emotionally to what I said and the songs I played. I felt connected with the audience, and I experienced the same emotions they were experiencing, or that I imagined them experiencing.

During my mundane period, however, I didn't connect with the audience at all. Instead of imagining people listening, I'd simply see the walls of the studio. Instead of talking to people, I'd talk to the microphone. Instead of allowing the power of the music and my own words to affect me, I'd allow it to immunize me against any such feelings. (Large dosages of things tend to nullify their own effects sometimes).

In short, I had lost perspective. And when I stopped experiencing the radio as a listener, my energy and enthusiasm eroded. Along with it went my ability to concentrate and pay attention. I sounded more robotic and I began making more mistakes. It's obvious how directly energy and enthusiasm contribute to performance and productivity. (I was only a disc jockey—my poor performance didn't really harm people. When you realize that the same can happen to surgeons or airline pilots, you understand how patients can die during a simple operation and planes can crash in good weather.)

Get a New Perspective

Once I realized that my perspective was off, and thereby adversely affecting my energy and enthusiasm, I knew what to do. I had to get a new perspective. I had to connect with the listeners once again. I had to regress in my profession—mentally go backward to a lower level of involvement. In this case, it meant experiencing the radio not as a professional broadcaster but as an average listener on the receiving end.

So I got in my car and I drove around the city. I looked at people walking along the street. I looked at people in their cars and lying at pools. I looked at homes and office buildings. And everywhere I looked I said, ''My voice goes to all these people in all these places. When I'm on the radio, people everywhere are listening.

I'm affecting people!'' I put myself in their shoes and imagined what they experience when they listen. And as I became one of them—as I experienced the radio like an interested listener—I felt the excitement once again. My energy and enthusiasm immediately came to life, and as a result my performance in the studio that evening improved dramatically.

You don't have to be a disc jockey to get a different, more exciting perspective. I've seen a number of people, in a variety of professions, get great results by adopting a slightly different perspective. You see, no matter what your job is, I can guarantee you four motivating things you'll see from your new perspective:

1. **You're affecting people.** The decisions you make, the actions you take, the words you use, and the alternatives you choose, each and every day, affect others. You're affecting people in your immediate workplace, which may be obvious at times, not so obvious at other times. But you're also affecting people both in and outside your company who you never have any contact with—people you don't even know exist.

   I don't recommend you do the following except as a hypothetical "what if" thought exercise. What if you made a fairly major error on the job tomorrow? Let's say you entered the wrong number in an important spreadsheet; you failed to screw in three key connecting screws; you lost an irreplaceable document; you shipped urgent materials to Milwaukee instead of Miami; you made some other major mistake in your line of work. And say your mistake went undetected through the system until some time later when it was too late to correct. What kind of effect would your mistake have on people? On people you don't even know? Would it be safe to say the consequences of your error would be severe and widespread? Would the repercussions ring on for some time afterward?

   As you can see, one small but significant error can affect many people. What may not be as obvious, however, is that your errorless work affects the same people with equal intensity, except in a positive way. You may not hear about it as much as you would a mistake, but your good work is getting noticed and is appreciated by many others down the line, inside and outside of your company. Everything you do on a daily basis is directly or indirectly affecting many other people.

To get a new perspective, you may need to touch base with some of the people your work affects. I know a seamstress who regularly attends fashion shows so she can see her work on public display. Sometimes an airline captain will stand in the cockpit doorway after a flight, bidding the passengers good-bye—what a great way to connect with the people who have just entrusted their lives to you. A computer operator will often observe various executives at his firm carrying, reading, and quoting the reports he turns out.

You will probably have to leave the confines of your workstation or office to touch base with some of the people your work affects. Think about where you might go, who you might visit, to get your new perspective. Do it periodically to stay in touch.

2. **You're in a position to influence others.** People are watching you; they're watching how you operate. They notice how you assess things and how you react. They note the conclusions, decisions, and moves you make. They pick up on your attitude and disposition. And to a degree, you influence their own attitudes, opinions, and subsequent actions.

You may have admirers who consciously latch on to you. But even if you're unaware of them, they're there. They may not consciously think of you as a leader or role model, but they're innately and subconsciously aware of your persona nonetheless. You are influencing them, whether they realize it or not.

What you must do is realize that this is happening. Understand that you are influencing people every day by your demeanor and behavior. When you do, your energy and enthusiasm will rise.

3. **There are people who wish they had your level of experience and expertise.** But they don't have it, and the only way they can get it is to put in the years. You have something now that some others can only attain someday. You can put that experience and expertise to work and produce much greater results than the people with less experience and expertise, provided you have a good deal of energy and enthusiasm to go along with it.

Your new perspective may involve working with less-experienced people. Take someone under your wing or teach a group of up-and-comers. Touch the people who wish they had your experience and expertise, and watch your energy and enthusiasm for having it come alive.

4. **There are people who aspire to be where you are now.** There are younger people who look up to you and dream about being in your position someday. There are older people who wish they had made some different decisions years ago, decisions that would have taken them down the path and into the position you're in now. Centered in others' aspirations and regrets is you. You, in this job at this time and place. Now. You're there, in position to make things happen.

Take a minute, an hour, or a day and get out of the office or plant. Watch other people, both younger and older. Image yourself in their position, aspiring to be in your position. Experience some aspect of your performance from their perspective. It will have a rejuvenating effect on your level of energy and enthusiasm.

UNEXPECTED HITS DESTROY ENERGY AND ENTHUSIASM

Dave had an incredible amount of energy and enthusiasm back when we went to high school together. Good grades really jazzed him, which is something most kids don't seem to experience. (He influenced me in that regard. Prior to meeting him, I didn't realize that earning top grades was important or fun. Once I caught his energy and enthusiasm, my grade productivity rose dramatically.)

Dave was on both the track team and the baseball team. While most of us didn't have even one job outside of school, he had two, which gave him enough money to buy a sharp car, complete with a jacked-up rear end, no muffler, and an eight-track tape deck (this was 1969, after all). The only reason he was not voted "Most Likely to Succeed" is because everyone figured he'd already succeeded. Hey, when you're 17 years old, have an excellent GPA, a little money, a hot ride, and the opposite sex hanging all over you, what more to life is there?

The last time I saw Dave was at our graduation ceremony. With diploma in hand, he chasséd into his car, cranked up "Born to Be Wild," waved good-bye, and peeled off into the sunset, powered by energy, enthusiasm, and a touch of style.

It's now 1989, and I'm mingling at the 20-year reunion. Suddenly I spot a familiar visage across the room. It's Dave, looking remarkably well preserved, though distinctly less energetic sitting by himself in the corner. "Hi Dave! How're you doing!" I greeted him. When he faintly replied, "Okay, I guess," I knew instantly that the melancholy-eyed Dave looking up at me was not the same wild-eyed Dave who used to fire me up 20 years ago. I sat down and we talked.

Twenty years ago Dave had two jobs. Twenty years later he didn't have one. Twenty years ago he drove a hot car, now he didn't drive any car. Twenty years ago he was every girl's dream. Now, after two messy divorces, he was too hesitant to even strike up a conversation with any of the women present at the reunion. Twenty years ago he had more energy and enthusiasm than the rest of the graduating class put together. Now he had nothing more than a drink in his hand and distant look in his eyes. The energy and enthusiasm was gone. Completely gone.

What happened? Did the ghost of high school past sneak into his bedroom one night, reach into his brain, and steal his entire supply of energy and enthusiasm? Did the surgeons perform an energy and enthusiasm–dectomy? Where did it all go? What happened?

As it happened, Dave was simply not prepared to deal with the toughness of life. Things came easy to him in high school, but out in the rough-and-tumble real world jungle it was another story. In the real world, he took a number of unexpected hits. The heavy-duty politics he encountered in the corporate arena came as a surprise, and he felt victimized. The pitfalls he encountered as an entrepreneur also caught him unprepared. And the constant effort necessary to keep a marriage together was a very rude awakening.

When the trials and tribulations of life blindside us, when we take unexpected hits, we become shell-shocked and we retreat. In many cases, the shock and pain we experience is so traumatic it decimates energy and enthusiasm instantly.

Do you know someone who tried something, experienced an unexpected hit, and subsequently lost energy and enthusiasm?

Has it ever happened to you? Let's discuss ways you can keep it from happening, or turn it around if an unexpected hit has zapped your energy and enthusiasm.

The Football Player Mentality

Compare Dave's experience to what football players experience. Football is a rough sport. You walk onto the field and encounter 11 people on the other side of the ball trying to make you fail. They're trying to block you, strip the ball from you, slam you into the turf. In a football game, you take lots of hits, literally. So why do football players want to go out onto the field? Wouldn't they be a lot happier sitting on the bench where life is a whole lot easier and safer? Evidently not. As I'm sure you've noticed, they can't stand sitting on the sidelines. Football players believe the more playing time they get, the better off they are. Why?

First of all, football players understand the nature of the game. They know the other team is trying to thwart them, and they expect to experience a certain amount of adversity. It's not like a player becomes scared for life because someone tackled him. It's not like a player runs off the field shockingly crying, ''That guy hit me and stole the ball right out of my hands! I'm never going back in there! I quit!'' That never happens because athletes know what to expect when they play the game. The hits they take are not unexpected.

In fact, football players, or athletes in any sport, not only expect adversity, they welcome it. They're motivated by the toughness of the task, by the difficulty of what they're trying to accomplish. I'm not describing some kind of plastic attitude an athlete might fabricate. I'm describing what naturally happens due to simple human nature.

Let me illustrate. Let's say we pit a professional football team against a high school team. After the first quarter, if it even got that far, the score would be 100 to nothing, or some ridiculous score reflecting the professionals' ability to trounce the high school kids at will. How motivated do you think the pros would be to get onto the field, to even play this game at all? Can you see that they'd have a decided lack of energy and enthusiasm knowing that it's so easy to score and win?

Now pit the pros against another pro team, a tough team that's at the top of its division. What happens to their level of motivation? Can you see how difficulty and adversity produce energy and enthusiasm? In fact, the more a team advances into the playoffs and encounters tougher competitors, the more intense and profound the players' energy and enthusiasm. As it turns out, energy and enthusiasm are directly proportional to the difficulty of the task, provided you believe you're capable of accomplishing it.

Some of us have it backward. We think that if a particular task or goal is easy to accomplish, then we'd have a lot of energy and enthusiasm to do it. Yes, we'd be motivated for the first five minutes. But unless there's some resistance there, unless there's some difficulty involved, we'd lose our interest quickly, and our energy and enthusiasm would erode.

Realization 11

Difficulty and adversity are the parents of energy and enthusiasm.

Once you understand that your tasks, goals, and aspirations should be difficult to achieve, you've empowered yourself greatly. Once you start welcoming adversity instead of cursing it, you've made the adversity work for you instead of against you. Once you start expecting to take some hits, the hits lose 90 percent of their destructive power.

I'm not advocating paranoia. I'm not suggesting you look for every possible snag or hiccup; that could spawn worry, which is the last thing you need. I'm simply advising you to recognize that some difficulty will exist. You should expect to encounter it and take hits along the way. Expected hits you can handle. It's the unexpected hits that can wreck you.

Show What You Can Do

Exactly how do you make the adversity you encounter work for you? Look at how professional athletes in any sport do it. They all cite the same reason when asked why they want to get into the game: "I want to show what I can do." It's a simple, logical statement, yet a very empowering one. Athletes want to show what they can do in the face of adversity, and that's exactly what you want to do.

Remember, if the task were easy, there'd be no point in showing what you can do. In fact, there'd be nothing to do. Other people would have already done it. But the toughness of the task, the difficulty of accomplishing it, the adversity that you encounter, is what drives you to show that you are capable of conquering it. Get in there now and show what you can do!

NEGATIVE REINFORCEMENT OR NO REINFORCEMENT

Negative reinforcement—or no reinforcement at all—causes your energy and enthusiasm to erode. Negative or no reinforcement comes from two sources: negative people and undesirable outcomes. And between the two, there's enough negative reinforcement running rampant in the world to drain the energy and enthusiasm from every one of us many times over. To keep that from happening to you, you must take deliberate measures to defend your brain from the ravages of negative or no reinforcement.

No Reinforcement

There will be many times throughout your life, perhaps once or twice each day, when you do something good and get no reinforcement for it—when no one takes notice, when no one takes the time to compliment you or express their appreciation, or when no one gives you some financial, material, or other form of reward. Such a lack of reinforcement tends to spawn the "what's the use" syndrome. Do enough good things without any subsequent reinforcement, and your energy and enthusiasm can disappear quickly.

There are two reasons why you don't get all the reinforcement you deserve, one justifiable and the other not.

First, many people unfortunately do not appreciate the actions of others or do not make the effort to express what appreciation they might harbor. Even simple "thank yous" don't get expressed like they should. If I asked you to name people who should have thanked you in the past but failed to do so, you'd probably have no trouble whipping up a long list of them, along with specific instances and your specific expectations of the form in which they should have expressed the thanks. Now, get ready for a real mindblower. Your name may very well appear on a lot of other peoples' thankless-jerk lists. "Maybe on one or two," you reluctantly admit. "But on many lists? Naw, not me."

Yes, you. The brain, you see, has a miraculous way of recognizing incidents of missed gratefulness. When someone else fails to reward you when and how you think is appropriate, you internally register an unmistakable pang of disappointment. But when you fail to show appreciation in a like situation, it doesn't occur to you at all that you should have acted differently—though you can bet the person deserving a show of appreciation feels it. After all, if you were cognizant of your opportunity to express appreciation, you probably would have exercised it. But quite often, when someone does something that warrants your expression of gratitude, you don't even realize it. (Appreciation varies from person to person, of course. Some people train themselves to express appreciation when warranted. They're never wanting for friends either.)

The second reason you won't ever get all the reinforcement you deserve is quite logical. Other people simply have other, more pressing things to do than to watch over you and cheer every time you make a move. In fact, no one, not even the best manager, parent, friend, or spouse in the world, is going to be tuned into you to the degree necessary to reward you whenever you deserve it. Great managers, parents, friends, or spouses do tune into you quite often and do reinforce your actions at times, but even that is probably a lot less than you need or deserve.

It's always nice to receive some kind of reinforcement from other people, in the form of praise, love, money, or something. But if you crave it or depend on it, you're going to go through life a very disappointed person. If you count on others to provide you with all the positive reinforcement you need, you're going to be miserable and resentful most of the time.

So who can you count on to reinforce you as needed? You. The only person who will be tuned into you to the degree necessary to reinforce you on demand is you. You are in the perfect position to recognize when you deserve reinforcement, and you're the perfect person to administer that reinforcement. Here are two ways of doing it:

Praise Yourself

Do you praise yourself whenever you deserve it? I learned how valuable self-praise can be from a radio time salesman I met years ago. He got into the habit of assessing his own performance after each sales call, saying things to himself like, "Wow, I was great in there," "I really explained things well," "I was confident, relaxed, and smooth," or "I listened well and talked just the right amount of time." Here's the interesting part: he would assess his performance with a *strong positive bias*. While he would make mental note of any mistakes ("I shouldn't have interrupted Susan that one time," or "I should have had more data to reinforce that point"), he did so with little emotion. Rather, he used his emotion, excitement mainly, to praise himself. The purpose of assessing your own performance is, after all, not to dwell on your mistakes but to reinforce your normally desirable behavior and make yourself feel good.

I praise myself at least a half-dozen times a day, sometimes twice that amount. Within the past hour, I praised myself for making a great ham sandwich, thinking of a new topic for one of my management columns, and remembering to call a friend on her birthday. Remember, self-praise is not ego fertilization or head inflation; it's merely a form of reward for executing the small decisions and actions you take daily.

How valuable is praise anyway? Take a look at professional athletes. One reason they perform so well on average is that professional athletes have one or more coaches talking to them all the time, sometimes yelling and cheering them on during the actual competition. Without such one-on-one coaching, and the positive reinforcement it provides, their productivity wouldn't be nearly as high.

Would your productivity increase if you had your own personal coach by your side all day long providing a constant stream of wisdom, direction, and cheering? Assuming you had a good coach, your productivity would likely increase, perhaps dramatically.

"But I don't have, nor am I ever likely to get, my own productivity coach," you point out. The impracticality of such an arrangement is obvious. In any company, large or small, the salaries, physical space, and organization necessary to accommodate all the coaches would be prohibitive. (Impracticality aside, the aggregate productivity of the country wouldn't increase under such a system even if every worker's productivity doubled, since half the workforce would quit being producers and become coaches.)

Praise helps keep negative emotions at bay and positive emotions alive. Praise is a very powerful energy and enthusiasm builder. But until you're ready to hire your own productivity coach, it's up to you to administer the praise on yourself. You may feel it's silly to tell yourself how great your last minor accomplishment was, but believe me, it's anything but. Only when you get into the habit of praising yourself regularly can you really appreciate the real benefits of self-praise. Try it. You'll like it.

Reward Yourself

Another way to positively reinforce yourself is to tie purchases to performance. I've said to myself that if I turn out six solid pages of writing before noon today, I'll treat myself to an exceptional lunch—and if I fall short of that goal I won't become angry or disappointed, but I will simply eat a banana instead.

You're going to buy things for yourself anyway, so you may as well tie those purchases to productivity. A saleswoman I know does so with all of her clothing purchases. "If I make a great presentation Friday, I'll buy a new pair of earrings," or "If I make my quota this month, I'll buy a new suit," are a couple examples of how she does it.

Tie some of your purchases to your accomplishments. Pick something you plan on accomplishing soon and decide what you'll purchase for yourself when it happens. Your reward doesn't have to be anything grandiose. In fact, small things you purchase for yourself anyway, like a new CD, magazine subscription, ice cream cone, or whatever, make great rewards when you attach them to accomplishments.

Negative Reinforcement

Two different television sitcoms from the late 80s and early 90s, "The Cosby Show" and "Married . . . with Children," depict family life quite differently. On "Cosby," the family members display respect and appreciation for one another. They see things differently and disagree at times, as family members will, but never lose the mutual respect and appreciation. And they express that respect and appreciation through verbal thank-yous and I-love-yous and through actions that help one another. "The Cosby Show" depicts a family that thrives on positive reinforcement.

Contrast that with the negative reinforcement depicted on "Married . . . with Children." The family members berate and insult one another in every other sentence. Of course, this is hyperbolic, fictitious nonsense written strictly for laughs. But what's so funny about mom, dad, and the kids constantly deriding one another? Instead of respect and appreciation for one another, they display the opposite. (It's also dangerous to depict such verbal abuse in the name of love. One reason abuse, either verbal or physical, among family members proliferates is that the abusers were taught such actions equal love.)

My question is this: In which household, Huxtable or Bundy, would you find the most productive people? The two shows stayed true to form in that regard. The Huxtable household had two professional parents, he a doctor and she a lawyer. And the kids' accomplishments were the subject of many episodes. In the Bundy household, you have a lazy shoe salesman and an apathetic housewife—not that there's anything wrong with those two careers; it's the characters' lack of energy and enthusiasm for their careers that's the problem. And the Bundy kids are totally unproductive.

Yeah, I know these shows are all fiction. But the amount of energy and enthusiasm—and subsequent personal productivity—of each family member correlates directly with their family's level of positive reinforcement, which makes both shows more true-to-life than we might think. Unfortunately, negative reinforcement—in the form of beratement, disrespect, distrust, and anger—exists not only in the home, but in the streets and the workplace. No doubt you've run into it here and there.

The Dead Battery

Beware of the "dead battery." Dead batteries are people who attach their jumper cables to you and suck out all of your energy and enthusiasm. How do they do that? Through constant negative reinforcement, by berating, chiding, and criticizing you, the company, the family, or the "system" in general.

Interestingly, dead batteries are usually people close to us, a parent, sibling, spouse, friend, or co-worker. They may even love you and wish you well. Yet they see fit to constantly denigrate you and/or the system. Dead batteries don't view their negativity as harmful to you. That's because they believe that if a negative attitude is good for them, it's good for you. It's a subconscious way of reinforcing the "correctness" of their negativity. They need you to adopt the same attitude to justify it in themselves, and they don t see that as harmful to you.

Have you ever noticed dead batteries never believe anything is their fault or responsibility? They blame everything that happens to them on other people, the system, or circumstances. They try to convince you that your energy, enthusiasm, and determination are useless because the deck of life is always stacked against you.

How do you deal with a dead battery? "I'll fire her up!" you exclaim. "I'll overwhelm him with so much energy and enthusiasm he can't help but catch it!" It's a noble intent, but it never happens. It always works the other way around; the dead battery drains your energy and enthusiasm rather than you energizing the dead battery. Why? Because the dead battery chooses to be a dead battery. He doesn't want to be charged up. This is quite different from a weak battery, which we all are from time to time. As a weak battery, we seek a charge and we get it from a friend, relative, movie, television program, book, tape, seminar, or wherever. But dead batteries don't want to be charged up; they only want to discharge you, so you're equal to them.

You must unhook yourself from your dead battery if you want to keep your energy, enthusiasm, and productivity, alive. One way is to mentally unhook yourself. To do that you have to learn to ignore them quite often, which can be difficult. Another way to unhook yourself is to reduce the amount of time you are in their physical presence. Sometimes this is the only way. You don't have to love them any less, but you can spend less time with them.

Here's another interesting thought: You may be someone else's dead battery, or your own dead battery. If you find yourself berating and chiding someone, or yourself, look out. You're destroying someone's energy and enthusiasm, and you're doing it to justify your own negative attitude.

Undesirable Outcomes

Negative reinforcement comes not only from people, but from undesirable outcomes. Like when you fail to convince upper management to adopt your proposal. Or when you interview for a job and get rejected. Or when you spend two hours trying to write a business letter that just doesn't seem to come together. Or when you try to beat your tennis partner and end up losing again. You get the idea.

Sometimes all it takes is one instance—one undesirable outcome—and you've been so strongly negatively reinforced, it's like a lightening bolt striking you down. I know one fellow who enjoyed getting up in front of people and speaking, until one day he made a presentation that bombed. That was 13 years ago, and to this day he's so terrified of public speaking he hasn't done it since.

The strategy for neutralizing undesirable outcomes, and keeping them from zapping your energy and enthusiasm, is to *bounce off of undesirable outcomes.* Look at the football player as an example. Let's say a wide receiver is going deep, and the quarterback throws a bomb right in the receiver's hands. And the receiver drops the pass. (No one screws up in front of more people than professional athletes. Imagine your last error witnessed by 70,000 people in a stadium, another 20 million watching on television, and highlight films replaying it forever!)

What does the player do after experiencing an undesirable outcome? Does he stagger back to the sidelines in bewilderment? Does he quit the game? It never happens. In reality, the player who has just experienced an undesirable outcome is even more determined to get back in the game. Why? So he can redeem himself. And a smart coach puts him back in soon and throws him a pass so he doesn't have to live long in the disappointment stage.

Bounce off undesirable outcomes just like professional athletes. Decide that you're going to redeem yourself. The desire for redemption is strong; it can produce lots of energy and enthusiasm. Remember, you're judged only on your average. It's only a matter of time before you produce a desirable outcome, provided you keep bouncing off of setbacks.

HAVE YOU LOST FAITH IN A BETTER LIFE?

The day you conclude your life is never going to get any better is the day your energy and enthusiasm vanishes. You show me someone who believes the future will never be as bright as "the good old days," and I'll show you someone with no energy and enthusiasm.

To create the energy and enthusiasm necessary to be productive, you must believe that your endeavors will enrich your life in some way, directly or indirectly. The enrichments you desire may be materialistic, such as a bigger house or better car. Or they may be nonmaterialistic, perhaps intellectual or spiritual. Or they may be a combination of materialistic and nonmaterialistic. Whatever they are, you've got to believe you'll attain them to have any energy or enthusiasm.

The Power of Expectations

Do you expect your life to improve with each passing day or week? Do you expect greater material, intellectual, or spiritual enrichment with each passing month or year? Your expectations affect your level of energy and enthusiasm greatly. If you have low expectations, you're going to have low energy and enthusiasm, and low productivity. Have high expectations, and you'll have high energy, enthusiasm, and productivity.

Realization 12

Your energy and enthusiasm rise and fall in direct proportion
to your expectations.

If it's that simple, why don't we all have the loftiest of expectations all of the time? Two reasons:

1. **We believe that no matter what we do, it won't change our life for the better.** "I've got a house I can't afford, astronomical child support payments, and credit card debt that won't stop growing. I'll be lucky to somehow maintain my existing lifestyle, yet alone ever enrich my life any," declared Stu recently. Does his assessment at all resemble yours? For many people, future expectations mean mere maintenance of mediocrity. Forget about a bigger house, faster car, college degree, or European vacation. Just get the bills paid each month—if you're lucky.

   In the 80s, people thought the way to acquire some of life's material pleasures was through debt. The gotta-have-it-now mentality of the prosperity-conscious yuppie spawned a lifestyle that made the monthly payment an instant American institution.

   Then at about the same time the Berlin Wall came down in Germany, in early 1990, a new wall suddenly sprang up in America, the Great Wall of Debt. All those payment princes and princesses who were cruising along the yellow brick road of upward mobility suddenly crashed into the Wall—and totaled their lifestyle. The same thing happened to a number of debt-laden companies, too. Paying the piper often necessitates doing with less instead of more. "Downshifting" your lifestyle is not the most pleasurable of experiences.

   So how are you supposed to have faith in a better life, and conjure up a great set of expectations, when the reality is that you've got to work your butt off just to keep your head above water? First, don't sell out to the debt devil. A better life is not attained by going further into debt. (I'm not really denouncing debt, which is a desirable financial vehicle for people and companies at times and under certain circumstances, but the abuse of it.)

   Second, increase your personal productivity. Notice I didn't say you need to increase your responsibilities or the amount of hours you work. Conquering the five productivity barriers, which you are in the process of doing this very moment, will cause your productivity to explode without working harder or longer. Accomplishment itself contributes greatly to a better life, for yourself as well as for others you affect. And the rewards accomplishment brings, such as recognition, advancement, love, and money, also make for a better life.

So you see, enhancing your lifestyle, materially, intellectually, and spiritually, is not only believable, it is inevitable. Your life will get better. How do I know that? Because you and I are discussing it all now. You're already moving ahead. Greater expectations, therefore, are quite appropriate.

2. **We're afraid of disappointment.** Many people choose to have low expectations to avoid the pain of possible disappointment. They see having high expectations as setting themselves up for a fall, or getting high on false hope. Have low expectations, they reason, and they're safe.

What's wrong with this reasoning? First of all, they're forfeiting one of the greatest energy and enthusiasm boosters, high expectations, when they chose not to have them. Second, having low expectations is actually the more unrealistic case.

Realization 13

Life naturally appreciates; it really does get better with age.

There is a natural appreciation built into life. Life gets better with age, provided you don't sabotage the natural process by making critically bad decisions along the way.

Having high expectations is consistent with the natural appreciation of life. And high expectations will not lead to disappointment if you remember three important things:

First, establish *moderately* higher expectations for the short run. Let's say you're currently making $44,000 a year. Should you expect to make $50,000 next year or $500,000? Which is more likely to lead to disappointment? A dieter doesn't expect to lose 40 pounds in one day; such would surely lead to disappointment. Expecting to lose four pounds a week for 10 weeks, however, is an empowering expectation.

Second, have *monumentally* greater expectations for the long run. Expecting to lose 40 pounds or make $500,000 a year is fine, as long as you give yourself plenty of time for that to happen. As long as you don't expect to leap from here to there in one fell swoop or by next Tuesday, your grandiose expectations aren't likely to be disappointing.

Third, keep your expectations *general*, not too specific or detailed. You might expect to be a manager someday, which is fine. But expecting to become the manager of your division, or even some other division of your present employer, is too specific. Keeping your expectations general is important when they deal with other people. You may expect your daughter to be a good student and graduate from high school on time; that's general and empowering. But expecting her to get an A on next week's history exam is too specific and problematic.

What Is "Realistic"?

Incidentally, whenever expectations are discussed, the words *realistic* and *unrealistic* inevitably pop up. According to conventional wisdom, you're suppose to have "realistic" expectations and avoid "unrealistic" ones. But my question is this: Who decides what is realistic and what is unrealistic? Who crowns one Arbiter of the Realistic and gives him the superhuman wisdom to correctly proclaim something realistic or unrealistic?

Think of someone who accomplished something great. It could be someone you know personally or a famous person living or dead. Now think back to when that person was just embarking on the endeavor and hadn't yet accomplished it. What if someone had said to her, "Be realistic! You can't accomplish that," and she had heeded the advice and never attempted—never accomplished? It's a good thing some people place no trust in realistic/unrealistic proclamations, or surely their accomplishments would have been mediocre (realistic) rather than great (unrealistic).

I believe that there is no such thing as realistic or unrealistic when it comes to expectations. After all, what appears realistic to one person may appear totally unrealistic to another. And no one, not even you, knows what is realistic or unrealistic for you or anyone else. Don't try to determine what is realistic or unrealistic for you or for others. Doing so is a rhetorical, futile exercise that produces no benefits. As long as you establish moderately greater expectations for the short run and monumentally greater expectations for the long run, and think in general terms, you'll avoid disappointment without getting caught in the realistic/unrealistic grinder.

STEPS IN CONQUERING THE EROSION OF ENERGY AND ENTHUSIASM

- **Step 1. Check your thrill immunity level.** Are you at all bored with something that once excited you? If so, mentally regress to a simpler, less involved time when you were excited. Think of a specific instance when your thrill level was high. Reexperience the excitement in your mind. This conditions you for executing the next step successfully.

- **Step 2. Get a new perspective.** Get out of your physical environment periodically and connect with the people your work affects. Connect with the up-and-comers who wish they had your level of experience and expertise. Connect with the people who aspire to be in your position. Realize you're influencing people, you're shaping their lives to some degree.

- **Step 3. Make friends with difficulty and adversity.** Recognize difficulty and adversity as the source of your sustained energy and enthusiasm. After all, if it weren't for toughness and adversity, there'd be no point in accomplishing what you want to accomplish.

- **Step 4. Show what you can do.** Everyone knows it isn't easy accomplishing things, even simple things, which affords you the opportunity to show that you are capable of accomplishing certain things that are important to you. Go ahead and surprise some, dazzle others. Pretend like the curtain has parted and you're in the spotlight. You know you can do it—it's now time to show it!

- **Step 5. Praise yourself often.** Depend on yourself for praise whenever deserved. All the little things you do successfully each day, from getting out of bed on time, to driving safely to work, to making the phone calls on your list, to having patience with the kids, deserve a bit of self-praise.

- **Step 6. Reward yourself often.** Fill in the blanks: ''If I accomplish (an item on your to-do list), I'll buy myself a (something you want).'' Rewards can be simple and inexpensive.

- **Step 7. Unhook yourself from dead batteries.** If people close to you are draining your energy and enthusiasm, you must unhook yourself. You may have to spend less time in their physical presence. You don't have to love them less, just see them less.

- **Step 8. Bounce off of undesirable outcomes.** Let an undesirable outcome be a source for your renewed desire. Get back on the horse and try again soon. The law of averages will catch up; you will succeed if you keep attempting.

- **Step 9. Maintain high expectations.** Your belief in a better life, expressed through your higher expectations, fuels your energy, enthusiasm, and productivity. Establish newer, greater expectations. Establish smaller expectations for the short run, greater expectations for the long run. Keep them general, not too specific or detailed. Forget about what is realistic or unrealistic. No one—including you—is in a kingly, officiating position to make realistic or unrealistic calls.

Chapter Four

Overcoming Your Negative Emotions

How many emotions have you felt in the past 24 hours? Did you experience the love, excitement, or laughter emotions? Did you feel any sadness, anger, or frustration? How about loneliness, jealousy, or depression? Since human beings are emotional creatures by nature, I'm sure you experienced a number of emotions in the past 24 hours, even if they weren't any of the ones I just mentioned, and even if your various emotional experiences were mere tinges of feeling. All emotional experiences needn't be major eruptions. We're always feeling something, it seems.

Human beings are not just emotional creatures, but *emotionally driven* creatures. The emotions you experience every minute of every day dictate your attitude, personality, words, and actions. This doesn't necessarily mean you're expressing your emotions outwardly all the time. It just means that emotions are driving your behavior, however that behavior might outwardly appear. Not only that, the emotions you wish to experience, or wish to avoid experiencing, dictate your personality and behavior just as much as those emotions you are actually experiencing.

Your emotions, whether actual, desired, or dreaded, affect your personal productivity to a very large degree. Negative emotions in particular, such as anger, frustration, depression, sadness, fright, despair, hate, jealousy, and others, are a major barrier to your productivity in many ways. In this chapter, you'll learn how negative emotions are created, how they affect you, and how you can effectively control them. Overcoming productivity barrier number three, *negative emotions,* not only lifts your productivity, it makes you feel a whole lot better, too. Let's begin.

WHERE DO YOUR EMOTIONS COME FROM?

According to a revolutionary new study, Dr. Alburt T. Scook has identified all emotions as living, biological organisms present in the air. These highly communicable, invisible organisms, or "emotites" as he calls them, enter and exit the human brain at will, often with lightning-like speed. Have you ever felt fine one moment, then suddenly felt angry, sad, or frustrated the next? Undoubtedly, one or more emotites infiltrated your brain and commandeered it for the duration. The only antidote, according to Dr. Scook, is to wear earmuffs and breathe into a paper bag. If the little rascals have trouble getting into your head, they'll move on to the next person instead.

You know I'm kidding. There is no such thing as an army of little emotites nor a Dr. Alburt T. Scook. Yet the idea of emotions existing outside of our bodies and somehow affecting us seems to make sense, doesn't it? It seems that way because it's a very good illusion, one perpetuated by two true, but misleading, conditions:

1. **You are not consciously creating your emotions.** Your conscious mind, that which thinks, reasons, and decides—that which is reading and evaluating these words now—knows it does not create any emotions.

   It's not as though you consciously decide, after all, to suddenly become attracted to another person or suddenly feel depressed. In fact, such conscious emotional creation is very difficult to do. Does a decision like "I will now become incredibly and irresistibly attracted to Harold" suddenly produce the love emotion? The love emotion, if is to be experienced at all, just comes out of nowhere whenever it's ready to come, without you deliberately creating it.

   Erroneous conclusion: Since we don't deliberately create our emotions, they must originate somewhere outside of our brain.

   Correct conclusion: Your emotions are created by the *subconscious* part of your brain. Your subconscious mind operates below your level of conscious awareness, which is why you may not realize that your brain is creating all your emotions. You may not be aware of all the other functions your subconscious mind performs day and night either, such as controlling your heartbeat, breathing, digestion, or body temperature.

The last time you drove home from work, did you consciously think about every movement of the steering wheel, gas pedal, or brake? Of course you didn't. You simply got in the car and thought about other things—what happened at work or what you're going to eat for dinner perhaps. The next thing you knew, you pulled into your driveway. Your subconscious mind drove you home. And that's just one example of how it's always working. Your subconscious mind actually handles about 80 to 90 percent of all your brain work, including the creation of emotions.

2. **Occurrences cause you to emote.** You're having trouble getting along with a co-worker and you feel resentful. Your neighbor's kid knocks a baseball through your picture window, and you become angry. Your girlfriend dumps you, and you feel distraught. You get passed over for a promotion, and you feel frustrated. Someone says something funny, and you laugh. Your ex-girlfriend calls a week later, and you become excited. Your supervisor praises you, and you feel proud. Your ex is only calling to get her hair dryer back, and you feel depressed. You're an emotional wreck, and it's all because of what's happening in your life.

Erroneous conclusion: Things that happen—various occurrences—create emotions.

Correct conclusion: Occurrences *trigger* emotions, but they don't create them. Your emotions lie dormant most of the time, waiting to be triggered or activated. When something happens, like that baseball crashing through your window, your subconscious mind evaluates that occurrence and reacts by producing a seemingly appropriate emotion.

WHO CONTROLS YOUR EMOTIONS?

Here's a question for you: If your emotions are controlling much of your behavior, who in turn is controlling your emotions? Think of it this way: The computer controls the printer—tells it how and what to print—but someone has to control the computer, right?

"Sure," you respond. "The operator controls the computer." Right. Getting back to the first question then, who controls your emotions? "The operator," you say? Very good. Next question. Who is that person, the operator who controls your emotions? Answer: You. You are the operator who runs your emotion-producing brain.

Realization 14

You control your emotions.
Nothing outside of your brain controls your emotions.

Here's the chain of command: Your behavior, including personality traits and actions, are controlled by your emotions, though you may not always be expressing those emotions outwardly. Your emotions, in turn, are controlled by the operation of your brain. You are the one who operates your brain—you're the one telling your brain what emotions to create at any given moment, although you do that subconsciously. You create and control your emotions without any conscious thought.

HOW YOUR SUBCONSCIOUS MIND CONTROLS EMOTIONS

The emotions that you feel are really a combination of electrical impulses and chemical secretions in certain parts of your brain. And it's your subconscious mind that controls this electrochemical activity, according to the instructions you have previously programmed into your subconscious.

Emotions are like spices sitting on a rack. Your subconscious chooses certain emotions and activates them much like a cook grabbing certain spices and sprinkling them in the dish.

Why does your subconscious choose the emotions that it does? Why, for example, does it choose anger instead of laughter at certain times? Or sadness instead of excitement? Two factors determine when and what emotions your subconscious mind creates:

1. Good-bad interpretation of occurrences. All forms of life possess an instinctive quest for survival. Humans, in addition to basic survival instincts, also have a higher-level quest for happiness and prosperity. Hence, your subconscious mind automatically interprets everything that happens to you or around you, or that in any way affects you, as either good or bad for you. Based on each such interpretation of each occurrence, your subconscious mind activates electrochemical activity accordingly, and you feel various emotions.

Example: You get out of your car and see a $10 bill lying in the parking lot. Your subconscious mind instantaneously interprets this occurrence on your good-bad scale, and depending on the interpretation, activates certain emotions. In this case, your subconscious mind determines that a new $10 bill in your possession is good for you. You feel a tinge of excitement and your facial muscles produce a smile.

Another example: You're presenting your ideas at an important meeting, and upper management is impressed. Then another employee, the same rank as you but from another division, mounts a counterproposal. As he's blasting holes in your plan, your subconscious mind, always interpreting occurrences on the good-bad scale, sees this occurrence as bad for you. Your subconscious activates certain electrical impulses and chemical secretions that make you feel defensive and angry. Your anger emotion in turn causes your facial muscles to tense, raises your blood pressure, and causes you to speak in a heated, incensed manner. And all this happens without you having to consciously think about it.

Yet another example: You're awakened by a bump in the night. You hear a louder thump, followed by a door creaking. Your subconscious mind wastes no time interpreting this as bad for you. Feeling frightened, you quietly descend a few stairs and peek into the living room, whereupon you see a dark figure entering through the front door. Instantaneously, your subconscious does its duty, and you become extremely frightened. Your subconscious, following its supreme directive to keep you from harm, may activate certain glandular activity. You may feel tense and freeze. Or you may feel scared and scream. Or you may feel extremely aggressive and attack the intruder. Or you may feel any combination of the above, all without any conscious thought on your part. (Your conscious mind may certainly realize this occurrence is bad for you too, but it isn't in control of your emotions. It's not like you consciously say to yourself, "I will now feel frightened," and somehow turn that emotion on like you do a light switch.)

Your subconscious mind is constantly interpreting occurrences as either good or bad for you, and to varying degrees. Then, through electrical impulses and chemical secretions, it creates the emotions you feel.

2. **Previously installed commands.** Your subconscious mind creates emotions according to the commands you have previously programmed into it. You may, for example, have a command in your brain that says, "If someone pulls out in front of me requiring me to hit the brakes to avoid him, I will become angry." Then, at some future date when a driver does exactly that, your subconscious instinctively produces anger, right on cue.

A computer can add a column of figures in a split second. How does it know how to do this? The computer has a math program in its memory. The program contains the instructions that direct the computer to perform the addition. When the computer receives your latest set of numbers, it adds them up without hesitation. Your subconscious mind works the same way, processing new information as it has been programmed to do.

Your subconscious receives certain information, such as a co-worker imposing her work load on you, and it produces an emotion—anger, let's say—without hesitation. How does it know it should produce anger when someone imposes on you? Why doesn't it produce fright, joy, love, or any other emotion? Why anger? It's simply following whatever commands were previously programmed into it; that's how it produces emotions so fast. It doesn't have to think about what emotion to produce, except in the case of completely new experiences. At some time in your past, you "told" your subconscious to produce the anger emotion if a coworker unduly imposes some of her work on you. You probably programmed this into your brain subconsciously, which means you didn't even know you were doing it at the time.

You may argue that, subconsciously or not, you did not program all these commands in your brain. You're right. The commands are in there, but you may not have been the one that put them there. Other people put a number of *installed commands* into your subconscious. And it's been happening, unbeknownst to you consciously, your entire life!

From day one, we learn. Children learn how they're "supposed to" feel in various circumstances. They learn by example from observing their parents. Children also acquire installed commands from teachers, peers, and from that supreme oracle of instantaneous learning, the television set.

Not all installed commands are "correct." When kids see cartoon characters falling off cliffs, slamming into trees, and getting their heads smashed between garbage can lids, and see other characters relishing the events, new installed commands instruct them to laugh or gloat at other's misfortunes. Or say you observe your supervisor expressing anger whenever a subordinate makes a mistake. Sometime down the road you're promoted to the supervisor's position. And what do you do when one of your subordinates makes a mistake? Without even thinking about it, you become angry.

Installed commands have entered your subconscious since the day you were born, and they're still entering. The idea is to recognize that this is happening and take control. You may want to change some of the commands currently installed in your subconscious. You'll find out how to do this a bit later.

POSITIVE AND NEGATIVE EMOTIONS

All of the emotions you experience fall into one of two categories: positive or negative. The positive ones, such as love, excitement, pride, joy, confidence, and security, make you feel good. The negative ones, such as sadness, fright, depression, anger, frustration, disappointment, and hate, make you feel bad. No single emotion is both good and bad. When you have mixed feelings, or ambivalence about something, it's because your subconscious is activating two or more emotions at the same time.

Positive emotions strengthen and empower you. It's easy to see that you will perform better when you're feeling excited, loved, or confident rather than bored, sad, or insecure. In fact, a slight difference in emotion can result in a major difference in performance.

Relationships with people at work and at home affect your entire psyche and your productivity. You're strengthening your relationships with others when you exude positive rather than negative emotions. And whether you realize it or not, you're exuding an emotional aura at all times. Even though you may not be expressing your emotions outwardly at times, your emotional state—positive or negative—seeps through your facade; it radiates from your body, your eyes, your voice. Others can innately detect your emotional state; so can animals. If you're giving off positivity, they'll be instinctively more attracted and cooperative. If you're giving off negativity, they'll be repelled and uncooperative.

There's more. If I asked you what you really want out of life, your innermost desire, what would you say? I'll bet you'd answer "happiness." Happiness is the ultimate human desire. It's been universal among all peoples around the globe since the beginning of the human race to the present. Next question: How much time and effort do you spend seeking happiness? "A lot," you say? I say a lot more than you realize. Practically everything you do day in and out is to bring about increased happiness. People watch television, call someone on the phone, get a new job, cook dinner, buy a new car, go into work every day, get married, get divorced, drink, dance, take the garbage out, collect baseball cards, get college degrees—I could go on and on—all to bring about more happiness.

Realization 15

The amount of happiness you experience is directly related to the amount of positive emotions you experience.

Positive emotions make you happy. Negative emotions, on the other hand, make you unhappy. They weaken you and disempower you. They block your creativity and productive abilities. (Negative emotions are not totally superfluous. They can be useful at times. Feeling a tinge of frustration, anger, or sadness may alert you to a problem that needs to be handled. Small—and I emphasize small—doses of a negative emotion can get us to do things differently. And sometimes even the most self-motivated of us can use a good kick, a negative-emotional awakening.)

The problem with negative emotions is that we simply overuse them. Our subconscious chooses them from the spice rack much too often and in much larger doses than needed. Think how your apple pie would taste if you put an entire cup of cinnamon in instead of a teaspoon. Too much cinnamon ruins the pie. Too much emotional negativity ruins our productivity, yet we overindulge with regularity. We've become a society of walking, talking, breathing negaholics.

The amount of negative emotions you experience, the length of time you experience them, and the intensity of those emotions is collectively called your *negative emotion usage level*, or *neul* (pronounced "neal"). Most of us have an unnecessarily high neul. We allow ourselves to feel anger, frustration, depression, jealousy, resentment, hatred, and a slew of other negative emotions all too easily and quickly. We even allow ourselves to rampantly display these emotions, often casting them forth with wanton vengeance like a berserk gunman shooting whoever enters his physical space.

What about you? Do you really want to live your life slopping through a cesspool of negative emotions day in and out? Do you really want to repel other people by radiating your excessive negativity? Do you really want to hurt the people you love by infecting them with your negative emotional displays? Do you really want to shackle your productive ability, making accomplishment more difficult? I don't believe you want any of those things. I believe you would opt for the opposite—living a life of positive emotional feelings and imbuing others with the same—if you only knew how.

Do you spend too much of your time feeling some negative emotion such as anger, frustration, or depression? If you have a higher neul than you would like to have, today is your lucky day. At least you realize your neul is running high and you're ready to back it down. Think about all those other people in the world who don't even realize how much they're hurting themselves and others with their excessively high neuls. They lead lives of shameful underperformance in just about every area. Or they might succeed in one area, such as making lots of money, yet fail miserably in another, such as in their relationships.

For you, that is about to change. Lowering your negative emotion usage level is not as difficult as you might imagine. It may have been difficult for you to change in the past because (1) you didn't understand how or why you kept experiencing all those negative emotions in the first place, and (2) you didn't know what to do to make things any different. As you learn the specific techniques that follow, you'll reduce your neul considerably and realize much greater happiness and personal productivity.

WHY YOUR BRAIN OVERUSES NEGATIVE EMOTIONS

Understanding how and why your subconscious keeps producing an excessive amount of negative emotions is a prerequisite for correcting the condition. Here are the five primary reasons your brain overuses negative emotions:

1. **Your brain interprets negative emotions as pleasurable.** Remember what we talked about in Chapter 2? You crave emotional stimulation, negative as well as positive. Quite often, your brain interprets negative emotions as pleasurable. Given the choice of experiencing no emotion or a negative emotion, your brain will most often produce the negative.

2. **You interpret occurrences as bad for you.** As we talked about earlier, your subconscious evaluates every piece of information it receives as either good or bad for you, and to varying degrees. Could it be you are interpreting a whole lot of things as bad for you? Remember, almost all occurrences are inherently neither good nor bad. They become either good or bad based on how you choose to interpret them.

   Years ago, I worked with a guy who was extremely sensitive to the weather. If the weather was anything other than sunny and warm, it was bad for him. As you might expect, he would display his bad-for-me interpretation without question. On rainy days, he'd walk around with galoshes, raincoat, and umbrella. That wasn't necessarily inappropriate, provided he removed all the rain gear upon entering the building. But he would keep the coat and galoshes on all day long, inside and out. He'd mope around all day, cranky and belligerent, blaming his fate on the "lousy weather."

One winter, during a heavy snowstorm, a number of people couldn't make it to work. I made it, along with a couple of others. The three of us were conducting business as usual when suddenly the door flew open and there stood a creature resembling the arctic monster in the 1951 sci-fi classic *The Thing*. Slowly the creature wobbled in, his legs so thickly wrapped in parka he could only walk by shifting his weight and swinging the free leg around. Over the next 45 minutes, The Thing gingerly removed his Eskimo armor, item by item, mumbling and grumbling with every arm stroke. When the goggles and ski mask finally came off, we could see it was indeed our fellow employee, who by then was barking and growling incessantly.

Let me tell you, this guy was absolutely miserable that day. He exuded depression and frustration. He not only complained about the "horrible weather" but about everything else that somehow seemed equally horrible to him (your interpretation of occurrences can spread rapidly if you let it). He actually caused himself to experience other problems, like spilling his coffee, losing his car keys, and accidently hanging up on the boss. "This is a terrible day . . . terrible," he whined. "I knew I should have stayed home. I should never have come in today. It's a terrible day, just terrible."

Normally, when the staff is short, people are elated when another co-worker shows up to share the work load. But when The Thing showed up that day, we all knew it was bad news (yes, we were interpreting his appearance as bad for us). Needless to say, his productivity was virtually nonexistent, and he was hampering everyone else's productivity. I encouraged him to knock off early that day, so as to "safely make it home without incident," which he did.

I not only encouraged him to go home, I encouraged him to move his home. He sought my advice one day about a job opportunity down south. Rattling off an equal number of pros and cons, he couldn't decide whether to accept the job or not.

I solidified his decision in three seconds. "The weather's great down there," I noted. "With sun-drenched days and clear-skied nights, how can you go wrong?" "Yes!" he exclaimed, with his eyes as wide as I'd ever seen them. The Thing has been living somewhere in Florida ever since (I lost contact with him years ago), presumably happy. The unfortunate thing is, he didn't have to move to a "better" climate to be happy. He could have simply changed his interpretation of colder weather.

I use this extreme example of interpreting an inherently neutral occurrence, the weather, as bad for you to point out the silliness and destructiveness of such interpretation. Perhaps you don't overreact to the weather, but you probably do overreact to a bunch of other equally innocuous occurrences.

Realization 16

Most of the things you think are bad for you really aren't.
Seemingly bad occurrences are often much better for you than they
initially appear.

Answer this: Is it good for you or bad for you when . . .

- A co-worker imposes some of his work load on you?
- Your company promotes someone else instead of you?
- Your spouse or date is late?
- You fail to complete a project on time?

If you are inclined to interpret any of these occurrences as bad for you, you are jumping to erroneous and destructive conclusions. I can tell you with absolute certainty that each of these occurrences is good for you. Don't agree? Hang in there. We'll discuss them in detail in a minute. Right now, let's continue discovering why your neul is so high.

3. **We have an abundance of installed commands that direct us to produce negative emotions.** Let's face it, the world is full of people with destructively high neuls. Like catching a cold, through no fault of your own, you probably caught a plethora

of installed commands that direct your subconscious to produce the same negative emotions as the people you caught them from. Social scientists have long ago discovered a direct relationship between adult criminal behavior and the same behavior in the parents of the criminals. Children of abusive parents tend to abuse their own children, for example.

I once knew a woman who consistently produced anger in response to her boyfriend and their relationship. He found himself in a no-win predicament, since she would become angry no matter what he did or didn't say, what he did or didn't do. Her frequent eruptions of anger kept the relationship in constant turmoil, until one day the guy had enough and broke it off.

Upon being questioned about her childhood, she revealed that her mother and father both verbally abused one another. They would express vehement anger, then follow that up immediately with expressions of love. The linkage of anger and love became installed in this woman's subconscious. She came to believe, subconsciously, that a tumultuous, anger-filled relationship equals love. She also believed that if two people didn't express anger toward one another, they must not love one another. Consequently, her subconscious produced excessive anger. It was her way of trying to establish love.

As twisted as this reasoning is, it's quite common. How many television shows or movies do you see in which two characters constantly display anger toward one another, yet are attracted to one another at the same time? Hollywood loves the anger-equals-love theme, especially in situation comedies. One, named "Hearts Afire," has John Ritter and Markie Post yelling and screaming at each other one moment and kissing the next, week after week. "Love And War" (at least the show titles are becoming more aptly descriptive) has Jay Thomas and Susan Dey doing the same (Annie Potts replaced Dey after the first season).

What kind of command becomes installed in your subconscious mind when you watch this stuff? That a tumultuous, anger-filled relationship equals love, that's what. The more you watch, the more the anger-equals-love command solidifies in your subconscious. Before you know it, you too find it increasingly difficult to reason that a stable, harmonious relationship can be a loving one. And that's exactly how destructive installed commands spread throughout the population.

In the Old West, cowboys had installed commands that directed their brains to produce instant anger if someone called them "yella" or a "mangy varmit." How did this command come to be installed in their subconscious? They learned it from watching others. They learned that if someone calls you anything but friend, you must become so angry you slug them or challenge them to a duel. Such behavior is so obviously silly when you look at other people in another time. But what about you in this day and time?

You'll find many of your own installed commands are equally silly if you stop and think about them. Have you ever noticed yourself reacting to occurrences the same way a co-worker or supervisor does, even though you believe that reaction is undesirable or unwarranted? In Chapter 3, I said that others are observing you and being influenced by you every day. It works the other way around too. You are observing others and taking mental note of their actions. All of this happens subconsciously for the most part. But you can end up adopting silly or undesirable installed commands simply by casual observation of others around you. It's a common occurrence in the workplace.

When you find yourself feeling a negative emotion, ask yourself if it could be due to a previously installed command you picked up from someone else. If you think for a while, you might be able to identify the actual person who or instance that influenced you.

4. **You use negative emotions to manipulate people.** Children learn that by throwing temper tantrums, or by doing the opposite like sitting cross-armed and ignoring everyone, they can get what they want. Adults often do the same thing for the same reason.

Watch people at work, especially people in management. When you see someone displaying a negative emotion, ask yourself if they're doing it to manipulate other people. Anger and guilt are the two most widely used emotions in manipulation. Unfortunately, many people are susceptible to anger and guilt manipulation, which makes those tactics quite effective. (Make sure you are not susceptible to either.)

5. **Negative emotions are easier to conjure up.** Let's try an experiment. See if you can create the joy emotion right now. Think of a time, an instance, when you felt joyous. Think of the circumstances, and the place, that contributed to your joyful feeling. Think of the people who were there; focus on one person in particular who contributed greatly to your feeling. Think about what that person did, said, and looked like at the time. Run the scenario in your mind like a movie. Think how you felt at the time, and feel the same way now.

Are you joyous right now? If so, how much? On a scale of 1 to 10, with 1 very low, and 10 very high, what level of joy are you feeling right now? Hold that answer.

Now let's see if you can make yourself angry. Think of a time, an instance, when you felt angry. Think of the circumstances and the place that contributed to your anger. Think of the people who were there; focus on one person in particular who contributed greatly to your feeling. Think about what that person did, said, and looked like at the time. Run the scenario in your mind like a movie. Think how you felt at the time, and feel the same way now.

Are you angry right now? On the 1-to-10 scale, where does your present anger rank?

Which emotion, joy or anger, ranks higher (1 to 10) in this experiment? Which emotion seems more real to you now? Which seems more contrived?

If you're like most people, your self-generated feeling of anger seemed stronger and more real than your self-generated feeling of joy. While your joyful state may seem somewhat plastic, your angry state may seem genuine. You were only pretending to be joyous, but you really felt angry, right?

We humans were born into a perfect world, at least in our minds. Even as adults, we still maintain a deeply instinctive belief in a perfect world. We expect things to be perfect, or at least pretty good. So perfection, or goodness, doesn't stand out nearly as much as imperfection, or badness. It's as though perfection is the white shirt, badness is the food stain. One is the backdrop, and the other stands out from the backdrop.

Think of it this way: You're having dinner at your favorite restaurant. You're pleased with the atmosphere, your table, the food, the service, and the prices. Then you dive into the dessert and discover a dead fly in your pie. How do you feel? If 99 percent of the dining experience was perfect, and only 1 percent, the fly, imperfect, do you feel 99 percent happy and only 1 percent unhappy? Of course not. You feel 100 percent unhappy. Perhaps even nauseous, irate, or angry. You'll spend the next 10 years avoiding that restaurant and talking about your horrible experience there. The bad stands out, not the good.

Negative emotions are easier to conjure up because they stand out more. They're foreground, not background. They're malignant, not benign. They're ripe for picking all the time. The brain chooses negative emotions so readily because it takes less effort to activate them than it does positive emotions. (With practice, it becomes just as easy to activate positive emotions. But few people develop the skill to do so.)

DON'T FIGHT YOUR IMPROVEMENT EFFORT

Your personal productivity and overall happiness are inversely correlated to your usage of negative emotions. In other words, when you take measures to reduce your neul, your productivity and happiness rise as a result. And they rise disproportionately; that is, a small reduction in your neul can produce much larger doses of productivity and happiness. And you don't have to wait at all for the results to show. When you stop a negative emotion in its tracks, when you snuff it out as quickly as it appeared, you experience greater happiness and productivity immediately!

Reducing you neul entails retraining your brain. It's not difficult to do, provided you don't fight your own efforts. Let me give you two examples of people who wanted to escape a painful life of negativity yet blocked themselves from doing so.

The Classic Negaholic

For many years, an old friend and business associate overindulged in sadness. Like your typical negaholic, she choose one negative emotion, sadness in this case, and used it with great regularity. (Remember, emotions are like spices on a rack. When you feel or experience an emotion, it is your subconscious that has chosen and activated it. Hence you are "using" the emotion, like you use paprika, cinnamon, or any other spice when you cook.) It seemed all our conversations included her whining about being so depressed, and quite frankly, I was tired of hearing it.

Over lunch one day, before the waitress even took our orders, my friend went into her sadness routine. After hearing a number of her "I'm having a bad day" and "I'm so depressed" statements, I decided to offer a solution. I explained how she herself was subconsciously creating all the negativity she was experiencing, and I began to give her the precise procedures for fixing the problem—when she stopped me in midsentence. "You haven't heard a word I said!" she snapped. "I said I'm having a bad day and I'm feeling depressed. And if I'm depressed, I'm going to be depressed!"

You see, some people want to continue experiencing any number of negative emotions, even though they complain about them. They're the classic negaholics. They overindulge in a negative emotion because they enjoy the sympathy and attention it garners. My gloomy friend wanted to become a happier, more productive person, but she mistakenly believed sadness was a legitimate means achieving that by instigating feelings of sympathy or love.

People who advertise their misery don't realize that the people giving them sympathy or attention really don't want to deal with them but do so out of some sense of obligation. Would you rather receive superficial sympathy by expressing negativity, or real love, respect, and admiration by expressing positivity? If you choose the negative route, you'll remain unproductive and block yourself from improvement.

The "That's Just The Way I Am" Club

Some people don't realize that it's possible to alter their emotions. The thought never occurs to them. Or, if they have given it some thought, they become an emotite believer. They believe their brain is not responsible for the creation of emotions, so therefore emotions cannot be controlled.

I remember one such fellow who overused the fright emotion, especially when it came to standing up in front of people and making a presentation. He was a fairly confident, self-assured guy otherwise, but when speaking before a group of people he'd turn into a scared, bumbling, stumbling goofball. A number of his friends offered many pointers for overcoming the problem, but he'd always brush them aside, saying "that's just the way I am."

This same guy was also going to night school, studying to become a CPA. Evidently he believed he could learn accounting, since he didn't justify his present non-CPA status by saying "that's just the way I am." He wanted to better himself; he wanted to become something he wasn't. And he was taking measures to do it. But he didn't realize that bettering his personality, becoming more adept at handling himself in front of other people, was a learning process just the same.

When someone says he can't change his emotions because "that's just the way I am," he's really saying, "I'm not willing to put forth any effort to better myself." That's-just-the-way-I-am-ers simply find it easier to accept whatever emotions their brain haphazardly creates instead of effortfully managing their emotions.

If, up to this point, you've been a dues-paying member of the "that's-just-the-way-I-am" club, quit. If you've ever learned how to do anything (like drive a car, balance a checkbook, speak English, take a shower, or hail a taxi), you can learn to manage your emotions. The first step in doing so, however, is to discard any tendencies to hold yourself back. You must be ready to improve yourself and willing to expend some effort to do so.

INTERPRET OCCURRENCES AS GOOD FOR YOU

The first step in reducing your usage of negative emotions, and unleashing your productivity in greater proportion, is to get in the habit of interpreting occurrences as good for you. It's much easier to do than you think.

Things happen. Your subconscious instinctively interprets all those things as either good or bad for you and activates your emotions accordingly. But wait. You can consciously interrupt your subconscious' interpretation if you don't like it. You can say to your subconscious, "Hey, you're creating anger (or whatever emotion) because you think this occurrence is bad for me. But I don't think it's bad for me at all. In fact, I believe it's good for me!" Do that once and you squelch the negative emotion quickly. Do that repeatedly, whenever you feel a negative emotion coming, and your subconscious will become deprogrammed—it'll cease producing the negative emotion in relation to that, or a similar, occurrence.

The Great Airport Escape

Here's how I first stumbled upon the power of interpreting occurrences as good for me instead of bad for me. It was January 2, 1983. I was flying from Detroit to Richmond and had a layover in Washington. I had heard that January 2 is traditionally the busiest flying day of the year, and when I got to National Airport in D.C., I believed it.

Baggage was everywhere, and I mean everywhere. Almost the entire floor area in the baggage claim section was strewn with luggage. You couldn't walk without stepping on someone's bag. Many bags had burst open. Shirts, socks, bras, panties, shoes, and who-knows-what decorated the floor. And it kept on coming. As the baggage return continued to spit out piece after piece, people were pulling them off the carousels and tossing them on the floor to allow the next new piece to surface. It was quite a sight.

The mass of confused, angry, frustrated people made the sight even more unbelievable. I saw people pushing, shoving, shouting, swearing, arguing, and crying. There were more negative emotions bouncing around than lost bags, and that was a lot.

It would have been understandable if I had felt some anger, don't you think? Would you have blamed me for saying to myself, "What's going on here? This is deplorable, an outrage! I don't need this headache," and the like? Everyone else, it seemed, was thinking that way, so anger must have been an appropriate response, don't you think?

Well, I didn't get angry at all. Not because I understood how to interpret occurrences as good for me; I didn't know about such a concept back then. But rather because I happen to have strong contrarian instincts that keep me from feeling or acting like everyone else. These instincts kicked in that day and caused me to think, "If this is bad for everyone else, it must be good for me." I have never had a problem believing that when the crowd goes one way, I'm best off going the other way. Believing that this baggage fiasco was good for me was not only easy, it was instinctive. (Had my luggage alone been strewn about, I might have very well experienced some anger. In that case, the lack of crowd anger wouldn't have triggered me to do the opposite.)

I decided to lean against a wall and observe the situation. While everyone else wandered about in mass confusion, displaying every negative emotion under the sun, I consciously repeated to myself, "This is good for me." I noticed that I was not only feeling no anger, I was actually feeling good! I was calm and collected, confident and strong. It even felt good to be feeling good at a time when most people chose to feel the opposite.

Eventually, I decided it was time to try to locate my luggage. After about 45 minutes of tiptoeing around the baggage-covered floor and failing to spot my two bags, I headed for the men's room. It was not easy walking around in there either, because luggage was covering that floor too. But once there, I happened to glance down at the floor near my right, and what did I see? There were my two bags, side by side, not five feet away from me!

With bags in hand, I strode past the grumbling throng toward my connecting flight gate. Unfortunately, the flight didn't wait for me to find my luggage. It departed on schedule, 10 minutes earlier. I went to the ticket window to arrange for another flight, only to find there were no more to Richmond that night on any airline (by now it was nearly 11:00 P.M.). This time, I did begin to feel a little negativity. I don't know if it was sadness, frustration, anger, or what, but I did notice general negativity rapidly replacing my positivity. It was a long day, and I was tired. I really wanted to get home and into bed.

I stopped to think. Rather than worrying or wondering what to do, I decided to first fix my feelings of negativity. Once again, my reason for doing so was not because I knew about lowering my neul back then, but because I simply didn't like feeling bad. I hated those yucky negative emotions! They made me feel lousy, and I was determined to get rid of them. Recalling what did the trick a few minutes earlier, I said to myself, "Missing that plane and finding no other flight is good for me." I didn't have any logical reason it was good for me, but I just decided that it was. Within seconds, I began to feel better. Within 30 seconds, I felt calm and strong again.

Next I made my way to the rental car area. Since Richmond is only a couple hundred miles down I-95 from Washington, D.C., driving home that night was a plausible solution. Plausible, but not probable, it turned out. The rental companies were being mobbed by disgruntled people, all pushing their way toward the counters, trying get one of the few remaining cars. Before I could decide what to do, the rental car employees all chirped something about "closing time" and began to shut down in rapid succession. When the mass of disgusted, angry people finally got the message and left, I walked up to the Avis window, the only one with an employee still in sight.

"I'm sorry sir, we're closed," said the Avis girl. I just stood there, grin and all, not knowing what to say. Asking for a car seemed rather stupid since a dozen people were just turned away and she just told me they were closed. So I asked for a plane instead, which sounded even stupider. "A 727 with AM-FM/cassette, preferably," I muttered. The Avis girl burst out laughing. She continued laughing over the next couple minutes as I relayed the story of my serendipitous men's room rendezvous with my luggage. "You're the first person who's made me laugh all day, and I needed it," she said. Then she added, "We're out of 727s, but I do have a Mustang if that'll do."

That accomplished, I went outside and waited at the Avis bus stop for the shuttle to arrive to take me to the rental car lot. As the bus was pulling up, I suddenly heard someone calling my name. It was the Avis girl, running toward me and waving her arms. When she reached me, she introduced a fellow running directly behind her. "This is Mr. Davis. He needs to get to Richmond too, but I don't have any more cars. I thought perhaps you wouldn't mind giving him a lift," she panted, out of breath from the run. "Be glad to!" I said, bidding him welcome.

Mr. Davis and I had a nice conversation on the road. It turned out he was a marketing VP of a major corporation in Richmond. When he found out I too was in marketing, he asked to stay in touch. Eighteen months later, when I started my own consulting firm, Mr. Davis's company became one of my first clients.

In thinking about the National Airport fiasco, I became convinced that my reluctance to experience negativity, and the subsequent positivity that empowered me, was crucial to (1) finding my luggage, (2) procuring a car, (3) being long gone while everyone else remained stuck in the thick of it all, and (4) landing a lucrative consulting project in the long run. That all happened because I said to myself, "This is good for me." I've since used the technique thousands of times, and all with great results. It never fails. All you have to do is interpret occurrences as good for you instead of bad for you and let your subconscious mind take it from there. You consciously and deliberately say to yourself, "This is good for me," and watch the magic happen.

Not Merely Positive Thinking

Don't mistake the good-for-me interpretation of occurrences as simple "positive thinking." While there's nothing wrong with positive thinking, I've found it's too nebulous a concept for many people to use effectively. As we all know, life has its difficult moments. In the face of a genuinely tough problem, positive thinking can appear to be an unrealistic, candy-coated attitude that reeks of ignorance. Hence, many people simply do not believe in positive thinking enough to make it work for them. (Kirstie Alley to George Wendt in "Cheers": "I tried that positive thinking stuff. I knew it wouldn't work, and sure enough it didn't!")

On the other hand, interpreting occurrences as good for you is a totally truthful, totally believable concept. It's simple logic. Occurrences are good for you because history proves it so. Give most any past occurrence the test of time, and it's quite obvious how and why it was good for you. How many seemingly bad things happened to you over the years that you now look back on and see as actually having been good for you? A good number, if you're honest.

Realization 17

The bad aspect of an occurrence tends to show itself immediately, whereas the good, and most often dominating, aspect tends to appear later.

The good aspect is there all along, albeit somewhat invisible at first. But since you know it's there somewhere, you are quite right in acknowledging it immediately. Regardless of how bad it seems at the time, know that a more powerful good aspect is also there, even if it's invisible at the time.

By saying to yourself "This is good for me" when you encounter a seemingly bad occurrence, you are putting the good forces of the occurrence to work for you immediately. In other words, you actually cause a bad situation to turn around quickly. You'll notice yourself feeling better faster, and the results of your positivity will appear a hundred times sooner than otherwise.

Realization 18

By interpreting occurrences as good for you, you cause the good aspects to surface sooner, and thereby turn seemingly bad occurrences into good experiences.

The Surprise Plan May Be the Better Plan

There's another reason why the interpretation of occurrences as good for you makes total sense. In many instances, a seemingly bad occurrence is actually a better alternative than the one you had in mind. In other words, your plan wasn't so hot to begin with. When things turn out differently than you'd planned, you may actually be in better shape because of it.

Realization 19

A seemingly bad occurrence may actually be a better alternative than what you had in mind.

We tend to experience negative emotions when things don't happen the way we had expected. But could it be what we expected was flawed? Is it possible the surprise occurrence is actually the better one? Darn right. Remember, different is not necessarily bad.

Why experience negative emotions just because something turns out differently than you'd planned? Why are surprises so bad? Why not interpret a surprise occurrence as good for you and then let it show you just how much better it really is? Lighten up. Surprise occurrences add spice to life and are often enriching and rewarding.

A Little Negativity Is Okay

Okay, you're buying my argument. Yet somehow you can't imagine yourself totaling your brand new car, let's say, waking up from a three-week coma, finding yourself mummified in traction, and saying, "Yes! This is good for me! Ha-ha-ha."

I'm not asking you to disavow negative emotions entirely, nor am I asking you to pretend like the bad aspects don't exist and become an emotionless robot. It's okay to react with sadness when you see a picture of a starving kid in Ethiopia. It's okay to feel frustration when you run your computer program for the 27th time and it still doesn't work right. It's just not good to overindulge in negative emotions. Once in a while, okay. Too often, and with too much intensity, no good. Go ahead and emote. Allow yourself some negative emotions. But abide by these two rules:

- **Don't wallow in negativity too long.** An initial allowance of some negativity, in some cases, gets it out of your system. It can allow you to move ahead to a more positive disposition sooner. Feel the negative emotion for 15 seconds or 15 minutes but not for 15 hours, days, or weeks. After an initial, short period of negativity, begin your good-for-me outlook. The sooner you adopt it, the sooner the good aspects will surface.

- **Don't cast your negativity toward the innocent.** Your theatrical outbursts seem totally ridiculous and inappropriate to others. In other words, you look foolish. You can also hurt innocent people and taint your relationships. People don't deserve to be on the receiving end of your negative emotional spears any more than you deserve to suffer theirs.

Interpretation Examples

Remember the occurrences I listed earlier: a co-worker imposes his workload on you, you were passed over for a promotion, your spouse or date is late, and you failed to complete a project on time? I asked you to interpret them on your good-bad scale. If these occurrences happened to me, here's how I would interpret them:

- **Co-worker imposes his workload on me.** Good for me. I can use his request to establish a new understanding between the two of us that can be mutually beneficial. Perhaps there's a way we can work together or help each other. We could learn more about each other's responsibilities and how they're performed. We could fill in for each other when the other is sick or on vacation. There are all kinds of possible arrangements that could benefit us both and the company. The door is open for discussion, and I plan to initiate some in a friendly and calm manner.

- **Passed over for a promotion.** Good for me. One of the key criteria for evaluating people worthy of promotion is to see how they react when they're *not* promoted. Here's my chance to separate myself from the pack, to demonstrate my ability to think like an owner of the company. By displaying understanding of the decision and willingness to support the promotee, I will distinguish myself far above those who would typically complain and pout. Who do you think will have the best chance for the next opening, me or one of the complainers? Things happen when they're ready to happen, and if this promotion passed me by, I can rest assured it was a blessing. Another one— a *better* one—may very well have my name on it.

- **Spouse or date is late.** Good for me. I have the opportunity to reinforce her opinion of me by demonstrating my understanding and gentleness, which is exactly what I would want her to do if the situation were reversed. If her lateness causes us to be late for some event, it'll be a more memorable occasion. Most people appreciate spontaneity and resourcefulness, and I can play off her lateness to create exactly that.

- **Failed to complete a project on time.** While it may be bad that I didn't complete the project on time, I can take care of that—

a delay probably isn't as big a deal as it seems anyway. There are aspects of this occurrence that are good for me. I can take this opportunity to figure out a better way of doing things. I can review this project and find out what went wrong. Did I take on more work than could realistically be done in the allotted time? Did I fail to allow time for possible snags? Did I waste time instead of getting down to business ? I can use this project to learn how to plan and perform better in the future.

In these examples, I've offered logical reasons I believe each is good for me. But when you get in the habit of interpreting more and more occurrences as good for you, you realize that you don't even need logical reasons to do so. The logical reasons occurrences are good for you may not be readily apparent at the time and may not come to light for some time later. But that doesn't matter. By knowing that there is good in most everything, you can confidently interpret occurrences as good for you regardless of the way things seem at the time.

Politicians and related political professionals have got it down pat. They interpret everything that happens under their leadership as not only good for them but good for their constituency as well. After debates, "spin doctors" interpret whatever happened as good for their side, even to the point where you wonder if the two opposing sides were watching the same debate. Now I ask you, are they wrong in doing so? Of course not. Since almost all occurrences are inherently neither good nor bad, one's interpretation becomes the primary source of potency in the occurrence. You can make just about any occurrence either work for you or against you, depending on your good or bad interpretation of it.

Try it. Say "this is good for me" the next time something happens. You will be amazed at how better you feel, how less stressed you feel, and how more productive you become.

CHANGE YOUR INSTALLED COMMANDS

Just because you inadvertently learned to produce anger when another driver cuts you off, or to produce depression when the love of your life fails to call, or to produce disappointment when the boss fails to compliment you, doesn't mean you can't do something about it. Just because you inadvertently caught various installed commands over the years that direct your subconscious to produce negative emotions doesn't mean you can't change the commands.

You can change the commands in your subconscious. You can replace the negative emotion-producing commands with positive emotion-producing commands. Once the old commands are gone and the new ones are in place, your subconscious will automatically react according to the new commands. You'll effortlessly experience a whole new world of tranquility, happiness, and productivity.

You can make any particular occurrence produce any particular emotion. It doesn't even matter if the association between occurrence and emotion makes any logical sense or not.

Joe, a radio time salesman, used to suffer from overuse of the disappointment emotion. When a prospect said "no," he'd feel disappointed. As anyone in sales knows, you're going to run into a lot of nos out there. As a consequence, Joe spent a lot of time disappointed.

But Joe learned how to change the installed command that produced the disappointment. From that point on, whenever a prospect said " no," he would automatically feel confident and smile. It sounds a little weird, a little inappropriate, I know. It doesn't seem logical, after all, to feel increased confidence when someone turns you down. But by installing a no-equals-confident command in his subconscious, Joe did exactly that. And his increased confidence allowed him to eventually turn many of those nos into yeses. Joe developed a reputation of being able to handle "difficult" accounts, quickly rising to be one of the top salespeople in his company. He raised his personal productivity tremendously simply by changing one installed command.

How would you feel if you paid way too much for something? Overpaying usually triggers feelings of sadness, despair, or anger in most people. But some people have reversed their installed commands, and they feel immense joy when they overpay. How so? Consider art auctions. The bidding may elevate the price way above its actual market value, but that doesn't matter to many.

When the bidding is over and the item is sold, attendees all clap in reverence to the "winner," who feels pride and joy despite paying a ridiculous price.

By changing your installed commands, you can cut down on your overindulgence of negative emotions. And it happens effortlessly once your new installed commands are in place. You simply feel less negative emotions.

Changing your installed commands is a two-step procedure. First, you must notice what type of occurrence brings about what emotion. You look for patterns, recurring occurence-equals-emotion relationships. For example, John noticed that whenever his boss asked him a question, he felt defensive. Carol noticed that whenever her husband left his clothes on the bedroom floor, she felt angry. Chris noticed that his brain produced the sadness emotion whenever he sat down at his desk each morning. Sometimes there's no obviously logical reason for some occurrence producing a particular emotion, so don't be concerned with why. Just become aware of your existing installed commands, whatever they may be.

Next, you link in your mind a new emotion to the occurrence. You do this before the actual occurrence happens. In other words, you imagine the occurrence happening and then imagine feeling the new emotion.

John imagined his boss questioning him, and then imagined himself feeling very confident. He said to himself, "When he asks questions, I feel confident!" while simultaneously envisioning himself conversing with his boss and having a confident look on his face. John repeated this statement and vision many times, over many days and weeks.

Carol imagined walking into the bedroom and finding her husband's clothes on the floor, then feeling laughter. She said to herself, "Frank's clothes on the floor look awfully funny." She helped herself see the humor by envisioning the clothes as miniature Franks, all huddled helplessly together, peering up at her like lost puppies. Carol repeated the statement and vision many times over, always being sure to feel the laughter emotion (which you can feel without actually laughing out loud).

Chris imagined himself entering his office and sitting at his desk in the morning and feeling invigorated. He said to himself, "When each new day at work begins, I feel invigorated and excited." He envisioned himself looking energetic and happy. Chris repeated his office-equals-vigor command many times a day for many days.

Linking new, positive emotions to occurrences is not a means of accepting whatever happens to you. By changing her installed commands from clothes-on-floor equals anger to clothes-on-floor equals laughter, Carol was not saying her husband's action was acceptable behavior. She was not giving up her desire for Frank to hang up his clothes. On the contrary, she was empowering herself to effect the change in Frank's behavior she desired. In her previous angry state, she only induced anger in Frank, which exacerbated the situation. But in her new, empowering state of lightheartedness, she was able to charm Frank into compliance. Within a matter of days, Frank's clothes-dropping behavior was reduced to an occasional sock here or there.

By changing his installed command from office equals depression to office equals vigor, Chris was not creating some kind of unrealistic fantasy world for himself. He was creating a very real, exciting environment by empowering himself to effect the changes needed to make it so. As his new installed command took hold, Chris found himself actually creating fun and excitement without even having to think about it, which is highly contagious in work settings, as you may have noticed. His co-workers soon caught the fun bug, and within a short time the whole office environment had changed.

By using positive emotions instead of negative emotions, you are better able to effect change in people and in situations. With positive emotions, you're able to inspire and motivate others. With positive emotions dominating your mental self, you will get much more cooperation than otherwise, and your personal productivity will rise significantly.

STEPS FOR REDUCING YOUR NEGATIVE EMOTION USAGE LEVEL

- **Step 1: Interpret occurrences as good for you.** When something seemingly bad happens, say to yourself "this is good for me." In some cases, you may allow yourself to use a negative emotion initially. Just be sure it runs its course quickly. Get into the this-is-good-for-me mode as soon as possible. Remember, occurrences really are good for you in some way, so immediately acknowledging the goodness makes total sense. It also makes the good aspect come to the surface much sooner. In addition, it could very well be that a different occurrence than what you'd planned is the better alternative. When you interpret occurrences as good for you, you can exploit them to great advantage.

- **Step 2: Become aware of your existing installed commands.** When you feel a negative emotion, notice what event or occurrence triggered it. If you have a recurring pattern of occurrence equals emotion, take note. Understand that many of the negative emotions you feel are triggered by installed commands that inadvertently snuck into your subconscious. They are changeable.

- **Step 3: Link a new, positive emotion to an occurrence.** Imagine an occurrence happening, and imagine feeling some new, positive emotion instead of the old, negative emotion. Induce the new emotion in yourself. Feel it, and see yourself expressing the new emotion outwardly through body and facial form, standing up straight or smiling, for example. Repeat this mental exercise five times in a row. Tomorrow, do another five repetitions. And five the next day. Then do your five reps three times a week for six weeks. And twice a month for the rest of your life.

- **Step 4: Verbalize your new installed command.** Link the occurrence and the new, positive emotion with a statement of command. For example: "When Ed teases me, I feel confident and relaxed," or "When the boss starts yelling, I feel calm and secure."

- **Step 5: When the actual occurrence happens, consciously feel the new emotion.** Consciously instructing yourself to feel the new emotion is part of what it takes to install this new command in your subconscious. When the actual occurrence happens, you may, for example, want to say to yourself, "I'm feeling confident now . . . confident." When the day comes that you automatically feel the new, positive emotion without having to consciously reinforce it, you know the new command has been successfully installed.

Chapter Five

Ending Action Avoidance

T o be highly productive, you must take action. Consistently. Yet there are probably a number of specific actions you could be taking, actions that would contribute greatly to your productivity, that you are not taking.

You may not be aware of your *action avoidance,* which is productivity barrier number four. You may be working hard, believing you are taking action, when in reality you're subconsciously avoiding taking the real action that produces results. Or you may be quite aware of your inaction, be displeased with yourself, but lack the understanding as to why you're that way. You may not know how to get yourself into action.

There are six main causes of action avoidance, and we'll explore them all in this chapter. If you execute the steps at the end of the chapter, you'll notice yourself taking real action on a regular basis, and your productivity will automatically rise as a result.

WHAT DOES "TAKING ACTION" REALLY MEAN?

People talk about "taking action" all the time, but few people actually stop to think what the term "taking action" really means. They assume it's clear-cut, self-explanatory. Action is action, plain and simple, requiring no further discussion, they believe.

But beware. The kind of action it takes to affect your productivity, to accomplish what you want each day, week, month, and year, may not be obvious at all. You may not be taking action because you may not know what "taking action" really means.

Or, the kind of action you are taking now may not be the kind necessary to boost your productivity and produce positive results.

I spent years working long and hard. I was acting, and I stayed busy. Yet I was getting nowhere. In fact, the harder I worked, the slower I got to nowhere. The only thing going fast was the years. I was getting older by the day, yet my accomplishments were few. I was on the proverbial treadmill, expending a lot of energy but standing still nonetheless. It was obvious something wasn't right, but I didn't know what. So I kept on working hard, and kept on accomplishing little.

One day, after a particularly long period of hard work and no significant accomplishment, I got up and left the office. It was a Thursday, and I told my secretary I wasn't coming back until Monday. I drove down to Virginia Beach, a two-hour drive from my hometown of Richmond, and spent the next two days lying on the sand and walking along the boardwalk. I was alone and deep in thought practically the whole time.

I recalled all of the motivational material I've studied over the years and found myself coming back to one particular point: the importance of taking action. All superproductive, supersuccessful people take a lot of action, so it's undoubtedly a key factor. Yet of all the motivational stuff that stresses the importance of "taking action," none of it bothers to explain exactly what that means. "What exactly am I supposed to do to take action?" I wondered. "I'm already working hard, which doesn't seem to be producing results, so perhaps the actions I'm taking are not the right ones."

I determined that if I could identify the *kind* of actions that produce positive results for others, I too might be able to produce positive results. By taking the right kind of actions, I hoped to increase my productivity to the point where all of my hard work turned into accomplishment and reward. I wanted to know what specific actions were necessary to do just that.

That Virginia Beach retreat turned out to be time well spent, as I ended up discovering what actually constitutes "taking action." I concluded that "taking action" is actually composed of three distinct types of activity. It takes all three components, or subactivities, to constitute real action. Eliminate any of the three, and you're not taking the kind of actions that increases your productivity, despite how hard and long you work.

Action Component 1: Talking to People

Your success, no matter what the area of endeavor or how it's measured, involves other people. Do you want to make a lot of money? Where's all that money going to come from? Other people. Want recognition? Where does that come from? Other people. Want to fall in love, get married, and raise a family? You can't do it alone. It takes other people to make it happen. Don't care about money, recognition, marriage, or raising a family? Want nothing for yourself but a life of total, unselfish giving à la Mother Teresa? Who do you give to? Other people. All roads lead back to other people as your ultimate partners in accomplishment.

Realization 20

To be highly productive, you need the cooperation, assistance, and recognition of other people.

Sure, there are some simple tasks you can accomplish without other people. You could write your report this afternoon or get the house cleaned today. Your productivity in those areas doesn't depend on others—or does it? You may depend on others to handle some other tasks so you can devote your time to writing the report. And you may need others to get out of the house for a few hours so you can clean it. Although you may not need the assistance of another with a particular task, you may very well need their cooperation.

You could move to some remote island, become a lighthouse keeper, and spend the rest of your life turning out the most artistic oil paintings known to man. You could be highly productive all by yourself. And you might become famous the world over. Your paintings might sell for millions of dollars apiece. You may be admired by many and considered a great success by most. And you did it all by yourself.

Of course, all the recognition, admiration, and fame would come one or two hundred years after your death. Since you spent your life in isolation, failing to interact with others to any appreciable degree, your accomplishments would likely go unnoticed or unappreciated. As George Bernard Shaw put it, "Talent is of no value unless recognized by others." What good does it do you or anyone else if your productivity is a secret? None.

Thomas Edison spent a lot of time working by himself, and he was a pillar of productivity. But his very first invention was a vote recorder that no one wanted. It worked fine, but since no one wanted it, he considered it unsuccessful. After that experience, he said he would never again invent something that no one wanted. In other words, his success as an inventor depended largely on other people—what they wanted and what they would buy.

To accomplish, you must interact with others. And the way you do that couldn't be simpler. You *talk to people*. In fact, the more people you talk to, the more you can accomplish.

How do highly productive people get so much done? You can trace it all back to the words that come out of their mouths. How, for example, did Ted Turner create Turner Broadcasting, a billion-dollar cable empire (WTBS, CNN, TNT), from nothing? Each move he made involved talking to people. His initial idea of putting WTBS, an Atlanta UHF television station, on satellite required him to pick up the phone and arrange to do so. In other words, he talked to people. Then, he had to convince cable systems to carry his new "superstation." Again, he talked to people. Then he had to borrow the money to launch CNN, hire a staff, and communicate to it what he wanted done. Each and every action goes back to the words that came out of his mouth.

How does a politician convince people to vote for him or her? By the words that come out of his mouth. How does a doctor explain what's wrong and deliver her advice? By the words that come out of her mouth. How does a tennis player make it to the U.S. Open? Wait a minute, you say. A tennis player gets there by playing tennis, not by talking. The game doesn't require words. In fact, some players like John McEnroe get themselves into trouble by talking, when shutting up might be the better alternative. True enough. But how does the player get into the tournament in the first place? Yes, that too is based on his play, but it also involves talking to the tournament officials, making his intentions known, and negotiating his entry. Okay, maybe the player's manager did that. But how did the player go about hiring his manager? And how does the player communicate with his coach? And how did the player arrange to get a coach in the first place? Without constantly talking to people, a potentially great tennis player might never get past the neighborhood court.

It's not the amount of words that come out of your mouth, or even the eloquence of your speech that's important, though the latter can have an effect. The better able you are to express yourself in conversation, the more profound effect your words can have. But even if you've got only a fifth grade vocabulary, you can still be very effective. Quantity is more important than eloquence, in this case. The real secret is talking to a number of people on a regular basis. The more people you talk to, the better. I'm not saying it's strictly the words you speak that will make you more productive. Other things besides talking are involved (as you will soon see), but those words and the number of people who hear them are an extremely important first step.

Talking to people was the missing component of action in my case. Ironically, I've always talked for a living. As a former disc jockey and newscaster, and a present day professional speaker and consultant, talking has always been a large part of my job. With speaking engagements and seminars, talking *is* the job. But because talking was my profession, I avoided talking in almost any circumstance other than when I was performing some professional service. I used to hate talking on the phone, for example. I'd avoid taking phone calls, and I'd return messages weeks or even months later. People would think I was either arrogant or mad at them. But the truth was, I simply hated talking on the phone and avoided it as much as possible.

As I was lying on the beach that week thinking about all this, I remembered an article or two I'd read about David Geffen, the record mogul. David turned nothing into a billion-dollar fortune over 20 years by discovering and signing such performers as Joni Mitchell, Jackson Browne, The Eagles, and Guns N' Roses. (He actually cashed in by adeptly selling his record label to MCA, then acquiring a large chunk of stock in Matsushita when that company bought the former.) David's obviously a productive guy, and he reportedly lives on the phone. One executive says that if he gets a call from David Geffen at 6:30 in the morning, he knows he's been the 10th person David's called so far that day.

What in the world does David talk about to all these people? "Hi. I know it's 6:15 in the morning, but my name is David Geffen, and I'm calling to find out what the weather's like on your end of the city. Cloudy there too, huh? Okay, go back to sleep—talk to you later." I couldn't imagine spending hour upon hour on the phone for even one day, yet alone day after day. But in looking at David and other highly productive people who seem to spend a lot of time phonejamming, I did conclude one thing: it must work. And the reason it works is because talking to people is one of the key components of action.

Once I realized that talking to people was one of the essential ingredients of taking action, I reversed my phone aversion. I began answering my own phone whenever possible, returning phone calls as soon as possible, and placing phone calls to people regularly. Whereas I used to spend no more than five minutes a day on the phone, if that, I began spending a minimum of one hour, talking to a minimum of five people a day. It's not exactly David Geffen's pace, but its a considerable improvement from my previous phone aversion.

Shortly after adopting my new phone strategy, guess what happened? Business began picking up. I began getting featured in more publications. Demand for my seminars rose. My phone began ringing a lot more than it used to. Now, by talking to more people as part of the action I was taking, results were showing up in ever-increasing magnitude. All that hard work was starting to pay off in accomplishment, recognition, and revenue.

All right, I *do* know what in the world David Geffen and others talk about. At least I know the two main categories of conversation, which are:

1. **Information gathering.** Say you're thinking of approaching a prospective customer about buying your company's services, or taking piano lessons, or having your house painted, or switching jobs. You must talk to people to acquire decision-making infor-

mation. You ask people inside and outside of your firm about the prospect's buying habits and criteria. You inquire what the piano lessons cost, and when they're held. You ask friends and neighbors what painting firm they might recommend, then you call a few firms and ask for quotes. You put the word out that you're "looking," and sniff out possible openings in other firms. And you do all this information gathering by talking to people.

2. **Influence or inspire.** You talk to people to influence them, to inspire them to act in some desirable manner. Remember, it's very difficult if not impossible to be productive, except with the simplest of tasks, all by yourself. You need the attention and cooperation of others. By influencing them, inspiring them, convincing them, your productivity rises exponentially as they respond.

Action Component 2: Committing Yourself

We've all known people who talk and talk and talk but never really accomplish anything. They're the "all talk and no action" contingent of the population. They'll talk your ear off, tell you all the great things they've done in the past (questionable, of course) and all the great things they're going to do (even more doubtful), but they never seem to be doing anything at the present time. Talking to people is important, but if talk is all you do, you're not taking action.

To really take action, you must *commit yourself.* You've got an idea that will make your department operate more efficiently, and you commit yourself to implementing it. You call a department meeting, explain your new idea, and get it up and running. You've been thinking of taking piano lessons, you've gathered the necessary information—now it's time to commit to doing it. It's time to sign up, to say "Yes, I'm in" and pay your tuition. You've checked into a number of housepainters and found one you like. Now it's time to commit, to give them the go-ahead and pay them accordingly. Your supervisor asks for a volunteer to head a new project, and you say "I will do it."

Committing to something means you bind or obligate yourself. Does that scare you? It shouldn't. There's nothing scary about putting yourself into an earning position. You were born to be productive in some area, perhaps in many areas, of endeavor. Your rewards, including recognition, admiration, companionship, love, advancements, money, and more, are awaiting. By committing yourself, you're simply stepping forward when your name is called. You're preparing to show what you can do and to collect your just rewards.

Commit to something, however small, every day. Each day, designate one thing on your to-do list a must accomplishment. Commit to it in the morning, and make sure you do it that day. Get in the habit of committing yourself, and you'll actually begin enjoying it. Before long, you'll be committing to bigger and bigger endeavors, accomplishing much more every day.

Action Component 3: Physical Movement

Talking to people gets you a third of the way there. Committing yourself gets you two thirds of the way there. The final third of the way is *physical movement*. Physical movement includes moving your arms, hands, or fingers. It includes moving your legs or feet. It includes moving your entire body from one location to another, such as when you travel to another city. Physical movement is any one or all of the above.

You're chuckling, and not without reason. It seems obvious that taking action involves physical movement. But here's the real laugh getter: Most people who think they're taking action habitually fail to follow through with some form of physical movement. They either don't understand that physical movement is a necessary part of taking action, or they refuse to admit it's up to them to engage in it.

I had a college roommate once who would lie on the couch all day long and watch television. He knew enough people, talked on the phone quite often, and had friends over almost every day. Talking to people was not a problem. Committing himself wasn't a problem either. I heard him committing himself time and time again to this or that endeavor. On one particular occasion he said to someone on the other end of the phone he'd ''be there tomorrow at three o'clock sharp.'' Guess where he was at three o'clock the next day? Where he was every day at three, lying in front of the television set.

Lazy people aren't the only ones who fall short when it comes to physical movement. I've known many ambitious people in the upper ranks of management who move no parts of their bodies except to put cigarette, drink, or food into their mouths. They put in eight hours a day, but fail to move the parts of their bodies that might make them more productive. The cleverest of them can create the illusion of productivity by attaching themselves to the wagon and riding others' productivity, but they themselves really don't accomplish much of anything.

After my first book, *Creating Demand,* came out, I noticed an interesting pattern of reaction from many people. It would seem that just about everyone is writing a book. At least they say they are. Most, of course, never really commit to such an undertaking, they're just the talkers. But I've known a few others who do commit to writing a book—they've got the semblance of a manuscript in progress—but fail to put in the keyboard time, which involves the physical movement of their arms, hands, and fingers, to complete the project. I have to admit there are more enjoyable things I could do with my time than sit at the computer for six hours a day punching the keyboard. But if my fingers weren't pushing the buttons now, these words wouldn't be here for you to read now. It all boils down to some form of physical movement.

Politicians have an image of nonaction, but when you look closely, you see that most really do take a good amount of action. They talk, of course. And they do often commit themselves to various proposals. Also, they physically move by traveling and by mingling with their constituency at meetings and social events in the streets and neighborhoods. In presidential election years, it's amazing how much physical movement the candidates engage in. They travel to numerous cities each day, day after day. They walk through the crowds. They shake a million hands a week it seems. No wonder these people rise to prominence.

Think of your job. Think of what it takes to be highly productive. Doesn't it involve some form of physical movement? Even if you have a desk job, you must move your arms, hands, and fingers to get the work done. Now think how easy it is to avoid that specific movement. The less you move your arms, hands, or fingers, the less you accomplish. It all boils down to physical movement.

Are you putting in the physical movement necessary to really take action? Think about a particular task or endeavor you want to accomplish, and think about what physical movements are required. Will you have to move your body, travel perhaps? Or move your legs, arms, hands, or fingers?

Realize that it's you who has to do this physical movement, not others. Even if you're in a managerial position, coaching others who do the more physical work, you still have to move yourself. Coaches move almost as much as the players, albeit off the field of play. The top CEOs in the nation aren't just sitting in their chair barking orders all day. They walk around the building and travel to their clients' and suppliers' locations. The late Sam Walton spent the majority of his time traveling to his Wal-Mart stores all over the country and walking through them when he got there. "Taking action" always boils down to some form of physical movement on your part.

Your Action Checklist

Whenever you aspire to take action to accomplish something, think of the three components of action: talking to people, committing yourself, and physical movement. Talk, commit, move. Talk commit, move. Talk, commit, move. Going through this action checklist will make it abundantly clear what you must do.

Each of these component activities, talking, committing, and moving, may not have a distinct end. You may, for example, continue talking after you've committed and begun moving. You may need to move indefinitely and continually reaffirm your commitment. Depending on your objective or the task at hand, you may engage in all three component actions simultaneously.

Incidentally, the three components of action do not come in any particular order, although the sequence that they were presented above—talk, commit, move—is the most common. You could, however, commit to something first, then physically move to gather information, then talk to people to execute the action. The sequence doesn't matter. What does matter is that all three component activities, talking to people, committing yourself, and physically moving, are present.

BREEZE PAST INDECISION

Another reason you may be avoiding taking action is that you're caught in a state of indecision. Have you ever noticed that a lot of time goes by between the point at which you determine you must take some kind of action and the point when you decide what actions to take? It's as though there's a mental Indecision Zone that you travel through. While you're in this Indecision Zone, time is moving but action is not. After all, you can't take action before you've decided what action to take.

The Indecision Zone—that period of time between wanting to take action and deciding what actions to take—inhibits action. While in the Indecision Zone, your productivity can grind to a virtual halt.

Realization 21

All action takes place after a decision. To take more action, make more frequent decisions.

Your objective is to spend as little time in the Indecision Zone as possible. Don't wander aimlessly through it, circling about like a forlorn cat. Enter the Indecision Zone and exit the Indecision Zone. In other words, pick up the pace at which you make decisions.

Here are two suggestions to spring you from the Indecision Zone:

1. Make decisions with limited information. Acknowledge there's no such thing as total certainty. Gather some information, then make assumptions and decisions based on those assumptions. It's better to be taking action with limited information than twiddling your thumbs in the Indecision Zone awaiting certainty.

A sign of weak decision makers is that they spend an inordinate amount of time gathering information, researching to death. They fail to realize that more and more information offers less and less incremental value—it's the old point of diminishing returns. With too much information, the pros and cons even out. On the one hand, I should do this; but on the other hand,

I should do that. Information is a great balancing rod, making things weigh out evenly. The more information you collect, the farther away from a decision you can go.

There's an old saying: "A person who wears one watch always knows what time it is. A person who wears two watches never knows what time it is." Collect too much information and you create greater confusion, greater doubt, which keeps you wallowing in the Indecision Zone, while opportunity windows are constantly passing you by.

Highly productive people gather some decision-making information. They rarely operate from a position of ignorance. But they know when to stop collecting information and when to start acting. There's a time to gather information and a time to act. If you keep gathering information, you'll suffer "paralysis through analysis" and avoid taking action.

2. **Reduce your options.** You remain in the Indecision Zone because too many options make your decision harder to make.

Back in high school, I worked summers at my father's printing company in Detroit. One day I waited on a customer who wanted to order some business cards but didn't have any idea what design he wanted. I whipped out a few sample cards, and when the customer couldn't decide, I brought out more samples. He kept hemming and hawing, so I kept bringing out more and more samples. Eventually, after an hour of looking and wavering, the customer said he'd come back later when he had a better idea of what he wanted. After the customer left, my dad pulled me aside and gave me some very useful advise. "You gave him too many choices. The fewer choices you give them, the quicker they'll make up their minds."

I had figured the opposite. I thought that if I kept showing the customer more alternatives, eventually he'd see one he liked and he'd make the decision to buy. But as I discovered, when you have too many alternatives, you may end up not liking any and never making the decision, or you keep questioning your decision once you make it. My father's advise made sense, and I couldn't wait to try it out.

It wasn't long before someone else inquired about business cards, and I said "Let me show you what we can do," displaying only six design samples. Then as we talked, I began *eliminating* some of the six, eventually narrowing it down to one design, which the customer bought. It took him only five minutes to make the decision. I've used the elimination-of-options strategy throughout my life. It's actually fun, like shooting down ducks at the arcade. Knock those options down in rapid succession, and the last one remaining is your course of action. Weak decision makers are forever trying to hold their options open. They are afraid to eliminate any options because they see that as weakening their position. They fail to realize that too many options are actually a heavy sedative. As a result, they spend their valuable time in the Indecision Zone, debating alternatives instead of moving ahead.

The next time you find yourself wandering aimlessly in the Indecision Zone, start eliminating options. You'll find it surprisingly easier to eliminate options than to choose one among many. Keep eliminating until you have but one option left. At that point, your decision has been made.

SELF-CONSCIOUSNESS MAY INHIBIT YOUR ACTIONS

Another reason you may be hesitant to take action is you're too self-conscious. You think a particular action may make you "look bad" or taint your image. It might invite criticism or laughter.

A couple years ago, I attended the birthday party for a little girl who was turning eight. The gathering took place at a miniature golf course. The birthday girl and a dozen of her friends were to play a round of golf, then go into the clubhouse for some birthday cake.

Watching these eight-year-olds knock the golf ball around with clubs as tall as they was quite amusing. I was paying particular attention to the birthday girl, who was taking about 20 or 30 strokes to get the ball in each hole (or it could have been one continuous stroke, since she discovered she could guide the ball in by pushing it with the club).

As the kids finished the last hole, they congregated in the clubhouse and anxiously awaited the cake. All except the birthday girl.

We found her sitting on one of the picnic tables outside with her head on the table wrapped in her arms. Her mother leaned down and asked her what was wrong. At first she didn't answer; she was too busy pouting to talk. A few seconds later, however, she indicated that she felt shameful because she "did so bad" on the course.

Let's pause the story for a moment. Did it really matter how well the birthday girl, or any of the kids, performed on the course? Was she, in your estimation, justified in feeling shameful? As an adult observer, you know that her golf performance mattered not one iota. You can also see that she really had no reason to feel shameful. This was her birthday party, she was suppose to be feeling joy, having fun. Yet to her, the feelings of disappointment and shame were very real that afternoon. To her, "looking good" in the eyes of her peers was very important.

Her mother leaned down and said, "Honey, it doesn't matter how you did. Your friends weren't paying attention to you anyway. They were only paying attention to themselves." After three seconds of silence, as the girl evaluated her mother's words, she popped up her head and smiled. She realized what her mother said was true. The others were simply not paying attention to her or evaluating her performance. She ran into the clubhouse excited about the cake and presents she was to open.

Realization 22

Other people aren't concerned with how you look,
they're too consumed with how they themselves look.

The truth is, other people aren't assessing you or your performance nearly to the fine degree you are assessing yourself or your performance. They're too preoccupied assessing themselves. People are subconsciously influenced by your attitudes, words, and actions, but they're not consciously judging you all the time. Ninety-nine percent of the people who see you aren't paying much conscious attention to you at all. Only a few key people—perhaps your spouse, parents, or boss—out of hundreds, thousands, or millions are scrutinizing you. And many times they're concerned with how you look because they think your performance reflects on them; you affect how they look.

You could dress in some crazy way and walk though the shopping mall, attracting attention, looks, and comments. People might talk about that "nut with the banana on her head," but no one would know it's you. Even if you bumped into someone who recognized you, so what? I know a woman who did exactly that. She said it felt incredibly liberating to do something a little looney without being concerned with what people thought. She even told some of her friends like me that she did it. Did we think less of her? On the contrary, I admire her independence of thought.

Few people cross over the hump and take action regardless of what other people think. You must become one of them, however. You've got to stop thinking about what others are thinking. Realize that the majority of others couldn't care less how you look; they're preoccupied with their own image. Use their indifference to your advantage. Take the actions you want to take, and let the image cards fall where they may.

Mistakes Quickly Dissipate

You hesitate to take action because you think you might make a mistake and be chastised for it. That could happen. But in time, and usually rather quickly, people forget either the mistake itself or that it was you who made it.

Realization 23

Most mistakes are quickly forgotten.

Back when I was a freshman in college, I made the mistake of sleeping through a final exam (why they scheduled those things

at the ungodly hour of 7:30 in the morning was incomprehensible).
I had no choice but to call the instructor, tell him what happened,
and hope he'd let me make up the exam. When he came to the
phone, I confessed that I had slept through the exam. After pausing
for a second, he said he would let it slide if I would come to his
office now and take it. As he graded the other exams, I sat in the
corner, alone, taking the exam.

The next term, I had another class with the same instructor. Sure
enough, the blasted final was at 7:30 A.M., and sure enough I slept
through it. "I got away with it the first time," I thought, lumbering
out of bed around 10 A.M. "But he's not going to let me off the
hook a second time."

Concluding that honesty is always best (after concluding he'd
never buy any of the harebrained excuses I was dreaming up), I
decided to call him once again and face the consequences, whatever they might me. The worst thing that could happen is I'd fail
the course. Not good, but not the end of the world either.

"I slept through the exam this morning," I said in a quivering
voice, fully expecting the worst. Then he said, "Oh, don't worry
about it. I had a student who did the same thing last term." There
I was 15 minutes later, sitting alone in his office taking the exam
and trying to look as different as I could from the last time.

We believe that if we make a mistake, history will forever flash our
name in searing, unforgiving light. We think we'll be forever ruined.
In reality, people forget much sooner than we give them credit for.
I'll bet you don't know who Edward J. Smith was. He made a rather
severe mistake once, yet no one remembers it was he who made it.
As Captain Smith sat on the bridge of the spanking-new ocean liner
Titanic, he was informed about dangerous icebergs ahead. Captain
Smith made the decision to plow through, and it was a bad one. But
history has long forgotten it was he who made it.

It's Your Average Success That Counts, Not Your Failures

Most of the time, no single item makes much of an impact on
people. It's the total amalgamation of your whole being or performance, over time, that makes an impact, not any one element like
your dress one day or an opinion you express the next.

Realization 24

You are judged on your average performance, not on any one
failure or any one triumph.

Except for the once-in-a-lifetime, extraordinarily tremendous or extraordinarily horrendous act you might commit, you are judged by your average performance. Think about it. At work, you are judged by the level of your average performance day after day, over the course of months or years. In relationships, you can't possibly judge your spouse, child, or whoever by any one single thing they do or say or by their appearance one day. It's the total person, averaged over time, who is judged.

The idea is to get your success rate up, to be productive on average. Don't be overly concerned with each and every little move you make, word you say, or mistake that results. To increase your success average, you must be willing to take a lot of actions, knowing full well many of them might not result in accomplishment. In other words, you might experience a little failure along the way. My guess is you would be willing to try lots of things that might not work out, to endure some mistakes, if you knew people weren't judging your every move. Guess what? They're not. They formulate opinions about you and evaluate your performance over time, averaging out all that you represent to them in their mind.

Realization 25

Your failures don't count. Only your successes count.

To accomplish more, and therefore raise your batting average, you must be willing to take lots of actions, knowing full well many won't work out. It's all a numbers game after all. As every successful salesperson knows, try 10 times, you succeed once; try 100 times, you succeed 10 times. What you may not realize is that all of life is a numbers game stacked heavily in your favor because your so-called failures don't count. "But if I fail 9 times out of 10, won't that bring down my average?" you ask. No. Your failures don't count. Remember, people aren't paying attention to your failures. They don't remember them, or they don't remember that you had anything to do with them.

Bruce Willis came to prominence as the male lead in the mid-80s television show "Moonlighting" and went on to become a major movie star. Yet in 1991, Bruce starred in one of Hollywood's biggest bombs, a movie called *Hudson Hawk*. The same thing happened to Julia Roberts. After starring in the blockbuster movie *Pretty Woman* in 1990, Julia reached superstar status, becoming Hollywood's most sought-after leading lady. Then in 1991, she starred in a movie called *Dying Young*, which went nowhere. And a few years earlier Dustin Hoffman and Warren Beatty starred in the mega-bomb *Ishtar*. Did any of these failures ruin the careers of Bruce, Julia, Dustin, or Warren? Not in the least. Each of these people is still a highly respected superstar, because they are highly successful on average. I repeat: Your failures don't count.

There is an exception. Your failures or mistakes do count if that's all you do. If a baseball player struck out all the time, he wouldn't last long. What makes your failures or mistakes inconsequential is your successes. As long as you're doing some good or great things periodically, you're negating the effects of your mistakes.

Action Outweighs Embarrassment

Let's say a baseball player makes a fielding error that results in a score for the opposing team. Okay, he looks bad for the moment. But he's still out there, still playing the game, still making an astronomical salary, still an admired celebrity. At the end of the year he's honored for his accomplishments not banished for his mistakes.

Is the baseball player embarrassed when a grounder dribbles right through his legs? Of course. What does the president feel when he says something slightly in error and it gets replayed umpteen times back on every newscast across the country? And when the stand-up comedians get ahold of it? Don't you think he feels tinges of embarrassment or humiliation from time to time? A little embarrassment and humiliation comes with the territory for those who consistently take action. Athletes or politicians make mistakes, in front of thousands, millions, tens of millions of people. But they're still there, day after day, in front of the world, taking action and experiencing a little embarrassment along the way.

Realization 26

If you're not feeling tinges of embarrassment or humiliation from time to time, you're not taking enough action.

What about you? Are you taking action and putting yourself in position to feel some embarrassment, or are you doing whatever you can to avoid anything that might lead to a little embarrassment? In many cases, it takes more effort to avoid an action than it does to take it. Put another way, you may be working hard yet holding yourself back by subconsciously avoiding taking key actions that might lead to embarrassment or humiliation.

I was recently addressing a group when a rather embarrassing thing happened. I was supposed to make a particular point about parents feeding their children, but somehow the words came out differently. Instead of saying parents must *feed* their children, I said parents must *eat* their children. The crowd burst out laughing, and I was a little embarrassed, to say the least. But I quickly recovered and went on without missing a beat. My talk went over big, and no one ever mentioned my error. In fact, I never let it bother me. I know from experience that taking action, accomplishing, and getting rewarded far outweighs a little embarrassment or humiliation.

YOU ARE DISCOURAGED BY THOSE IN AUTHORITY

You may avoid taking action, or stop taking action, when someone tells you your actions are useless or ridiculous. Or someone in authority may deny you the opportunity to take a particular action. Unfortunately, a lot of people give up taking action because someone presumably "in authority" discouraged them. The sad thing is they were listening to people who didn't know what they were talking about.

Realization 27

People in positions of authority who deny you don't know what they're talking about.

You know you've reached a milestone of maturity when you realize that people in authority are wrong half the time. There is nothing more fallible in the world than human judgment. Even animals get it right more often. But humans can think, and they can think wrong. Humans can reason, and they reason incorrectly. Humans exercise judgment, and they misjudge things more often than not.

When Janet Jackson decided to pursue a recording career, she first went to the record company her brother Michael recorded for, CBS Records (now Sony Records). CBS rejected her, as did a bunch of other companies. But A&M saw her potential and gave her a contract. The rest is history. After her *Control* album sold over five million copies and her *Rhythm Nation 1814* album over six million, lifting Janet to superstar status, a writer for an industry trade publication asked an executive at CBS Records why they rejected her a few years earlier. "We were schmucks," he answered. (Janet has since signed a $35 million, three-album deal with Virgin Records.)

Mariah Carey's debut album sold over six million copies, making her a so-called overnight success. In June 1992, when her single "I'll Be There" reached the top of the charts, she surpassed even The Beatles by setting the record for the number of consecutive number one songs in a row ("I'll Be There" was her eighth). Yet little more than a year earlier, after sending her audition tape to virtually every record company in existence, all she got was rejected. One day at a Hollywood party, she was introduced to

Tommy Mottola, president of what was then CBS Records, and handed him her tape. Tommy played it on his way home, heard that incredible voice, and immediately went back to the party to find her. This time the CBS people were the geniuses, and all those other record company people were the schmucks.

My favorite story of people in authority not knowing what they're talking about involves film star Arnold Schwarzenegger. In 1977, after having been in the United States for only seven years, Arnold decided winning bodybuilding contests and dabbling in movies and television wasn't enough. He wanted to be a full-fledged movie star. And he made his intentions known publicly, saying "I am confident I will be the best actor around."[1]

Arnold put together a plan to become a movie star. He took acting lessons, voice lessons, and even accent removal lessons. Then, as he recalled years later, "I ran into incredible resistance." It seemed no agent would even take him on as a client. Most laughed him right out of their offices. Finally, one agent at least talked to him and offered him a piece of advice. If Arnold wanted any chance at all of ever landing a role, which was doubtful at best, he'd at least have to change his name. No one, after all, could possibly make it in the movies with a goofy name like Arnold Schwarzenegger, the agent said.

But Arnold didn't believe that this agent, or all the others who wouldn't even talk to him, were right. Despite that all these agents had years of experience in the business and he had little, Arnold believed they were wrong and he was right. He believed he could become a movie star despite what the authorities said.

Of course, we all know that Arnold went on to become a major movie star, and he didn't even have to change his name. But let's go back to the days when he was rejected by all those agents and answer this question: Were the agents correct when they told him he had almost no chance of making it in the movie business? Consider the facts. Arnold had virtually no acting experience. He was unknown except in bodybuilding circles. He had a heavy accent, and he did have a goofy-sounding name. Were the agents correct when they assessed his chances as slim to none and told him so?

---

[1]A&E's "Naked Hollywood" series, 1991.

Here's the answer, and it's important: The agents may have assessed his chances accurately; they may have been "correct" to tell him he had almost no chance. But their assessment, as "correct" as it may have seemed at the time, was actually wrong. Why? Because they were only assessing Arnold's chances based on the current facts, what existed at the time. They failed to assess his chances based on what can be in the future, what he might become. Put another way, they lacked vision. They couldn't see Arnold *developing into* a major movie star. Only Arnold could envision himself doing so.

Realization 28

Even when people in authority are "correct" in denying you, they are wrong. They are basing their assessments on what is today, not on what can be tomorrow.

When someone in authority discourages you, when they tell you it can't be done, or you're not the person to do it, you must not let their assessment affect you. If you believe them, you'll lose your desire to act. Instead, do what Arnold Schwarzenegger did and what everyone else who accomplishes difficult things does. Don't pay attention to the doubters, even if they are in authority. Remember, they're most likely misjudging your abilities. And if they're correctly judging your abilities, they're doing so without vision. They don't see that your abilities can improve. Either way, they're wrong in denying you. Keep on taking action.

If you want proof that people in authority most often don't know what they're talking about, observe how often they disagree. You can watch economists, stock market advisors, politicians, entrepreneurs, doctors, lawyers, and corporate CEOs all speaking from experience and positions of authority but all saying different things.

I began to grasp the realization that people in authority don't know what they're talking about when I began my radio career in college. One day while I was on the air, the studio door flew open and the program director marched in, leaned over to me, looked me straight in the eyes, and said, "Ott, you're never going to make it in this business!"

I was 18 years old, it was my first radio job, and he shook me up. I could barely finish my shift. But somehow I knew he was wrong. In fact, his discouragement inspired me to work harder to prove him wrong, which I did. Within six months of his curt proclamation, I had gone from college radio to the professional ranks, and he ended up working for the postal service.

Then I had another eye-opening experience. A few years later, I decided to look for a job at a bigger radio station in a bigger market. I put together an audition tape and sent copies to two Top 40 stations in different parts of the country. After a week or so, I called the program director at the first station to find out if he liked my tape. "You have too much energy," he said (the term *energy* in broadcasting refers to the intensity or punch of the disc jockey's delivery). "You talk way too fast. You're not what I'm looking for." Then I called the program director at the other station. "You don't have enough energy," he said. "You don't talk fast enough. You're not what I'm looking for." Remember, these two guys, in authority to hire and fire at their respective stations, listened to the exact same tape of me but had totally opposite judgement of me, meaning one of them had to be wrong. (The program director at the second station ended up hiring me after I kept calling him back and talking so fast on the phone he couldn't understand what I was saying.)

When was the last time someone in a position of authority misjudged things and blocked you from accomplishment? It happens every day, in every walk of life. Bank loan officers make shaky loans to third world countries with virtually no chance of repayment, yet they deny others a much smaller loan to start a business. Coaches cut players who eventually turn into first-rate performers on another team. Doctors misdiagnose things. I know a fellow who had a complete physical exam one week, with the doctor telling him he's in perfect health; then he died of a heart attack the next week.

Bo Schembechler, the legendary head football coach at the University of Michigan, once told a guy trying out for quarterback that he'd never play on the team. After the guy made the team as quarterback, Coach Schembechler told him he's the worst quarterback he's seen in 40 years.[2] Luckily, Jim Harbaugh didn't believe his coach, despite the coach's undeniable ability and experience. If Jim had allowed the coach's discouragement to affect him, he may not have gone on to become the starting quarterback not only at Michigan, but for the Chicago Bears.

This discussion is not an indictment of people in authority. It is, rather, simply a recognition that human judgment is fallible *on all levels*. The point is you have no reason to believe those people who block you from taking action. And you have every reason to continue taking action to prove the doubters wrong. I'm not saying you should rebel against your supervisor or undermine the management of your company. That is a different matter entirely. Management deserves to have the job done as they see it. And your superiors will make some judgmental errors, the same as you. If you expect them to let some of your errors slide, you've got to do the same of them.

Incidentally, off-base judgment by people in authority doesn't always work against you. Sometimes you're the beneficiary of their misjudgments. On listening to some of my early audition tapes when I was just starting out in radio, I find it quite amazing that people actually hired me. Perhaps they exercised poor judgment, or perhaps they had vision and felt I would develop in time. You can benefit the same way as long as you keep taking action, keep putting yourself in position to advance.

BLAME AND FAULT GRIND ACTION TO A HALT

When two or more people are working in close proximity in an office, plant, or wherever, blame and fault tend to proliferate. Every day you can witness someone blaming someone else for something. When people blame one another for this or that, action slows down. Your personal productivity and the productivity of the company are adversely affected by blame.

There are two things you should do to sidestep the blame syndrome and keep the action alive. First, be very slow to assign

---

[2]ESPN's "Gameday," October 11, 1992.

blame or fault to another. People make mistakes, including you. The last thing anyone needs is you aggrandizing their mistakes, making them feel lowly, and placing the weight of the problem on their shoulders. You don't appreciate anyone doing that to you, so don't do it to others.

Second, when others are standing idle, blaming one another, step forward and offer a solution or solve the problem yourself if possible. Think how you can personally grab the reins and steer the conversation away from blame and toward a solution. Let it be up to you to refocus attention on solving the problem and maintaining productivity. The idea is to keep the action from getting bogged down with blame, which it will probably do unless you direct it otherwise.

YOU THINK YOU'RE TAKING RISKS WHEN YOU'RE REALLY NOT

When Martin Snead and I started our management consulting company in 1984, I was amazed at the number of people who asked about the risk we were taking. The word *risk* kept coming up, but until it did, I hadn't even thought of it. I really didn't understand what people were referring to when they'd say, "Gee, aren't you guys taking a big risk?"

What risk were we taking? If the company failed, we could always get another job. Is it really that big a deal? Is it really a risk to quit your job and start your own company? Sure, we put some of our own money on the line as start-up capital. I suppose we could have lost it all. So what? What else would I do with my money—buy a car that depreciated to zero in eight years or invest in someone else's company? Why not invest in *my* company? Investing in yourself is always the best investment you can make. Besides, money is replaceable. It wouldn't take Martin or me long to make it back even if we did lose it. We simply didn't see the risk.

I know a fellow author who has a completed book manuscript ready to submit to publishers. But instead of submitting it, he keeps on revising it. One day I put him on the spot, asking him why he was afraid to send the manuscript in. He paused then said, "I guess I'm reluctant to take the risk."

Risk?! There's that word again! What risk?! If you're placing some irreplaceable item, like your life's savings, your right arm, or your life, in jeopardy, you're taking a risk—like high school kids take when they get drunk on Saturday night and stand on the trestle within arm's length of speeding trains. But when you've got little or nothing to lose, there's simply no risk involved.

"I risk losing my dignity, which would happen if they reject my work," the reluctant author said after I asked what risk he could possibly be referring to. Let me tell you what I told this guy. Losing a mental state, like dignity, for example, is no loss at all. Mental states are just figments of your subconscious mind. They're totally harmless and completely replaceable.

How long do you suffer a loss of dignity anyway? As long as you choose to, I suppose. This guy could have had his manuscript rejected by any number of publishers and chosen to spend the rest of his life in some miserable, dignityless stupor. (Remember what we discussed in Chapter 4. You experience negative emotions to the degree you choose to.) It's a self-inflicted wound if there ever was one. On the other hand, he could have chosen to feel a loss of dignity for all of 10 seconds, or maybe not at all.

Taking action is like playing chess. If you hope to win, you've got to move your pieces. And if you move your pieces, you're going to lose some of them. Conversely, if you're afraid of losing your pieces, you'll be reluctant to move. And you won't win. Oh how exhilarating it feels when you realize you're not really taking the risk you thought you were. Now you can make your moves with confidence and determination. When you cut yourself loose of those sandbags called risk, your actions become remarkably easier to take.

HOW TO BURST THROUGH THE BARRIER OF ACTION AVOIDANCE

Here is a step-by-step procedure for conquering the action avoidance barrier and boosting your personal productivity:

- **Step 1: Talk to people.** The more people you talk to the better. Ask them questions, and gather information. Inspire people to act. Influence them. Build relationships.

- **Step 2: Commit yourself.** Say to yourself or to others, "Yes, I will do it." Put yourself on the line. You were born to step up to the plate, so commit yourself to do just that. It will feel very comfortable committing to things once you realize you're capable of following through and achieving.

- **Step 3: Engage in physical movement.** All real action eventually works its way down to your arms, hands, fingers, legs, or feet. One or more of those body parts has to be moving to constitute real action. Realize that it's you who must do the moving, even if you're in a managerial or coaching position.

- **Step 4: Make decisions with limited information.** Gather some information, then make assumptions and decisions based on those assumptions. Remember, it's better to act on limited information than remain idle awaiting greater certainty.

- **Step 5: Reduce your options.** Too many attractive options will keep you from deciding on one and acting. By eliminating your options, even good ones, and even if you do so arbitrarily like flipping a coin to see which gets rejected, you can arrive upon your chosen course of action much sooner.

- **Step 6: Take action in the face of judgment.** People are not scrutinizing you nearly to the degree you think they are. They don't care about how you look; they're too preoccupied with how they look.

- **Step 7: Welcome a little embarrassment.** Once you experience a tinge of embarrassment in the line of duty, you realize it's really not so painful after all. In fact, you can get to the point where it rolls off your back without any lingering scars at all. Go ahead and laugh at yourself. Once you accept that real action entails a bit of embarrassment from time to time, you'll actually start to feel good when you feel embarrassed. And you'll negate your aversion to certain actions that you perceive as potentially embarrassing.

- **Step 8: Don't believe people who discourage you.** Even if they're in a position of authority, and even if they seem correct, prove them wrong. By taking action regardless of the amount of discouragement you receive, you will become better, more proficient. What once caused people to discourage you will soon cause them to claim they were your mentor. (Agent before actor becomes star: "You haven't got a prayer, kiddo." Agent after actor becomes star: "I knew you were destined for greatness the moment I first saw you!")

- **Step 9: Sidestep blame.** Be very slow to assign blame and fault to others. When the blame is flying, step forward and redirect attention to the problem. Offer a solution, or solve the problem yourself. Let it be up to you to keep the action going.

- **Step 10: Denounce the risk.** Ask yourself, "Is whatever I'm risking replaceable?" If the answer is yes, then you're really not taking any significant risk. Remember, life is like a chess game. If you move your pieces, you're going to lose some of them. But at least you're playing and have a good chance of winning. Fail to move your pieces because of the perceived risk of losing some, however, and you're out of the game—destined to lose.

Chapter Six

Cure When Disease

W hen will you be promoted? When will your singing career take off? When will you finally complete your paperwork? When will you find the person of your dreams? When will you make your next big sale? When will your biggest problem go away? When will you get the bigger office you were promised? When will you acquire that brand new boat?

When will it happen for you? I know you're working smart and hard day after day, year after year, and deserve to accomplish your objectives and reap your rewards. But I want to know when all that will happen. Think of one particular endeavor you're working on presently in your life, and tell me when you'll achieve it. I want a date. A month and year. When will you achieve your goal, and when will you get rewarded?

That was a string of trick questions. The correct answer to any "when" question is that there is no answer. You don't know when you'll be promoted or become the next singing sensation. You don't know when you'll make your next sale or become financially independent. Who knows when you'll achieve a goal or get a reward? No one knows when.

Yet we keep asking ourselves rhetorical "when" questions over and over. We can't seem to function unless we know when we'll achieve and when we'll get the reward. So we keep asking ourselves "when" questions and keep coming up answerless. Or we fabricate answers—we name a date on which we expect results. And we become frustrated and angry when things don't happen "when they should," either of which causes our personal productivity to slow or stop altogether.

Productivity barrier number five is *When Disease*, the overconcern with when things are going to happen. When Disease is a common affliction, based on a natural tendency to want to know when situations will change for the better. You probably have When Disease to some extent.

THE WHEN MONSTER

Some people have it bad, really bad. We call them When Monsters. They're easy to spot because of their constant rhetorical wailings: "When are they finally going to give me a raise around here?!" "When are they going to promote me to the position I should have been in years ago?!" "When will people start recognizing my talent and buy my paintings?!" "When will the right person come along?!" "When will I have the money to buy that new car!?" When, when, when.

When Monsters sabotage their own success by focusing on the one question for which there is no answer: When is a particular something going to happen? They keep trying to force things, and they keep producing disastrous results. In that sense, their notion of unmet accomplishment and unjust reward becomes a self-fulfilling prophecy. When Monsters live in a perpetual state of frustration, never feeling things happen when they should.

Whether you have slight, recurring When Disease tendencies or are a full-fledged When Monster, you've got to cure yourself now. Only when you fully clear the When Disease barrier and rid yourself of all its symptoms can your true productivity become unleashed.

There are many different angles to When Disease, and our discussion of each will contain specific remedies for your full treatment and recovery.

THE FORCES OF THE UNIVERSE DICTATE WHEN

You have a great deal of control over what you accomplish throughout your life by how you choose to spend your time and energy. And you can choose to spend your time and energy on whatever tasks or endeavors you like, from starting your own business, excelling at your job, climbing mountains, getting one or more college degrees, raising a family, inventing something better than sliced bread, or whatever you like. You control what you accomplish. But the one big variable you have almost no control over is *when* you accomplish and *when* the rewards arrive.

Realization 29

There are an infinite number of forces at work in the universe that affect when you accomplish a particular endeavor and when the rewards arrive. You can't control when.

There are many forces at work in the universe that affect when you can accomplish a particular task or endeavor and when you'll get your reward. Trying to control when, therefore, is futile.

The term *forces of the universe* may connote something spiritual or metaphysical to some, which is okay. But it really refers to the combined effect of numerous concrete variables over which one has no control. Such variables include the decisions of other people, including people you never meet firsthand, that affect you; laws that change, sometimes even totally reversing the circumstances you've grown accustomed to; the shifting sentiment of the population at large, or of consumers who buy your company's product or service; plain old luck, both good and bad; and even the weather, which can affect everything from the food you eat to your travel plans day by day. There are an infinite number of ever-changing, uncontrollable variables that affect your productivity. Their combined effects constitute the forces of the universe.

Make Things Happen by Aligning Yourself with the Forces

The forces of the universe run their own agendas; they do not conform to your agenda. When you try to fight them by forcing things to happen, you lose every time. On the other hand, when you align yourself with the forces—all those uncontrollable variables—you glide to accomplishment, and get your rewards with much less resistance. There is a big difference between making things happen and forcing things to happen. Making things happen is good and usually produces a favorable result. Forcing things to happen almost always produces either something you hadn't wished for or undesirable side effects.

I could cite examples of people who for years fought with everything they had, overcoming major obstacles regardless of what it took to do so, to finally achieve some notable accomplishment. Implicit in that kind of story is that it's good to forge ahead relentlessly, regardless of the resistance you encounter or the side effects you cause. Perhaps. But that sounds a lot like working harder, not smarter, doesn't it? For each person who fights like mad to achieve something (forcing things to happen), there's another who waits until the forces of the universe back her up (making things happen) and achieves the same or greater success with much less resistance, less severe side effects, and in much less time.

How do you tell the difference between making things happen and forcing things to happen? The answer may both disappoint you and excite you. It may be disappointing in that you're probably hoping I hand you some new, high-tech computer that confidently flashes either "making" or "forcing" whenever you enter a prospective endeavor, which I'm not going to do. But it'll be exciting when you find out that you already possess such a computer, albeit not new or high-tech.

Realization 30

If something doesn't feel right, you're out of alignment with the universal forces; you're forcing it to happen. If it does feel right, you've got the forces with you; you're making it happen.

Your *instincts* tell you the difference between making things happen and forcing things to happen. Your instincts are a super-computer that takes all the information you know, combines it with the forces of the universe (to which your instincts are linked), and tells you whether you're forcing or making.

Groan if you like. Trusting your "feels right/doesn't feel right" instincts seems vague and impractical, I know. It usually takes a number of years of unrewarding hard work to finally realize that your instincts, as vague and impractical as they may seem, are indeed the key to aligning yourself with the forces and improving your productivity. You can save yourself years of grief by accepting Realization 30 now and tuning into your instincts. Through practice, you'll develop sensitivity to and trust in your instincts. Your "feels right/doesn't feel right" instincts will begin to seem not only solid and practical but indispensable.

Perhaps you or someone you know spent years in a profession that they eventually abandoned, having finally acknowledged the profession just didn't feel right. I know one such fellow who actually completed medical school and became a full-fledged M.D., only to quit medicine entirely and become a geologist. "All the time I was pursuing my M.D., I was trying to force something that just wasn't meant to be," he explained in retrospect. "I knew deep down it just didn't feel right, but I let logic outweigh my feelings. Then one day I stopped fighting my instincts, and I just did what I really wanted. It feels great!"

Your instincts will lead you correctly not only when it comes to major career decisions but in lesser, everyday situations. Sharron, along with four other managers in her firm, had to prepare a short summary of their "objectives, opportunities, and problems" for a meeting with the corporate heavies the following afternoon. The other managers were planning on preparing their material the following morning, which afforded plenty of time since the meeting wasn't until 4 P.M. But Sharron noticed herself "just not feeling right" about letting it go until the following morning. Her instincts told her to prepare the material that evening, which she did.

The next day turned out to be one of those crazy days when everything broke loose. One of the vice president's schedule changed; he had to be on a flight at 1:00 P.M., so the meeting got moved up to 10:00 A.M. Guess who was the only one thoroughly prepared, the only one who made a first-rate, impressive presentation? Sharron paid attention to her instincts, did what felt right, aligned herself with the forces of the universe, and racked up a tremendous victory.

What about you? If something you're trying to accomplish is

just not happening, despite tremendous effort on your part, it's probably because you're not in alignment with the forces—too many of the uncontrollable variables are working against you. I'm not saying you shouldn't face adversity or rise to the challenge of difficulty. Most of your aspirations won't come easy. Adversity is normal, to be expected. You will have to put forth effort. But I am saying you should trust your instincts. If it instinctively feels right to engage in a certain activity at a particular time, then you're in alignment with the forces; you're making things happen, despite the difficulty you encounter. But if it doesn't instinctively feel right, you're out of alignment with the forces. Continued pursuit of that endeavor at such a time is forcing it, which isn't good.

Making things happen by aligning yourself with the forces of the universe is very simple. Stay sensitive to your instincts. When you get a "doesn't feel right" signal from your instincts, put that particular activity, task, or endeavor on the shelf; delay its pursuit until it does feel right. That feeling may come an hour, day, month, or year later, or many years later, or never. You can't control when; the forces of the universe run the agenda. Forget about when you will accomplish it or when the rewards will arrive. When the forces of the universe are with you—when the relevant uncontrollable variables shift in your favor—you'll get a "feels right" green light from your instincts, and your productivity in that particular endeavor will be very high.

"But I Can't Wait for the Forces"

I hear you. You're telling me you seldom have the luxury of waiting for the good old forces of the universe to fall into alignment one fine day. You've got to produce today, right now, this minute, regardless of what the forces are doing. Let me offer you three insights that will help:

- **More than likely, you *are* in alignment with the forces already.** Most people instinctively do what I described above, they end up following the innermost directives of their instincts, even if they don't consciously acknowledge doing so. The job you have now, the tasks you're involved in day to day, where you're living, the friends you hang out with, all come to be because you are following your "feels right" instincts. Instinctively aligning your activities with the forces is a default condition that exists most of the time in your life. It's only when When Disease takes hold, and you become unduly anxious for some result, that you start to ignore your instincts and begin fighting the forces.

- **There will be many things you have to do in relation to your job or personal life that you don't like doing.** That's just the way life is. Just because you dislike a particular task or prefer another course of action instead of the one you're engaged in doesn't mean you're out of alignment with the forces. The "feels right" or "doesn't feel right" condition doesn't necessarily activate itself with every little move you make. In the absence of a very strong and sustained "doesn't feel right" instinct, you're doing fine despite your immediate displeasures or discomforts.

- **Conforming to the agenda of the universal forces rather than your own agenda doesn't mean you idly waiting for something to slap you in the face.** You can be consistently active and highly productive by simply engaging in tasks or endeavors that do feel right at the time. If you have enough aspirations or things on your to-do list, there are always many that are in alignment with the forces at any given time.

THE PRODUCTIVITY-REWARD TIME LAG

Earlier in the book, I noted that highly productive people seem to get abundant reward throughout their lives—recognition, respect, admiration, advancements, promotions, or money, to name but a few. What I didn't mention is that the rewards don't always come the second we think we deserve them. Sometimes—many times— you can accomplish something and get no reward whatsoever. At least it seems like you got nothing because no reward arrived on time. Whatever reward you might have eventually gotten sure took its good old time in arriving, it seems.

There exists what I call the *productivity-reward time lag*. Simply put, it means the rewards of productivity don't usually arrive during or immediately after accomplishment. They arrive some time later, after most or all of the work has long been done. Because of the productivity-reward time lag, it usually takes a continuous stream of steady accomplishment before you reap rewards. Even then, they can show up in small measure. The truth is, it takes a series of continual accomplishments, sustained over a span of time, to get the really big rewards coming in.

Realization 31

There exists an inherent time lag between productivity and reward.
Sometimes it can be a very unfair time lag.

Sometimes, the productivity-reward time lag expands, becoming a very *unfair* time lag. In tough times, such as the deep recession of 1991–92, the productivity-reward time lag widened so far that many people are still waiting for their rewards to arrive. Not only were raises sparse for many during that time, but advancements and promotions were even sparser. As many companies downsized, thousands of people found themselves promoted right out the door, as their positions suddenly ceased to exist. And whole companies ceased to exist, leaving many entrepreneurs ruing the day they struck out on their own. Sometimes the rewards move in the wrong direction, distancing themselves from you instead of embracing you.

You're familiar with the problem. When the rewards of accomplishment—recognition, admiration, advancements, money, and all that good stuff—are late in arriving, we tend to become discouraged. We start asking "when" questions out of frustration. We can become When Monsters in no time.

The productivity-reward time lag isn't going to go away. It's just the way the world is. Don't be disheartened. Feel great that you're now getting a handle on the situation. Feel excited that you now understand how rewards behave. Now you understand that worthwhile rewards are naturally late in arriving, so it makes little sense to question their tardiness. Now you're ready to turn it all around and make the productivity-reward time lag work for you instead of against you!

Now Rewards for Now Work

The world's most successful people, whether you measure success in financial terms or any other, have learned to sidestep the ravages of the productivity-reward time lag completely. How do they do it? How can you do it?

First, don't wait for others to reward you. Reward yourself. And do so continuously. We talked about self-praise and tying your purchases to performance as two ways of rewarding yourself back in Chapter 3. You may want to review it if you've forgotten how that works.

Here's a third way of rewarding yourself that we haven't discussed yet. Create *now rewards* that you enjoy *during* the productivity process. It's a way of making the actual work a little more enjoyable now, at the time you're producing, thereby taking some pressure off the end reward to keep you motivated.

Right now, as I'm writing these words, I've got the stereo blasting away here in the computer room. As I'm typing, I'm dancing, clapping, and singing along to George Michael's "Too Funky," which happens to be playing at the moment (I write standing up quite often). Why should I wait to get some reward? When you write a book, the rewards usually don't come for months, even years after it's published—long after the work is done. It's good when it comes, but what about now, when I'm doing all the work? I've created a little now reward for myself as I produce, and I'm enjoying the writing process a lot more because of it.

Carol is an advertising sales manager for a weekly newspaper. On one particular Friday, she had the salespeople stay in the office all day and work the phones, selling ads in an upcoming Valentine's Day issue. Since the end rewards, in the form of sales commissions, wouldn't come for many weeks down the road, Carol created some now rewards for herself and her staff. She created a party atmosphere, complete with pizza, soft drinks, and music. As each salesperson got another verbal commitment from an advertiser, she tossed a $20 bill into a hat and did a little cheering as well. At the end of the day she divided the hat money, which had grown to a few hundred dollars, evenly among the salespeople. It was a now reward for now work.

Let's face it, not every task or endeavor you undertake is so intrinsically enjoyable that you don't care about getting some bigger, more enjoyable reward at the end. Most of your motivation for accomplishment may, in fact, be attributable to the reward you expect to gain afterward. For instance, say you voluntarily work four hours longer Wednesday evening just to complete your paperwork. It's not that you love the paperwork so much you can't pull yourself away, it's that you expect a little extra recognition and a bonus. Because of the productivity-reward time lag, however, the recognition and bonus may not arrive for some time afterward.

By creating some now rewards that you experience during the productive process, you're making the work itself a little more rewarding than it otherwise might be. This makes it easier for you to be patient during the productivity-reward time lag, when the end reward has yet to arrive.

Use now rewards only when conditions allow. There will obviously be times when now rewards like those in the above examples are impractical. Blasting the music and dancing while you work may disturb others in your workplace and may not fit the corporate culture. Now rewards work best in either a solitary environment or in one in which everyone present can partake equally.

Ignore the Time Lag

Another way of making the productivity-reward time lag work for you is to simply *ignore* that the rewards are slow in arriving. You may not have been able to ignore the tardiness of reward in the past because you had no reason to believe they ever would arrive. To you, a slow-arriving reward was no reward. If it didn't come immediately (meaning whenever you expected it), you panicked and pouted, thinking life gave you the old shaft once again.

The productivity-reward time lag will often delay your rewards, but that delay doesn't mean they're not coming. The rewards will arrive eventually and in great abundance, provided you sustain your productivity in the meantime. You must continue to produce with vigor, knowing full well that the rewards will arrive eventually when they're good and ready to. And they will, without fail.

Realization 32

In time, you always get your just reward.

You've heard Realization 32 before, only you may have a tough time believing it. Here you are, producing like crazy year after year and patiently waiting for your illusive rewards to arrive someday. And all the while you notice a lot of seemingly incompetent, inept bumblers basking in undeserved reward here and now. Yes, the rats do win the rat race at times. But, given enough time, the really substantial rewards do find their way to the deserving. The karma may not be instant, but it will get you eventually.

When the rewards are nowhere to be found, remind yourself of Realization 32. When you know your just rewards will arrive eventually, you are better able to ignore their tardiness, keep up your productivity, and avoid catching When Disease.

By the way, the word *reward* does not necessarily mean something desirable. Remember the saying "Every day, the world turns over on someone who was on top of it." People who display wanton disrespect for others or allow their egos to storm through all in their path are candidates for an eventual downfall. The rats may win the race at times, but it usually doesn't take long for them to self-destruct. Remember, Realization 32 is always in effect and always takes affect in due time.

EXPECTATIONS INSTEAD OF GOALS

If you're doing what many goal practitioners recommend—establishing goals for the next year, the next 5 or 10 years, or your entire life, writing them down, looking at them each day, and visualizing their attainment—if you're doing all this and are happy with the results you're getting, good for you. I'm not going to recommend you do anything differently. You may want to skip this section. But if you've had trouble either establishing goals or making them work for you, this section is for you.

Good Theory, Not So Good Practice

The theory behind the setting of goals is sound. Goals give you a target, something to shoot for. They give you a sense of purpose and direction. They can excite you and motivate you into action. And most important, if you burn them into your subconscious, they'll guide you toward their attainment even when you're not thinking about them. A set of clearly defined goals can be very beneficial to your daily productivity and can have a profound effect on what you're able to accomplish over the years.

Goals Can Warp Your Priorities

So what's the problem? There are two problems, to be exact. First, your goals can become more important than you. You can inadvertently and harmfully mess up your priorities when you focus so strongly on your goals.

When the long-term welfare of the masses is at stake, it may be justifiable for a goal to be more important than any particular people. If a company can't attain the success it craves with the people it has, it will get new ones who do bring about success. The goal is more important than the people. If a baseball team can't win with the players or coaches it has, it will hire, fire, and trade to get the right people who can produce a winning team. The goal is more important than the people. Sometimes a country will send soldiers into battle knowing full well many will not come back alive; but it feels the importance of the goal eclipses people's lives. The goal is more important than the people.

But your goals are not more important than you or the people you love and care about, are they? I think you'd agree that you and the special people in your life are more important than any of your goals. Not that your goals and your loved ones are necessarily mutually exclusive. One of your goals could be to spend one hour a day with the kids, for example. But for some strange reason, few people seem to establish relationship-oriented goals—New Year's resolutions perhaps, but not goals. Most people's goals center on career, money, and material possessions, it seems.

By constantly focusing on your goals, you can raise them to a level of importance they may not really deserve. Your priorities can get out of whack. Your goals begin to overshadow other, more important things, such as your health or relationships, that don't ever make it onto your goal list. Do you know people who want to make a certain level of income and have established some desired figure as a major goal? Sure enough, the goal guides their behavior, and they do whatever it takes to attain it. Unfortunately, their marriage can crumble or their kids can get into trouble through neglect; or their friends and business associates may feel used and abused, relegated to second-tier status compared to the goal.

Goals are things, either tangible or intangible, that you have yet to attain. When you focus so feverishly on them, you can become obsessed with what you don't have and unappreciative of what you already do have. Isn't it sad that so many of us have so much goodness in our lives—health, wonderful children, a nice home, a decent education, delicious food on the table, a great country to live in, the list could go on—yet we're unhappy because we're oblivious to it all and instead are obsessed with what we don't have?

You are more important than your goals. Your family and close friends are more important than your goals. The things you presently have in your life, material, intellectual, and spiritual, are more important than your goals. A goal is not worth attaining if it wrecks your life in the process. What I'm saying here is that you need to keep things in proper perspective, you need to maintain healthy priorities. But when you focus so much on your career, money, or material goals, you tend to subconsciously alter your priorities and spend less time maintaining the great things you already have. Watch out. Goals can warp your priorities.

Goals Can Be Discouraging

The second problem with goals is that they seldom happen within the time frame you've allotted, which makes you extremely susceptible to When Disease.

After keeping a goal list for many years, I began to notice a rather disheartening pattern developing. Day after day, month after month, I'd work on my goals, yet as each year ended I noticed only about 1 out of 10 of them coming to fruition. And I don't have lofty goals. You won't find walking on Mars, making it to the top of *Forbes* list of richest Americans, or replacing Jay Leno as ''Tonight Show'' host among them.

What happens when you look at your goal list one day and see that they're just not happening? All the bad things we've talked about in this book so far begin to take hold. Negative emotions, headed by frustration and anger, begin to flourish. Your energy and enthusiasm erode. When Disease takes hold. The next thing you know, you're a prime candidate for the When Monster of the Year award.

Trade Goals for Expectations

You could keep all those bad things from happening by tearing up your goal list and forgetting about goals entirely. But by doing so, you forfeit the positive benefits of goals; that is, they give you targets to shoot for and instruct your subconscious how to guide you. The good goes out with the bad.

There is a way to retain the positive benefits of goals yet keep them from screwing up your priorities and discouraging you when they fail to happen. There are two things you should do. First, don't call them goals. Call them *expectations*. We talked about the power of expectations in Chapter 3, you'll recall. Expectations draw you toward their attainment just like goals yet don't demand supreme reverence.

The word *expectation* is much softer and friendlier than *goal*. The word *goal* bespeaks a certain feistiness that demands to be achieved at any cost. Since the word is used in many sports, it implies a win-lose state—you win if you achieve the goal, you lose if you don't. But the word *expectation* is much easier to deal with. It implies that it already exists in some form; it's something you fully, completely, and unequivocally expect to materialize in due time. The certainty of an expectation gives you great power to make it happen, yet it doesn't require your unequivocal devotion.

Get Rid of Deadlines

Second, don't attach deadlines to your expectations. Get rid of your one-year goals, five-year goals, and the like. Have one master list that you add things to and scratch from (when they're attained or no longer of interest to you) year after year. Look at your list of expectations frequently, burning them into your subconscious. But instead of telling your expectations which ones you're going to work on when, let them tell you. Certain ones will feel right at certain times, and certain ones won't feel right at certain times. At any given time, you work on the ones that feel right, without attaching deadlines to their attainment.

Without deadlines, your expectations are unencumbered and unimposed. They are free to be affected by the forces of the universe and not your self-imposed agenda. The forces of the universe are so many times more powerful than you that you will notice yourself achieving your expectations faster when you let them tell you when they're ready to be acted on. Certain expectations that may have been dormant will suddenly jump off the paper and cry out to you for nurturing. That's when the forces of the universe are behind them; that's when you'll encounter less resistance in their attainment than at any other time. By refusing to attach deadlines to your expectations, you allow the tremendous forces of the universe to run the show. And you end up accomplishing much more in less time!

THOSE DASTARDLY DEADLINES

As long as we're on the subject of deadlines . . . self-imposed deadlines, whether they be aimed at accomplishment ("I want to be a vice president by my 33rd birthday") or reward ("I want to be making $60,000 a year within two years"), work against you most of the time. Realization 29 says you can't control when something is going to happen. Establishing deadlines is a futile attempt to change the way the universe works. And the immutable laws of the universe always prevail. Deadlines don't work. (There are specific conditions under which deadlines can be beneficial. We'll discuss those later.)

Did Thomas Edison say, "I've got to invent the electric light bulb by June 18"? He didn't attach any deadline to it. He worked vigorously, believing he would be successful eventually but never knowing when it would happen nor feeling it had to happen by a certain date.

Think of someone you know and admire for having accomplished something notable. It could be a friend or a well-known person. Now think about this: How many things had to happen in order for that person to accomplish whatever? That person may have worked smart and hard over many years, but it also took some luck didn't it? Luck, one of the many universal forces that affect when, comes when it pleases. You can keep yourself in position to be the beneficiary of luck when it appears, but you can't make luck appear on demand.

Bill, a middle manager with a large apparel manufacturer, used to attach deadlines to everything he wanted to accomplish. He had specific deadlines for when his division would reach a certain level of sales, when his office would get a new computer system, and when he would be a vice president. And Bill frequently felt frustrated because things seldom worked out by deadline time. It was only after becoming a When Monster, and driving himself and others around him crazy wondering about when, that he decided to take a radically different approach.

One day, Bill decided to cast his deadlines aside, although—and this is very important—he did not cast aside his aspirations and desires. He continued to take action toward accomplishment every day, without worrying about when the end result might happen. What did happen as a result of Bill's new, deadlineless agenda? First, he felt a sense of great relief; the weight was off his shoulders. He became a calmer, happier person, and a brighter, warmer demeanor began to emerge. Second, he noticed himself and his subordinates working much more efficiently; they seemed to get more done in less time as Bill's productivity leverage was improving. Third, the accomplishments of the office were indeed many, though they weren't happening in any preset order. Bill concluded that by allowing accomplishments to happen when they will without deadlines, they happen much more often and with greater ease.

Why don't things usually happen by deadline time? Because there are a multitude of variables, including the decisions and actions of other people, that affect things. You can't control all the variables enough to meet deadlines.

When to Use Deadlines

Some people believe deadlines are good in that they spur you forward, they provide pressure that helps motivate you. This is true, but only under very specific conditions.

If you are in control of completing a particular task, a deadline may be of benefit to you. But deadlines seldom work when it takes more than one person to do the work necessary for completion. Watching a building go up provides a primary example. If you've ever seen one completed by the originally scheduled completion date, you've witnessed a miracle.

Realization 33

Deadlines are beneficial only when they're attached to simple tasks under one person's control.

This doesn't mean people can't work together toward a common objective. A team effort can be highly effective, as long as each team member has a separate or different section of the task to accomplish and is not directly dependent on others to complete their sections by the deadline. An effective team effort is, after all, nothing more than a number of people doing their individual parts. Team members may help one another, but not to the dereliction of their own duties.

Deadlines also do not work when whatever you wish to accomplish is more than a simple task. Do you want to become a world-renowned singer with a smash album on the charts? There's nothing wrong with that, as long as you don't attach a deadline to it. Think what might have happened to Bonnie Raitt had she set a deadline. Bonnie recorded for years with only moderate and fleeting success. Most people hadn't even heard of her, and that was after many years of singing professionally. Surely, had she a deadline for stardom, it would have passed without having been met (does anyone set a deadline for massive success in excess of two years?). And she might have given up in disgust; unmet deadlines have a way of doing that to the best of us. But Bonnie kept on going, and eventually big-time results kicked in when her *Nick of Time* album won a slew of Grammys and sales exploded, catapulting her to stardom "overnight."

The "Shoulda Happened by Now" Deadline

Sometimes we never really set a deadline, yet we wake up one day and feel as though a deadline has passed nonetheless. We feel as though something "shoulda happened by now." Shoulda gotten promoted by now. Shoulda had that new product fully developed and on the market by now. Shoulda been married by now. Shoulda bought a home by now. Shoulda been assigned a better work shift by now. Shoulda had that report written by now. Shoulda been a millionaire by now. Shoulda finished reading this book by now.

Okay, maybe you could have accomplished more of your expectations by now. Maybe you could have been more productive in the past. Calm down. You are in the process of correcting that now by learning this material. In the future, you will be more productive. But you've got to stop attaching deadlines to things you want to accomplish and to the rewards you expect to receive. Stop feeling as though you're behind schedule. Let the all-powerful forces of the universe work for you instead of against you by letting them happen as they naturally will. You do your part—keep on taking action—and don't burden yourself with the weight of a deadline to meet.

The Imposed Deadline

What if someone, your supervisor for example, imposes a deadline on you? As long as you alone are in control of whatever has to happen by deadline time, you're okay. You may have to turn in your written report by 5:00 P.M. Friday, or get 75 cartons loaded by midnight tonight, or have placed 10 phone calls by tomorrow afternoon. In each of these examples, it's a relatively simple,though not necessarily easy, task that you are in control of accomplishing. The deadline that has been imposed on you will motivate you to complete the task on time, despite any inconveniences or hardships it might also provide.

But what if someone imposes a deadline on you that isn't under your control to meet? Let's say you're a shoe salesperson and your supervisor decides you must sell five pairs of shoes by the end of the day. Does the "end of the day" deadline help or hamper you? Since the selling of shoes requires other people to buy the shoes, selling x pairs by a certain deadline is not under your control. Is it possible you could do an absolutely exquisite sales pitch and a prospect might not buy, despite your brilliant performance? Of course. It happens all the time. For various and innumerable reasons, everyone you talk to today may walk out without buying; you might not sell any shoes by the end of the day. Or you might sell 10 pairs, or 2 today and 8 tomorrow, or whatever. When your success depends on other people, and for most things it will, deadlines are counterproductive.

Are you imposing harmful deadlines on yourself or others? The Mafia is not known for its enlightened, productivity-boosting management style, yet many well-meaning managers adopt its "do or die" deadline approach anyway. At one radio station a number of years ago, the general manager told the salespeople to "come back with a signed contract by the end of the day or don't bother coming back." What happens when you put people under that kind of deadline? In this case, they all returned that day with signed contracts. Only they had to lie to do it and ended up never collecting on any of them. (One creative salesperson sold a remote broadcast to a gas station, promising the owner a razzle-dazzle, crowd-drawing event rivaling that of the Ringling Brothers Barnum & Bailey Circus. When the disc jockey showed up on remote day with no more than a sign in hand, the gas station owner went into shock. "Where's the balloons, the clowns, the mobile studio with sound and lights?" he asked, dumbfounded. "They promised you all that?" the jock chuckled. "We don't even have a mobile studio.")

The Difference between Deadlines and Time Lines

Say a company decides in January it wants to do $5 million in sales during the year and assigns each salesperson a sales budget, representing the portion of the $5 million that person must bring in. Are the December 31 deadline and the monthly incremental deadlines good or bad? Do the deadlines help the salespeople or hinder them? Would the company be better off saying "we want to do $5 million in revenue *someday*," instead of stating a specific date—a deadline—for accomplishment?

The rule we discussed earlier, that deadlines are dysfunctional if attached to something out of one's control, applies here. No question about it, a salesperson or sales staff could work 18 hours a day, seven days a week, making absolutely brilliant sales pitches, and still walk away without enough sales to meet certain deadlines.

Once again, let me clarify what I'm saying. People can control *what* happens. Salespeople can control, to a large enough degree, what amount of revenue they bring in. But they can't control *when* they'll bring it in. There are too many factors out of a salesperson's control to guarantee *x* dollars in sales by a particular date. Therefore, establishing a deadline, and pretending as though one does have control over it, is almost always detrimental to productivity.

Having said all that, let me throw you a slight curve. Deadlines may be detrimental to productivity, but *time lines* can be helpful to productivity. Time lines are simply the matching of specific occurrences with specific points in time, usually projected into the future. That may sound like a deadline, but it's actually quite different.

There are three big differences between deadlines and time lines. A deadline:

- Limits the amount of time available for completion. Time runs out on a certain date.

- Includes an undesirable consequence if not met. (That's why its called a deadline—you're dead if you don't meet it.)

- Is static. Once established, it doesn't change.

A time line, on the other hand:

- Does not limit the amount of time available for completion. Time never runs out.

- Includes no undesirable consequences if certain occurrences do not happen by certain dates.

- Is dynamic. The matching of occurrences and dates can, and does, change as time goes on.

A company that decides it wants to do $5 million in revenue this year could simply establish a time line instead of a deadline. It can use the time line for planning purposes and as a basis for decision making. The time line is like a map to aid the company in its travels from here to there.

With a time line, the company doesn't stop selling if it happens to fall short of its $5 million projection by December 31. It continues selling into the next year without missing a beat. Time doesn't run out. (Accounting periods run out, reflecting what amount of revenue has been achieved by what date, but that doesn't stop the company from existing and functioning beyond.) And the company doesn't create any negative consequences for itself as a result of falling short by a certain date. I'm not saying the company doesn't make adjustments in its product or marketing, but it doesn't fold the business and fire everyone. Instead the company celebrates doing $4.8 million or whatever figure it did attain by the end of the year.

And it made adjustments along the way. Six months into the year, the company may have decided to adjust the amount of revenue, upward or downward, that it reasonably expected to achieve in the following six months. With a time line, the matching of particular occurrences and particular points in time change periodically. Altering the time line is no big deal; it happens often.

Time lines are great planning tools. You can use them yourself. As you begin taking action to make some of your expectations happen, go ahead and attach time lines to the process. Anticipate what will happen when, including the incremental steps that lead to the end accomplishment. Just be sure to keep them from becoming deadlines. To do that, make sure you don't stop working when something doesn't happen by a particular point in time—most things won't, you know. And don't create any negative consequences for yourself or others, such as anger, beratement, punishment, or the like, when something doesn't conform to the time line. Finally, keep altering your time lines to fit changing circumstances; for example, you once expected to travel to the Phoenix office in May, now you expect to do so in June.

THE JET EFFECT

Your perspective can warp when you're in the heat of productivity. Your perception of time and your rate of accomplishment can seem quite different than they really are. Often, it seems as though you're not accomplishing things as fast as you really are.

When you're flying in a jet at cruising altitude, how fast does it seem like you're traveling? When you look at the inside of the plane, you see no evidence of movement at all. When you look out the window, you see clouds slowly drifting by or land slowly passing underneath. Although your plane is streaking through the sky at an incredible speed, around 400 or 500 miles per hour, it seems like you're barely moving. Only when you touch down does it appear you're moving fast, yet the plane has slowed considerably by that time.

Realization 34

You are accomplishing faster than you think you are.

The Jet Effect distorts your perception of speed. It makes it seem as though you're moving slower than you really are. Have you ever felt you're not accomplishing things as quickly as you should be? If you have When Disease, it'll seem this way often. In reality, you may be accomplishing at a good clip, but the Jet Effect makes it seem as though you're not moving nearly as fast. In other words, the Jet Effect is one of the causes of When Disease.

Of course, perhaps you really aren't accomplishing as quickly as possible. Your productivity may be stunted by any combination of the five productivity barriers, which you are now in the process of overcoming. But there's an equal chance, however, you may very well be accomplishing at a good rate, but the Jet Effect makes it seem otherwise.

Over the years, I've had many business executives express concerns about their company's lack of performance. Yet in many cases, after examining the situation, I found the company performing quite well. But the Jet Effect makes executives feel otherwise. They have a hard time judging just how well they're actually doing. (Behind every nervous executive is always some degree of financial desperation. Financial pressure will exacerbate the Jet Effect and often cause people to look at the wrong end of the situation for answers. Instead of looking down the line for performance inadequacies, they should be looking up the line, or in the mirror, to the source of the financial pressure. There's where they'll find the problem. Nine times out of 10, the person initiating the financial pressure does so out of impatience, not for a justifiable reason.)

From our own perspective, it may seem like we're not moving fast enough. But other people may see that we are moving quite rapidly. I was once asked to address a graduate-level research class about how radio stations use research. At the time, I was the marketing director of a major station in town. I was also in graduate school myself, no older than the students I was speaking to. When they found out I was their age (I was 27 at the time), many seemed astonished at what they saw as commendable accomplishment for a person their age. One person even asked me how it felt to have "accomplished so much at such a young age." That absolutely astonished me, because I had never thought of myself as someone who had accomplished much at all nor that my age was really that young. But it got me thinking. Maybe their assessment was more accurate than mine. Could it be I was indeed accomplishing more than it seemed?

One of the causes of the Jet Effect is that results tend to show up after you complete a task or endeavor rather than incrementally as you progress. Unlike painting a house, in which results show up with every brush stroke, many endeavors hide their results until completion. With many tasks or endeavors, the results show up all at once, in the end—or taking the productivity-reward time lag into consideration, sometime after the end. That makes it seem as though you're not progressing during the actual work period.

To overcome the Jet Effect, you need to mentally land and assess your performance from the ground. Instead of looking forward, focusing on what you want to accomplish, look backward and see how far you've come. Take note of the things you have accomplished in the past month, year, or four years. By mentally landing and looking backward, you can clearly see how far you've traveled over time. But when you're in the air, looking forward in anticipation of accomplishment and reward, it'll seem like you're not moving fast enough.

Thirty Percent Is Great

Years ago, a wise man told me that if I accomplished 20 percent of what I set out to, I was doing just fine. I always wanted to do better than fine, so I determined that if 20 percent was fine, then 30 percent must be great.

It's true. You will never be able to accomplish all things you set out to, unless you live to be 300 or so. About one day a year, I actually get done all of the things on my to-do list for the day. The rest of the time, I operate somewhere between 20 and 40 percent, averaging about 30 percent. What happens to the items on my daily to-do list that don't get done? Most are carried over to the next day, and the next after that, and so on until they do get done. Some I scratch off the list completely, realizing that they really don't need doing after all. But if I can get 30 percent done each day, I know I'm really cooking.

Realization 35

If you accomplish 30 percent of what you set out to accomplish, you're doing great.

One major cause of When Disease is expecting to accomplish more than 30 percent each day. The most notorious When Monster I've ever known drove herself to the edge by expecting to accomplish 100 percent of the things on her to-do list every day. She was one notch away from cracking when I happened to mention that I accomplish only 30 percent of the things on my daily to-do lists. "Only 30 percent?" she said, astounded. "Is that okay? Can you really live like that?" It's not only okay, it's great. Absolutely great.

THE FUN FACTOR

People with When Disease are always wondering when the fun will begin; when their lives will be more exciting. They're constantly perplexed and frustrated by the belief that fun times are passing them by, while others are basking in fun day and night. Consequently, they're on a constant mission in search of fun yet never seem to find it anywhere.

I've got news for you: The fun has already begun. Not only are you accomplishing more than you think you are, you're also having more fun than you think you are.

Have you ever gone on a vacation and had what you thought was a mediocre time, yet you recalled the experience some years later and felt it was a lot more enjoyable than you thought at the time? So much so, that you wish you could relive it? Think back now to your high school or college days. Does it seem like you really had a good time? Some people say those days were the best of their lives, yet they also remember not recognizing them as anything extraordinary at the time.

Realization 36

You are having more fun than you think you are. These are great days!

If you disagree with Realization 36, it's because your brain is playing tricks on you. Your brain tends to discount pleasurable experiences and heighten unpleasant experiences at the time they're happening. Then, your brain will do the exact opposite when it recalls experiences some time later, heightening the pleasurable and softening the unpleasurable.

Think back to a former job you had years ago. It may be that you remember some bad times, but I'll bet you also remember a lot more good, fun times than bad. Remember some of the people you worked with back then? Remember some of the projects or assignments you and the others were involved in? Does it seem like you were having fun back then?

Have you ever noticed yourself thinking about an old relationship with fondness, even having strong, pleasurable feelings for the other person some years later? Rationally, you know the relationship was faulty and destined to end, yet you tend to remember only the good parts of it. Your mind is magnifying the good times in retrospect.

As horrible as war is, veterans will often reunite with the people they served with and reminisce about the good old days. Even though their war experiences may have been negative, they look back on those times and feel the positive aspects. The fun times, which happen even during the horrors of war, stand out in time.

There's a tendency for your mind to discount the amount of fun you're having in the here and now. In reality, today is just as much fun as any time in your past. Someday you will think back to today and remember the great times. You'll remember the people who you're working with, the building you're working in, and the various projects you're spending your time on now. The trick is to recognize the great times now, while you're experiencing them.

Make Fun Memories

One of the reasons you remember the past so fondly is because you have memories of specific occurrences. You don't remember everything that happened to you when you were 20 years old, but you remember certain occurrences that stand out. You can recall exactly where you were and who you were with when something happened. You may gather with old friends years later and talk about "that night" or "the time Jerry got lost and ended up sleeping in his car."

Specific occurrences are entering your memory these days, occurrences that you will recall with great fondness for the rest of your life. Instead of letting them happen randomly, why not create memorable occurrences? Why not do something today that you and others will remember?

Most of the specific occurrences you recall with fondness are usually very simple things: a look on someone's face; something someone said; or a funny situation that happened at work, at home, or at school. You don't have to travel around the world to create a fond memory. Keep it simple yet uniquely different in some way.

Make memories for yourself and others. Create fun situations, happy occurrences. I know of no company in the world that wants its employees to be unhappy or melancholy. Why not take it upon yourself to create a few fun occurrences from time to time in the workplace? These are fun times for you, so realize it and maximize it!

HOW TO CURE WHEN DISEASE FOR MAXIMUM PRODUCTIVITY

Here is a summary of the steps you can take to stop your harmful obsession with when:

- **Step 1: Align yourself with the forces of the universe.** Trust your instincts. Don't try to force things to happen. If it doesn't feel right at the time, you're out of alignment with the universal forces, or the multitude of uncontrollable variables that affect you. Wait until a particular endeavor feels right before you undertake it. By waiting until the forces of the universe give the green light, you'll accomplish much more, with less resistance and in less time. Realize also that you are naturally in alignment with the forces most of the time. It's only when you ignore strong "doesn't feel right" instincts that you succumb to When Disease and knock yourself out of alignment.

- **Step 2: Reward yourself.** Praise yourself many times each day as you accomplish simple little things. Tie your purchases to accomplishments. Create now rewards—little pleasures you experience while working. The idea is to provide yourself with some reward now and take the pressure off the end rewards that may be late in arriving.

- **Step 3: Ignore the productivity-reward time lag.** Make the tardiness of reward a nonfactor. Know that you will get your just rewards eventually, even though you may have to wait a while. Keep up your productivity regardless of when the rewards arrive.

- **Step 4: Establish expectations instead of goals.** Have one master list of all your expectations. You may loosely prioritize them, but refrain from attaching deadlines to them. Let each expectation jump out at you when it's ready to be worked on.

- **Step 5: Attach deadlines only to simple tasks under your control.** Deadlines will help you only under these strict conditions. Attach deadlines to simple tasks on your daily to-do lists. Do not attach deadlines to any of your expectations that require the cooperation, assistance, or compliance of others. Most of your expectations will fall into this category.

- **Step 6: Use time lines instead of deadlines.** Use time lines to aid in planning and decision making. Make sure you understand the differences between time lines and deadlines.

- **Step 7: Assess your performance by looking backward.** Because of the Jet Effect, you'll underestimate your rate of accomplishment. To compensate for that and to assess your productivity accurately, look at what you've accomplished over the past month, year, or four years. See that you really have accomplished a lot.

- **Step 8: Make fun memories.** These are the best days of your life. Today. Now. Do fun, unusual things that you and others will remember. When you acknowledge the greatness of the moment, you'll stop asking when the fun will arrive and start enjoying the fun that's present.

IGNITING YOUR PERFORMANCE WITH THE FIVE PRODUCTIVITY THRUSTERS

Chapter Seven

Patience and Relaxation to the Rescue

N o matter what it is you're trying to accomplish, whether it be finishing a particular task by five o'clock this afternoon or acquiring a million-dollar house someday, you'll achieve your objective much easier and sooner if you remain patient and relaxed during the productive process.

Productivity thruster number one is *patience and relaxation*. When you have patience and relaxation, you operate from a position of tremendous strength. With the power and strength of patience and relaxation behind you, your performance improves dramatically. Your efforts have much greater impact, and your productivity sky-rockets.

So why don't I just recommend you be patient and relaxed, and end this chapter right here? As you know, it's not quite that easy. Patience and relaxation can be very elusive at times. In fact, most people don't even know how to go about bringing those states into their lives. And those who do know how usually run into strong opposition when they attempt to be patient and relaxed. We've got a lot to talk about in this chapter.

To bring patience and relaxation into your life in a major way, you've got to first reduce your resistance to them. We'll begin by discussing why patience and relaxation are so difficult to attain and what you can do about it. Then you'll be better prepared to bring patience and relaxation into your life in a big way.

WANTED DEAD OR ALIVE: TENSION AND STRESS

There are two villains determined to keep you from experiencing patience and relaxation. Throughout your life, you'll be constantly dogged by two lowly outlaws called *tension* and *stress*. These dynamic agitators do their best to prevent you from being patient and relaxed.

Tension and stress can't stand seeing you in a patient, relaxed state.

"Lookie there, Stress. I think good ol' Mike is starting to relax while he works."

"By golly, you're right, Tension. Let's make our presence known and gum up the works royally now!"

The next thing Mike knows, he's feeling uneasy and strained. Then, as tension and stress turn up the heat, Mike feels distress and anxiety coming on strong. And his productivity is decreasing inversely as tension and stress rise to prominence.

Tension and stress are the flip side of patience and relaxation. To the degree you reduce tension and stress, you gain patience and relaxation. We'll work on reducing tension and stress first, then deal more directly with patience and relaxation later.

HOW TENSION AND STRESS AFFECT YOUR PRODUCTIVITY

Tension and stress are formidable foes. They're strong and powerful, with unrelenting drive to keep you from feeling patient and relaxed. Here are the three main ways tension and stress affect you:

- **Tension and stress make you anxious.** Tension and stress trick you into believing time is running out faster than it really is. When you think time is closing in on you, you act in very unproductive ways. You make precipitous, ill-conceived decisions. You panic, shooting wildly into the darkness. You lose patience and jump the gun, ruining the deliberate, methodical progress you had been making. Anxiousness does not become you. When you display it, your productivity ebbs quickly.

- **Tension and stress breed negative emotions.** Tension and stress are great agitators; they love to stir up negative emotions. They goad your subconscious into creating negative emotions in good measure, as your subconscious believes it's doing the right thing by complying. Let's give credit where due: tension and stress are good at their job. And your subconscious is always vulnerable to clever persuasion.

  Besides lowering your personal productivity, a display of negative emotions lowers your productivity leverage, as other people are turned off by your emotional antics. Other people, who aren't being affected by tension and stress quite the same as you, may very well shake their heads and run for cover (and laugh behind your back) as inappropriate emotions indiscriminately fly off your persona. Tension and stress strike again.

- **Tension and stress shake your confidence.** Tension and stress are master intimidators. They make you think the task or undertaking is greater than it is and your abilities are less than they are. This cuts down your confidence and becomes a self-fulfilling perception; that is, when you lack confidence, your abilities really are reduced.

  Magnification of the task or endeavor and reduction of your abilities are simple deceptions performed by the great illusionists tension and stress. While you're shaking in your shoes, staring up at a task that seems mountainous, tension and stress are backslapping and cackling, congratulating themselves for having successfully fooled you once again.

THE FIVE VULNERABILITIES THAT ATTRACT TENSION AND STRESS

Tension and stress are like burglars. They cruise the neighborhood looking for vulnerable homes to violate, and they avoid homes that appear well secured. Your mind and body is your home, and it's level of vulnerability fluctuates.

(You may be wondering why I've chosen to personify tension and stress, why I depict them as outside forces that assault you, the opposite approach I took when explaining negative emotions. The truth is, tension and stress are also created by your subconscious mind, no differently than any negative emotion. But because tension and stress involve rather severe physical changes in addition to rather extreme mental states, I'm treating them differently for purposes of this discussion. I think it would be more useful for you, not to mention a little more fun, to think of tension and stress as outlaw characters who harass you. We'll let usefulness override accuracy in this instance.)

Tension and stress are actually mental and physical reactions to worry, acute uncertainty, performance pressure, relationship disharmony, and change. Let's discuss each in detail and see how you can make yourself less vulnerable to tension and stress and thus more receptive to patience and relaxation.

Worry

In Chapter 2 we discussed why we worry and how we can vaporize worry whenever it pops up. In that chapter, I noted that worry can cause tension and stress, as well as other maladies like heart attacks, ulcers, and diseases. I list worry here to remind you that it is a primary cause of tension and stress, all the more reason to master those six worry-vaporzing steps.

Acute Uncertainty

You're trying to fall asleep, but questions keep swirling around in your mind. What will happen at tomorrow's meeting? Will I be included in next month's round of employee cuts? Does he like me or not? Will she say yes? Will I pass the exam? When will this problem go away? Why did he do that? Will it work out for the best? What will I be doing a year from now?

Sound familiar? Every now and then some of life's uncertainties become acute. They grow in intensity like winds that develop into a tornado. When you've got an uncertainty tornado swirling through your mind, tension and stress run rampant, preventing you from being patient and relaxed.

Realization 37

Life is supposed to contain a great deal of uncertainty.

Uncertainty itself is not a problem. Life is supposed to contain a good measure of it. Think of what life would be like if there were no uncertainty, if everything that was to happen were known to us in advance. What would life be like if at birth we were all given the date on which we will die? Can you imagine what it would be like knowing that little piece of information? We'd be totally preoccupied with the time passing. "Oh no, I've only got 22 years left!" "Only 97 days, seven hours, and four minutes left! What am I going to do?" "Thirteen minutes to go! Twelve minutes, 59 seconds! Twelve minutes, 58 seconds . . . "

We'd go crazy if we knew how much time we had left. People who do have a good idea how much time they've got left, such as prisoners on death row or the terminally ill, spend their remaining time either doing nothing or traveling the world. They usually don't embark on productive endeavors. ("What, doc? I've got six months to live? Gee, I think I'll enroll in college and work on a masters!") It's not knowing that keeps us going, that makes us productive members of society.

What would it be like if you knew which team would win the baseball game? In a world of total certainty we'd all know who would win, so the games wouldn't even be played. No sports would exist, since there would be no uncertainty to exploit. No movies or television shows either, at least none containing an element of uncertainty, like mysteries or game shows.

What if you were certain what other people were thinking? An episode of "The Twilight Zone" depicted such a situation. For one entire day, this fellow was able to read minds. He could hear, in his mind, what everyone else at the office was thinking. It drove him crazy; it was the worst experience of his life. Believe me, you're better off not knowing a lot of things.

Uncertainty's natural state is latent. It's like the wind—always present to some degree, but usually latent, not hampering our life to any appreciable degree. Only when it kicks up and transforms into a tornado does it becomes acute and dangerous. That's when you become obsessed with it, when you allow uncertainty to commandeer your mind and consume your thoughts.

Here are three things you can you do to keep uncertainty latent, to keep it from transforming into an obsessive tornado:

1. **Make assumptions.** We talked about this in Chapter 5 as a means of taking action. Remember: Gather some information; then make assumptions; then make decisions based on those assumptions. What if your assumptions prove to be incorrect? You adjust them—make new assumptions—as new information makes itself known to you over time. Remember, it's better to act on assumptions than idly wait for certainty.

2. **Make plans.** People get it backward all the time. They think they can't make plans (to do whatever) because they lack certainty regarding various other variables.

   I dated a woman a few years back who always had a difficult time making plans more than 30 minutes in advance. On Wednesday, for example, she'd suggest we go to a concert on Saturday but hesitate to commit. She'd say "I don't know if I can go because I don't know what I'll be doing Saturday night." I replied, "If you make plans now, you will know what you're going to be doing Saturday night." No, this woman did not have a frog-sized IQ. She was as sharp as they come; yet for whatever reasons, she couldn't commit to anything until uncertainties were reduced.

Realization 38

You make uncertainty latent by making plans.

Instead of waiting for greater certainty to make plans, create certainty by making plans. With plans, you make uncertainty latent and render it harmless.

Have you had a period in your life when you felt very uncertain about your future, wondering where you'll be or what you'll be doing? Most of us do experience such "lost" feelings more than once over the years. During one of my lost periods a number of years ago, I experienced a great deal of tension and stress, as questions about my future danced through my mind.

Then I had an interesting thought. I recalled a time in my life when there was also a great deal of uncertainty, yet I did not feel any tension and stress. It was my college days at Michigan State University. If there ever is an anything-can-happen environment, with uncertainty in abundance, it's college. Classes come and go. Roommates come and go. You meet new, wacky people every day. You live in different rooms or apartments over the years. You're always under pressure to produce papers and study for tests. You're constantly taking exams and being graded. There is a lot of uncertainty. So why didn't I feel any tension and stress at the time? Do they only afflict those over 22?

The answer I came up with is very simple. In college, I knew what my future was going to be, at least for the four-year duration. I knew I'd be a student at Michigan State for four years. My future, I felt, was set in stone for that period. So all the other uncertainties didn't really count. They were latent uncertainties. Tension and stress didn't bother me because I had total certainty about my four-year future. Only when I graduated did tension and stress show up, as my future was then once again uncertain.

During that lost period, as I reflected on my tension-and-stress–free college days, I decided that planning your future in four-year increments makes a lot of sense. So I put together a plan of what I would be doing for the next four years. It took a while for me to convince myself it was valid, but eventually I began to feel confident my plan was the way things were going to be. And miraculously, tension and stress left when my next four years were determined.

Plan your future now. Decide where you'll be and what you'll be doing for the next four years. And don't tell me you can't do that because of various uncertainties. Of course there are uncertainties. But you're in the process of rendering those uncertainties latent right now with the plans you're making. You'll be amazed how therapeutic that can be.

Don't confuse making plans with the attachment of deadlines. With deadlines, you're taking a particular event and deciding when it has to happen by, like saying, ''I want a promotion by July first." When you make plans, you're doing the exact opposite. You're taking a particular point in time and deciding how to use that time, like saying, "Monday, I'll examine the Johnson proposal." Deadlines are bad, plans are good.

3. **Visualize results in advance.** Imagine whatever you want to accomplish before you actually accomplish it. See the end result in your mind, and play it over and over again. When tension and stress see you thinking ahead like this, they know they're going to have a harder time messing with your mind, so they tend to leave you alone. Visualization is such a useful and effective technique, I devote an entire upcoming chapter to it. You'll learn exactly how to visualize then.

Performance Pressure

Another vulnerability that invites tension and stress is performance pressure. Whether it comes from people or circumstances, performance pressure always amounts to the same thing: you must do something within a certain, limited period of time. And you must do that something well.

Why does such a condition invite tension and stress? More than likely, you lack experience in whatever task or endeavor it is you're attempting. If you were experienced, and had accomplished the same or similar task before, the pressure wouldn't result in much tension and stress. In that case, the pressure would be your friend, providing valuable motivation.

That is exactly what happens sometimes, doesn't it? Think back to a time when performance pressure felt good, exhilarating, and exciting. You rode the pressure wave brilliantly and accomplished the task well and on time. You worked well under pressure that time because your experience guided you confidently and surely. Only when you lack experience and question whether you can perform the task in the allotted time does performance pressure abet tension and stress.

The obvious way to handle performance pressure is to gain experience. Here are three helpful hints:

1. **Gain experience incrementally.** Don't take on monumental tasks or endeavors that require you to make a major leap in ability or performance in one fell swoop. So many college graduates expect

to do this and think their newly acquired degree entitles them to be hired as a CEO. Instead, first commit to tasks and endeavors you believe you can accomplish fairly easily. Then gain experience by taking on slightly more difficult tasks in succession. Build your experience incrementally. Stretch yourself incrementally. Challenge yourself to accomplish more than you have in the past incrementally. That's how you keep gaining experience and growing without inviting tension and stress along for the ride.

2. **Practice.** Entertainers and athletes appreciate the value of constant practice like no others. For every hour of performance, an entertainer or athlete spends several hours, even several days, practicing. In the 1992 summer Olympics, one of the synchronized swimmers, who won a medal for her two-minute routine, said she spent an average of seven hours a day in the pool, seven days a week, practicing. That practice-to-performance ratio is well over a million to one—no wonder she's one of the best in the world and turned in a superb Olympic performance.

Practice is a great tension and stress reducer. And it's not reserved strictly for entertainers or athletes. You are free to practice anything you desire. Try it next time when you find a particular endeavor stressful. Cynthia, for example, found herself feeling a great deal of tension and stress when it came time for her six-month performance review. So she practiced the review session at home, ahead of time. She actually sat on her couch the way she planned to sit in the conference room at work on review day. She practiced answering questions and speaking in a confident, relaxed tone. By the time the actual review happened, Cynthia had reduced her tension and stress considerably, and she performed very well in the review.

Lou found himself victimized by tension and stress whenever he had to lunch with his supervisors. So he practiced at home. He practiced walking confidently into the restaurant, sitting up straight without fidgeting, and listening intently. Practicing his movements and facial expressions, as silly as it may sound, actually reduced his level of tension and stress measurably and made each lunch go much smoother than the last.

For Steve, the process of buying a new car was filled with tension and stress. So as practice, he visited showrooms and talked to salespeople regarding cars he had no intention of buying. By the time he went in to purchase his car of choice, he had worked tension and stress out of his system.

When you find yourself facing a task or endeavor that engenders tension and stress, why not do a little practicing? It may seem rather odd at first, but that's only because it's a new idea. Get in the habit of practicing, and you'll experience a lot less tension and stress in your life.

3. **Delay judgment until after the action stops.** Don't judge yourself as you're performing. It slows down your thinking, makes you tentative, and invites tension and stress. Instead, evaluate yourself or the results you're getting only after completing a task, or a segment of it, never while the action is in progress. (Actually, your subconscious mind will make instantaneous evaluations and instruct you to adjust your actions accordingly while it's all happening. This is fine. It's conscious evaluation that invites tension and stress.)

Relationship Disharmony

I don't know of any condition that makes you as vulnerable to tension and stress as quickly and forcefully as disharmony in a relationship. It may be a personal relationship with your significant other, a family member, a friend, or a professional colleague, supervisor, or subordinate. When disharmony flares up, and it will from time to time in even the best of relationships, tension and stress have a field day at your expense.

There are four things you can do to keep your relationships harmonious and greatly reduce or assuage the disharmony you experience from time to time:

• **Don't be a turmoil creator.** Yes, it's true. You may very well be the cause of the turmoil. I know it doesn't seem that way; it never does. But without realizing it, you may in fact be instigating the disharmony. It could be you're subconsciously trying to stir up negative emotions. Or perhaps you're subconsciously attempting to get back at someone who you think hurt you in some way. Or perhaps there are a few installed commands in your subconscious that make your personality somewhat contentious.

Take a look at your behavior when interacting with others. Are your words or actions causing greater disharmony? Why are you doing that? Why not do and say different things, things that calm people down and make them feel good instead? The last thing you want to do is invite tension and stress to take up permanent residence in your home or workplace by instigating disharmony in your relationships.

- **Listen intently.** Listening is not easy. It takes effort. You've got to deliberately tune out all distracting thoughts; you've got to hear everything the other person is saying as well as feel the emotions he's conveying. You will be amazed at how proper listening reduces disharmony. It allows effective communication between you and others. When you really hear what another person is saying and feel what that person is feeling, a special rapport develops that automatically reduces disharmony in your relationship.

- **Reduce your usage of negative emotions.** You learned how to do this in Chapter 4, and you're implementing the techniques we discussed to reduce your negative emotion usage level. As your neul declines, so goes the amount of disharmony you experience in your relationships.

- **Associate with people with like values.** Most conflicts can be resolved, with one big exception. Values, those innermost principles and standards we all live by, can clash irreconcilably. Putting two people with opposite values in the same room for any extended period is like caging together two wild bobcats. Disharmony isn't even the word; havoc is more accurate.

  You will naturally gravitate toward people with like values. Just make sure you don't inadvertently marry, go into business with, or work for someone with values very different from yours, or you'll be inviting disharmony at the deepest level.

Change

You can add change to the list of life's only guarantees, behind death and taxes. Change is a natural part of life; things are changing all the time. With some things, such as the aging of your body, the constant change is slow enough that you can see the results only after a significant amount of time goes by. But the change is occurring anyway, every second of every day, like clockwork.

Everything is constantly changing. The geography, including roads, buildings, bridges, and landscape, changes over time. In your place of work, people are hired, promoted, fired, and retired. Companies themselves are born, grow, and sometimes die. Political leaders serve and leave. Fashion trends and fads come and go. Everything is changing all the time.

If change is so prevalent, so normal and natural, why do we get so upset by it? Why does change invite so much tension and stress into our lives? Change, as common and pervasive as it is, is also a threat. We tend to equate change to danger, since its very nature can upset the comfort we've collected over the years. Therefore, aversion to change is a natural defense mechanism. Unless you're the one instigating the change, you will inherently find it unsettling and threatening to some degree.

Change courts tension and stress, which are actually defined in some psychological circles as a physical reaction to change. But since change is unavoidable, does that mean the tension and stress it causes are also unavoidable? Is there anything you can do to lessen the threat of change?

You don't have to do anything to render change harmless; it's already harmless. The harmful aspect of change is largely a mirage. Even when you experience a change that does harm you, you can be sure there will be another change forthcoming that helps you. Change as a whole balances out and is basically harmless. Most of it, better called *progress*, is actually beneficial.

George became incensed when he found out his company was planning to rearrange some divisions, putting him into another division. The change so upset him, he became a haven for tension and stress. George couldn't eat or sleep because of tension and stress. He fought the change like crazy, speaking to his supervisor and his supervisor's supervisor, trying to keep himself from being affected. Was George harmed by the change? Some minor things changed for the worse, some for the better. But they all averaged out, with no net effect on George whatsoever—all that aversion to a change that didn't harm him in the least.

Do you find yourself suddenly feeling tense or stressed when a change is proposed or when one occurs? In business situations,

I've always been able to make change work in my favor because I don't look at it as a threat. You should do the same. Think about Realization 39, and notice how true it is in your life.

Realization 39

Change as a whole is good for you. Even negative changes are always balanced out by positive changes that render the negative harmless.

WHAT ABOUT NERVOUSNESS?

Like tension and stress, nervousness is both a physical and mental reaction. But nervousness differs from tension and stress in two important ways.

First, nervousness is almost always caused by one thing: performance pressure. More specifically, it's caused by you being judged by others on your performance. Put another way, your performance wouldn't make you nervous if you weren't being judged by others. It's the judgment of others that makes you nervous.

The second difference between tension and stress and nervousness is the level of severity. Tension and stress are at the dangerous end of the scale; nervousness is not.

Although the physical symptoms of tension and stress and nervousness are similar, including tight stomach, rubbery legs, shaking hands, dry mouth, and excessive sweating, their differing levels of severity make them quite different in actuality. When you're only nervous, the outward symptoms are largely superficial. They make you feel lousy, but they really aren't hurting you. But when you're affected by tension and stress, the symptoms are usually just the tip of the iceberg; underneath you can be suffering from any number of genuinely harmful ailments (such as ulcers, heart irregularities, eating disorders, mental breakdowns, and so forth.)

How can you tell the difference between tension and stress and nervousness? You can be nervous and happy at the same time. But when you're affected by tension and stress, you can't be happy. I've never been more nervous than when I sat down at the microphone for my very first radio job when I was 18 years old. I was so nervous, sweat was oozing out of my hands, which were shaking like a paint mixer. But I was elated to be there. It was my burning desire to be on the radio, and now it was finally my chance. I was extremely happy—and extremely nervous. How about you? Have you been happy and nervous at the same time? I'll bet you have, but I'll also bet you've never been tense or stressed and happy at the same time.

Nervousness is not necessarily good, but it's not necessarily bad either. A number of experiences throughout your life are going to make you nervous. It comes with the territory if you're alive and productive. You've got to learn to operate, to perform productively while you're nervous. It's not easy, but you must do it. Otherwise, nervousness will get the better of you and prevent you from accomplishing. Don't give more credit to nervousness than it deserves. Nervousness is just a sideshow, a minor distraction. Accept it or ignore it, but don't acquiesce to it.

BRING IN THE GOOD GUYS

Okay, you've taken the above measures to reduce your vulnerability to tension and stress. You've softened these two lugs up. What do you do now? It's time to bring in the good guys, patience and relaxation. Once tension and stress have been weakened, patience and relaxation are ready to ride into town and clean up.

PATIENCE WHIPS TENSION AND STRESS

Let's discuss both patience and relaxation separately, starting with the former.

Remember, we said tension and stress love to distort your perception of time, tricking you into believing time is running out faster than it really is. When you think you have less time, you become anxious, which really screws up your productivity. Patience hits tension and stress precisely in this area, righting your perception of time and reducing your anxiousness. Thus, tension and stress have been foiled, as their primary weapon, time distortion, is disarmed by patience.

Realization 40

Time really isn't running out as fast as it seems. You have more time than you think to accomplish what you desire.

The key to bringing patience into your mind is to understand that time really isn't running out as fast as it seems. You have more time than you think to accomplish what you desire. Yes, there are exceptions. In some cases, time is of the essence. But even then, it's often not as critical as it would seem. It may be that your team is behind by two touchdowns in the final two minutes of the game, but there's always another game, always another year of games. Even if it's your last game, remember it's exactly that—a game. Life goes on. It's never as critical as it seems at the time.

Linda hadn't gotten a raise in a while and felt she was due. The more she thought about it, the more she felt unfairly compensated. Tension and stress began to take hold, caused by the acute uncertainty of not knowing whether she was ever going to make more money. As tension and stress intensified, her anxiousness rose. Linda determined that the longer she waited to approach her supervisor, the worse were her chances of getting a raise.

As Linda's sense of urgency rose, she became anxious to meet with her supervisor. She called him to ask for a meeting, but couldn't reach him immediately (his office was in an adjacent building, not readily accessible in person). When he didn't return her call that day, she began to panic. She felt tremendous tension and stress, and her anxiousness rose accordingly. She could hardly sleep that night. The next morning she left two more "important" messages, and not getting an immediate reply, she finally burst into his office that afternoon requesting an "urgent meeting" to discuss a "severe problem."

Thinking it was something monumental, the manager delayed a meeting with an important client, leaving the client waiting in the reception area. He invited Linda in to discuss the problem right then and there. Upon learning it was a raise request, something that could be addressed at a more appropriate time, he became a bit perturbed. She had embarrassed him in front of the client, and had exercised poor timing. It turned out the company had been considering Linda for a promotion at a substantial raise; but it now began reassessing her judgment. Had Linda understood that time was not running out on her, that she really could better herself by not trying to beat the clock in requesting a raise, she would have had the patience necessary to avoid her anxious mistake.

Some people declare they just don't have any patience; they say that's just the way they are. That's because they always feel they're short of time. But when you take Realization 40 to heart, and understand that time isn't running out nearly to the degree it seems, patience automatically appears.

It may help you to think ahead in time. Think a month ahead, six months ahead, or a year ahead. Think about what things will be like then. Say to yourself, "September (or another month down the road) will arrive without doubt. By then, I'll be over this problem and things will be much better. That being the case, I can be more patient now. I know everything will work out just fine in time." By thinking ahead, you better understand that today, this hour, this minute is not as critical as it seems. When you think ahead, patience appears and tension and stress further disappear.

RELAXATION KNOCKS OUT TENSION AND STRESS

Patience's partner, relaxation, is equally adept at running tension and stress out of town. Remember, when the foes square off—a weakened tension and stress versus a strong patience and relaxation—the latter two always win the battle.

There are two types of relaxation, one you're familiar with and one you may not be so familiar with. Let's discuss the familiar one first.

Unproductive Relaxation

Perhaps you're in a very relaxed state right now as you read. You might be sprawled out on the couch, with the fireplace going and soothing music in the background. Or sitting by the pool, drenched in sunshine, piña colada in hand. Or sleeping with this book under your pillow, allowing it to osmotically seep into your brain (good luck with that one). In any of these or similar cases, you're definitely relaxed. But you're not exactly productive. Reading a book, watching television, or consuming food and drink, is valuable in its own right, but it's not really productive endeavor. We call it *unproductive relaxation.*

Unproductive relaxation is an important part of your well-being. It allows your brain and body to shift into neutral and cruise a while. It allows you to recharge your mental and physical energy; in fact, the ultimate in unproductive relaxation is sleep. It can also be fun.

To engage in unproductive relaxation, most people alter their body position. They sit or lie down, consume food or drink, and slow down their body movement. Some people do all these things to excess, including the overconsumption of food (all the wrong kinds) and drink (the alcoholic kind, usually) in the name of relaxation. Excessive unproductive relaxation diminishes your productivity, but the right amount of unproductive relaxation benefits you immeasurably. How do you know what amount is excessive and what amount is right? One way to tell is to do an honest check of your productivity level. I know one guy who spent an average of five nights a week partying. One day he realized that the years were going by, but his career was going nowhere. He cut his partying back to one night a week, and within six months his career miraculously began to move ahead.

Everyone has favorite ways of engaging in unproductive relaxation, such as reading the newspaper, watching television, lying out at the pool, whatever. Regardless of your favorite, these three suggestions will help you implement them:

- **Once a day, spend at least one hour straight in unproductive relaxation.** Remember, this will include altering your body position. It also includes reducing your brain activity and cruising. You shouldn't have to do much thinking or moving when you're in unproductive relaxation. The obvious time to do this during your workday is lunch time. Or if you have a working lunch, do it over dinner when you get home. Or after dinner, if you prefer.

- **Twice during your workday, engage in eight-minute unproductive relaxation respites.** Take time to slow down your thinking and body movements for these short breaks.

- **Spike your personal to-do list once in a while.** About once every two or three weeks, I take my personal to-do list for that day (as opposed to my job to-do list), which is usually loaded, and toss it aside. In other words, I do absolutely nothing productive that day. I'll watch television, read, go to the movies, the park, or the beach, or do whatever interesting thing comes to mind at the time. But I don't do anything that requires expending much mental or physical energy.

  Ever wonder why football players spike the ball so often after scoring a touchdown? It's their way of demonstrating superior power over the football—an object they're taught to treat with supreme reverence during the game. You should do the same with your personal to-do list once in a while. Remember, you are master of the list, not the other way around. If you feel like doing nothing one day, spike your list and relax. There's always tomorrow.

  Obviously, you may not be able to do this with your job to-do list. But that's okay, because your job to-do list is not really the one that needs spiking. After all, you're not supposed to engage in unproductive relaxation while you work. It's your personal to-do list that needs spiking once in a while. Your personal time is supposed to contain a good amount of unproductive relaxation. Yet many people drive themselves even harder when they're off work, jamming their evenings and weekends with monumental task loads. Take a personal day, a Saturday or Sunday, and spike your to-do list once in a while. You deserve, and need, the break.

Productive Relaxation

The other type of relaxation is *productive relaxation,* and it's as crucial to your overall productivity as unproductive relaxation. Productive relaxation is what you do *while* engaging in some productive endeavor.

If the term *productive relaxation* sounds oxymoronic, consider this: Professional athletes say the two things they try to do mentally during a game are concentrate and relax. Relax? Do they plan to go out there and lie down on the field with a cup of spiked Gatorade? I don't think so. The type of relaxation they're talking about is totally compatible with concentration, intensity, and aggressiveness. In fact, productive relaxation heightens your concentration, intensity, and aggressiveness.

Realization 41

You're supposed to be relaxed while you work or perform.

Productive relaxation is the state in which you are at ease or loose. In the productive relaxation mode, you concentrate with your conscious mind, and you make decisions and act with your subconscious mind. You know when that happens because you don't have to think about what you say or do. Your moves all come naturally and instinctively.

When you've got your conscious mind concentrating on the task at hand, and your subconscious mind making decisions, you've reached the pinnacle of productive relaxation. In this state, tension and stress are nowhere to be found. You feel energetic and confident, excited and forceful. The words tumble out of your mouth effortlessly. Your body movements flow freely. Your actions string together like a well-choreographed ballet. You're cooking, baby!

Getting into productive relaxation at will can be done, although it will take practice. Follow these tips:

- **Realize you're supposed to be relaxed while you work or perform.** Some people don't understand the concept. They think that if they're engaging in some productive activity, they're supposed to be tense and tight. Some people even work themselves into a tension frenzy in preparation for productive activity. They grit their teeth, growl, and attack the task like a mad dog. Realizing that it's not only okay but desirable to be relaxed while productive is half of what it takes to get in that state. Make the realization, and you're halfway there.

- **Breathe deeply.** Relaxation is part mental and part physical. A neat little maneuver that addresses both aspects is deep breathing. Take a deep breath and hold it for three seconds. Exhale slowly, and as you do, tell yourself to relax. Believe it or not, you're relaxing yourself this way. Deep breathing tends to slow down your heart rate; and the intake of oxygen soothes your nerves. Breathe deeply anywhere, at any time, when you want to be more relaxed.

• **Smile.** Another nifty relaxation technique is based on the incompatibility between tension and stress and smiling. A tense or stressed mind will not produce a smile. Conversely, a smile will negate a good amount of tension and stress during its duration. Don't count on a smile to happen automatically. Like I said, tension and stress will prevent you from smiling. You will have to deliberately put the smile on your face, even if you're feeling tense or stressed. Then, the smile will relax you, and tension and stress will diminish. You may have to hold the smile for a few minutes for it to take effect. Don't worry, it looks good on you.

• **Let your subconscious guide you.** Have faith in the directives of your subconscious and leave the driving to it. Know that your subconsciously controlled decisions—the ones that come without your having to consciously think about them—will lead you correctly.

HOW IT ALL RELATES

Let's take a minute to summarize how all the elements we've talked about relate to one another. The accompanying chart is helpful. It shows your relative productivity potential under four different conditions.

Patience and relaxation cause your productivity to increase tremendously. But becoming patient and relaxed is not easy. Why? Because anxiousness, negative emotions, and weakening confidence prevent patience and relaxation from taking hold.

What causes anxiousness, negative emotions, and weakening confidence to proliferate in your mind? Tension and stress. Those guys were born to make life difficult for you.

Who then invited tension and stress to the party? They crashed your party. Sensing some vulnerability in you, they busted in. The vulnerabilities that attract tension and stress are worry, acute uncertainty, performance pressure, relationship disharmony, and change—any one or in any combination.

What do you do about all this? You execute a two-pronged strat-

Productivity Potential Chart

Tension and Stress	Nervousness	Productive Relaxation	Unproductive Relaxation
Symptoms	Symptoms	Symptoms	Symptoms
• Tight muscles. • Quick, shallow breathing. • Rapid heartbeat. • On edge, high-strung. • Tentative. • Anxious. • Low confidence level. • Low energy level. • High negative emotion usage level.	• Unfocused energy. • Tentative. • Superficial physical changes (sweating, butterfly stomach, rubber legs, etc.).	• High energy level. • Focused energy. • High concentration level. • Subconcious decision making. • Deliberate, flowing moves. • At ease, loose.	• Slow or no physical movement. • Low thinking level. • Low energy level.

Shaded areas represent productivity potential under each condition. Productive relaxation is by far the most desirable state for maximum productivity.

egy. First you soften up tension and stress. Then you call in patience and relaxation. You implement this strategy by executing the following steps.

STEPS IN ACQUIRING PATIENCE AND RELAXATION

These 10 steps will guide you through the entire process of becoming a much more patient and relaxed person. Each step will result in increased productivity for you.

- **Step 1: Make plans.** When you establish plans for your future, you render uncertainty latent. Make short-term plans for the next day, week, or month. Make long-term plans for the next four years (in general terms, where you're going to be and what you're going to be doing). To aid the planning process, make underlying assumptions whenever necessary. As time goes on and new information becomes available, you may alter your assumptions. You may subsequently alter your plans. Having a flexible plan is far superior than having no plan.

- **Step 2: Gain experience.** Learn and perform incrementally, as opposed to leaping ahead all at once. Take on tasks and endeavors that teach and challenge you a bit more each time. Before you jump into a new endeavor, practice. Practice is a great tool for reducing tension and stress and building confidence. Think of new ways you can practice something, then spend a little time doing it.

- **Step 3: Bolster relationship harmony.** Say things that calm and relax others. Make people feel good about themselves. Listen intently. When you hear every word and feel what the speaker is feeling, you automatically build rapport, attraction, and harmony.

- **Step 4: Welcome change.** Change is ubiquitous; you can't avoid it. So don't fight it. Embrace it instead. When you welcome change, you put yourself in position to benefit from it. Remember, even harmful changes are eventually neutralized by subsequent positive changes.

- **Step 5: Operate while nervous.** Nervousness is really harmless. That old deodorant commercial had it right: "It's okay to be nervous, just don't let 'em see you sweat." Perform like you're not nervous. Nervousness goes away much quicker when you take action in the face of it.

- **Step 6: Acknowledge the existence of more time.** When you're feeling anxious, look ahead in time. See things as you would like them to be in a week, a month, or in six months. Time is not running out nearly as fast as it seems.

- **Step 7: Engage in unproductive relaxation daily.** Spend at least one waking hour a day in unproductive relaxation. This will entail a reduction of mental and physical activity. Treat yourself to two eight-minute unproductive relaxation respites during your day. These are like pit stops that allow you to refuel as you perform.

- **Step 8: Spike your personal to-do list once in a while.** Show that you are master of your aspirations, not a slave of them. One or two days a month, do nothing productive, or at least nothing on your list as it relates to your personal life. Get out of your routine; live a little differently for that day. Don't worry about falling behind. When you spike your to-do list once in a while, you're actually empowering yourself to accomplish more in the long run.

- **Step 9: Remind yourself daily that you're supposed to be relaxed while you perform.** By constantly telling yourself to relax, you're simultaneously blocking tension and stress from entering and escorting relaxation in.

- **Step 10: Breathe deeply and smile.** Both deep breathing and smiling are outward, physical signs of patience and relaxation. You must consciously and deliberately take deep breaths and put a smile on your face; don't wait for them to happen on their own. You may also have to hold your smile for a while, for a few minutes at a time.

Chapter Eight

Get into Highly Concentrated Attention

Highly concentrated attention is exactly that. It's a highly focused, deeply intensive mental state of attention, like the state kids go into when playing video games. It's also highly explosive. When you're in highly concentrated attention mode, you can blow past obstacles and cut through a task with laser beam precision. It's what highly productive people do, and what you will soon be doing.

Highly concentrated attention, productivity thruster number two, is high-powered thinking that produces high-level results. When you concentrate, your personal productivity can elevate rapidly. You can accomplish twice as much in the same amount of time, or the same amount in half the time, or a combination of both. And it doesn't cost you a cent. If you picked up this book hoping to find just one simple technique that can simultaneously raise your productivity and save you time, at no cost, this is your chapter.

IT ISN'T EASY TO CONCENTRATE

Admit it—you really don't spend a lot of time in deep concentration, do you? Neither do I. No one does. Concentration is rare; we do it infrequently. Some people can actually live their lives day in and out without ever concentrating on anything.

If concentration is such a beneficial, productivity-lifting state, why do so few of us spend even a little time doing it? Why isn't it standard procedure instead of a rarity? Three main reasons:

1. **The brain defaults out of concentration.** Our brains instinctively avoid expending any more energy than they have to (which

some members of society demonstrate ever so eloquently). As a means of self-preservation, the brain naturally gravitates toward a relaxed, low level of thinking. In the absence of certain stimuli specifically designed to kick the brain into high gear, the brain defaults into low gear. It will remain in low gear, out of concentration, as long as no stimuli to the contrary exist.

2. **Concentration guzzles brainpower.** When you're concentrating, you're burning mental fuel at a high rate. It's not unusual for someone to feel mentally and physically tired after a period of deep concentration. In other words, concentration is not an easy state to maintain. Do you spend your entire day running wherever you go? Not likely. It would be too physically draining. The same is true of concentration. It's too mentally taxing to engage in full-time.

3. **Distractions abound.** To concentrate, you have to tune out all the other, nonrelevant stimuli that reach your five senses. This is supremely difficult, especially when such distractions as other people, the television, the phone, the refrigerator, or who knows what constantly beckon for your attention.

ANYTHING-CAN-HAPPEN (ACH) MODE

If we're not concentrating most of the time, what are we doing? Most often, we operate in a mental state halfway between concentration and sleep. We spend most of our waking time in light-duty thinking, not in deep concentration.

Most of the time, your brain operates in anything-can-happen (ACH) mode. In ACH mode, your brain meanders along, reacting to whatever stimuli reach it through the senses. And all kinds of different stimuli do reach the senses. All kinds of sights, sounds, smells, and touches are constantly diverting your attention one way and the other. In a hectic anything-can-happen environment, anything can and does happen.

Consider, for example, a typical day at the office. Anyone can stick his head into your office at any time and blurt out something just to get your attention. "Hey Ed—check this out!" you hear, as a trade publication containing a picture of the blurter lands on your lap. Any number of others can blurt out anything all day long. (Don't attempt to stick a "do not disturb" sign on your door. You'll spend the next month explaining to everyone that there's really nothing wrong with you, that you're just trying to get some work done. No one ever buys that argument. Evidently the notion of someone working in isolation is so unusual it strains credulity.)

The phone may ring at any time, and it may be anyone in the world calling. It could be your best client, someone selling a dubious offshore investment scheme, a wrong number, a fan from halfway around the world just calling to say "hi," or a friend asking for your help with a personal problem. Anything can happen. (Anything *does* happen. I experienced each of these phone calls this morning alone.)

Any number of fires can flare up on a moment's notice that require your immediate attention. One of your subordinates needs help with a problem. Your supervisor calls an emergency meeting to discuss a customer defection. A co-worker doesn't show up for work, and you must assume some of his duties. Members of the top brass are coming in from out of town. There's a bomb scare in the building. Anything can happen. (Even when anything doesn't happen—I didn't experience any of these things recently—their potential to happen constitutes an ACH environment.)

Most of the time, we operate in an ACH environment, with our brain in ACH mode. Here are the typical characteristics you exhibit when you're in ACH mode:

- **You're highly reactionary.** Something happens and you react to it. I'm not talking strictly about putting out fires, though that in itself can take a lot of your time. Routine work moving through the pipeline may simply require your reaction. Your co-workers continue to plop more reports on your desk, which you must read and approve. Your supervisor calls a meeting and you attend. A customer calls and you service her. Other people initiate things— or some things, like a bursting water pipe, initiate themselves— and you must react. And your reaction becomes an initiated action that someone else must react to. You're part of a reactionary chain, in which each person's action must be reacted to by someone else. No matter what happens, it all shakes out the same: In ACH mode, you spend almost all your time reacting to things.

- **Time accelerates.** When lots of different things happen in your presence—people talking, phones ringing, fires flaring, meetings transpiring, people coming and going, and so on—time seems to go by faster than it normally does. In the whirlwind of an ACH environment, what seems like four hours may have actually been eight hours. And you don't even need to be having fun for time to fly. The hectic, fast-paced environment will warp your perception of time in direct relation to the number of things that happen and the pace at which they happen.

- **You think laterally.** Most thinking that occurs in ACH mode deals with things that are happening in the present. You're thinking about what's happening as it's happening, as opposed to thinking about something else in the past or in the future. Lateral thinking is good; you're supposed to be paying attention to what you're doing.

There's nothing wrong with ACH mode. You could operate in it your entire time at work and be a productive, well-thought-of employee. But your personal productivity would be about average. Since most people operate in ACH mode most of the time, you're like most people: moderately productive.

HIGHLY-CONCENTRATED-ATTENTION (HCA) MODE

Highly-concentrated-attention (HCA) mode is the mirror image of anything-can-happen mode (coincidentally, the letters ACH and HCA are reversals of one another). When you learn to operate in HCA mode, a whole new world of productivity and reward opens up to you.

The characteristics of HCA mode are:

- **You're highly creative.** I don't necessarily mean creative in an artistic sense, although that may be. When you're in HCA mode, you can create something from nothing with the greatest of ease. The right words come to you when there might otherwise be silence. You put your pen to the paper and that letter you've been meaning to write for weeks suddenly materializes in a matter of minutes. Solutions to problems suddenly come to mind. New ideas pop into your head. When in HCA mode, your creativity explodes way beyond your average.

- **You think at warp speed.** In HCA mode, your brain is thinking much faster than it normally does. Ironically, while thinking rapidly, things seem to happen in slow motion.

    In the 1992 winter Olympics, a woman skier who had just set the course record was asked by a reporter if she knew she was doing so well during her run. "I knew I was having a good run because it seemed like I was moving in slow motion," she answered. She was in such deep concentration, her brain was moving faster than her body, which seemed to be going slower by comparison.

    Morten Andersen, the highly successful field goal kicker for the New Orleans Saints, expressed the same feeling: "When I hit the ball, it travels up . . . toward the goal . . . and [when] it all goes in slow motion, I know I've had a great kick."[1]

    Television and movie directors have found a way to depict the slowing of an event that one experiences in HCA mode. They use slow motion to depict something that is actually happening very quickly. The first time I saw this technique used was in the 70s television show "The Six Million Dollar Man." The Steve Austin character, played by Lee Majors, would supposedly run at incredible speed, which they'd depict by showing him running in slow motion. The technique has since become a staple and can be seen in numerous television shows and movies.

- **You think ahead.** Remember what we said about anything-can-happen mode: We tend to think laterally; we think about things as they're happening. But in highly-concentrated-attention mode, the brain actually shifts forward, thinking *ahead* of what is actually happening.

    O.J. Simpson, the legendary running back for the Buffalo Bills, once said the secret to his great running ability was that he thought ahead of where he actually was on the field. In other words, he would think about the spot down the field where he

---

[1]ABC's "Monday Night Football," November 23, 1992.

wanted to be, which changed instantaneously as he ran, instead of where he actually was.

In HCA mode, the time difference between your thinking and what is happening can be but a split second, hardly noticeable by any measure except your performance. When you feel things are "clicking," when your moves are graceful and flowing, it's because you're thinking ahead of your moves by a split second.

The time difference between your thinking and what is happening can be much longer than split seconds. When you're in HCA mode, you can envision the future, you can think minutes, hours, days, even years forward. HCA mode is a great tool for future planning. It's great for creating your future.

- **Your motions quicken.** Because you're thinking ahead in HCA mode, your movements are able to happen quicker than they normally would. Because O.J. Simpson was thinking ahead of himself as he ran, he actually ran faster. Think about what happens when you type. If you're thinking about each letter as you push the corresponding key, you type slowly. If you think ahead by a split second, if you think of an entire sentence and not the individual letters, your fingers miraculously push each appropriate key in rapid succession. It's as though your fingers are chasing your speeding mind, which is exactly what's happening.

BENEFITS OF HIGHLY CONCENTRATED ATTENTION

Since you normally spend little time in HCA mode, I'm going to talk you into changing that. Let me take a minute to enumerate the benefits you will gain by thinking in HCA mode.

- **You'll get great ideas and solutions.** You'll think of new ideas and solutions that will make your job easier and more pleasurable. You'll think of fun, exciting things that will enrich your life and the lives of others close to you. People will naturally be attracted to you, as they see how resourceful and fun you are.

- **You'll have more free time.** Since you'll be accomplishing in less time, you'll have time remaining for other enjoyable activities. It's like creating extra time in each day.

- **You'll treat yourself to one of life's finest pleasures.** The brain-power you expend in HCA mode is not exhausting, it's exhilarating, invigorating, and refreshing. It's the mental equivalent of a physical workout, beneficial and pleasurable all the way.

- **You'll stimulate your career.** Remember, most everyone else at work will be operating in ACH mode, turning in average performances. But as you spend regular amounts of time in HCA mode, your productivity surpasses that of the others. Before long, you'll look like a miracle worker. Who do you think the company is going to promote?

THE CATCH

At this point, you probably either (1) can't wait to find out how to get into HCA mode and unleash yet another round of your personal productivity, or (2) can't wait to hear the catch. We'll get to the how in a minute. First, the catch.

You will encounter a great deal of entry resistance as you attempt to go into HCA mode. When a rocket blasts off, a lot of fuel is expended and a lot of thrust is required to get the thing off the ground and out of the Earth's gravitational pull. The gravitational pull impeding your shift into HCA mode is your brain's instinctive desire to avoid expending excessive energy.

There is an exception. You can go into HCA mode immediately and with no resistance if you experience a traumatic event. Say you're driving on a winding, icy road in the middle of winter. Suddenly your car begins to skid. You lose control, and the car is heading for a cliff. What will happen to your level of concentration? Instantaneously, your brain will shift into HCA mode and become fixated on the situation at hand. Your brain will shift into overdrive as it attempts to handle the immediate problem. As your car skids and your brain races, it will seem like everything is happening in slow motion.

In a matter of seconds, you regain control, and avoid the cliff, and the traumatic event is over. As you slowly shift out of HCA mode, you can replay the experience back in your mind, recalling every detail of the dangerous landscape, the skidding car, and your feelings at the time. The whole experience seems like it took a few minutes in retrospect, when in reality it took only a few seconds.

Your brain will assume HCA mode in a flash if it senses danger or any other condition that warrants your supreme attention. But traumatic events are not the norm. You can't wait for a traumatic event when you want to shift into HCA mode and be more productive. You must instigate HCA mode yourself. Yet when you do, your brain may choose not to cooperate. Remember, the brain likes to avoid expending undue amounts of energy. It'll kick and scream as you try to get it into HCA mode. If it were easy, everybody would be in HCA mode all the time instead of ACH mode. You have to be willing to put forth a good deal of effort to get into it. Sometimes it takes several minutes of forced concentration to slowly work your brain into HCA mode. And sometimes, after spending several minutes getting to the brink of HCA mode, your brain will snap out of it and you'll have to start all over.

Here's two pieces of good news. First, your brain can become conditioned to go into HCA mode more readily as you experience the mode more often. Like a dog being trained, your brain eventually gets the idea and begins to cooperate. It gets easier with time.

Second, once you're in HCA mode, maintaining it is not as difficult as getting there. Take that rocket I mentioned earlier. Once it's out of the Earth's gravitational pull, it can keep moving on considerably less fuel.

If your brain instinctively fights HCA mode, are you violating the natural laws of human nature by contorting it into HCA mode? No. The truth is, your brain was designed to operate in HCA mode occasionally. The state is as natural as ACH mode.

Realization 42

Your brain likes operating in highly-concentrated-attention mode, even though it fights going into HCA mode.

HCA mode is the mental equivalent of physical exercise. Just as the human body was designed to engage in limited amounts of physical exertion, the brain was designed to engage in limited amounts of mental exertion. Why do some people, or all of us some of the time, take great pains to avoid physical exertion? Because it's work, it requires expending excessive energy. But what happens when we do it anyway? Lo and behold, a great physical workout turns out to be exhilarating and refreshing. And it keeps the body in good physical condition. Do it with some regularity, and the body begins to crave the workout. It really does want to expend the energy, even though it leads you to believe otherwise initially.

As you get used to HCA mode, your brain will begin taking a liking to it. It'll put up less and less resistance getting into HCA mode, and it'll enjoy the mental workout during and afterward.

HOW TO GET INTO HCA MODE

Here is the step-by-step procedure for getting yourself into HCA mode upon demand:

- **Step 1: Reduce distractions.** Either alter your ACH environment by turning off the phone, television, or whatever, or leave your ACH environment for a more secluded place. Notice this step recommends you *reduce* distractions not *eliminate* them. If you believe you must eliminate all distractions, you'll end up concentrating on the distractions more than the intended subject. On a remote, exotic island with nothing but you and nature, the birds or the wind will become a distraction if you think every little thing is a hindrance.

- **Step 2: Allocate special time for HCA mode.** Both Martin Snead and I will often come into work an hour or two early or on Saturday afternoons. We devote this off-hours time strictly to HCA mode. Without the phones ringing and people buzzing around, it's much easier to engage in HCA activity. As you might expect, we each get much more work done in two hours of HCA time than we do in six hours of ACH time.

- **Step 3a: Put the object of your desired concentration into motion.** Motion commands concentration. Video games demonstrate this very vividly. They suck you into HCA mode because there's constant movement on the screen, with multiple things happening all at once and in rapid succession. Take the video games away from your kids and give them books instead. Watch what happens to their levels of concentration.

If whatever you're trying to concentrate on is moving, like a person walking by, a movie, an airborne baseball, or an assembly line, you're in luck. But what if the object of your desired concentration is inherently stationary, like a book? Then you must move instead. Move your eyes rapidly across the words—you're not trying to speed-read; you're just warming up and getting yourself into HCA mode. You've got motion one way or the other, whether the words are moving past your eyes or your eyes are moving past the words.

Motion doesn't always involve sight. Sounds can be put into motion too. Is it easier for children to concentrate on a random string of words mentioned one at a time or a nursery rhyme? When the words are in motion, as in a nursery rhyme or song, they attract deeper attention.

—Or—

- **Step 3b: Engage in physical movement.** Sometimes the object of your desired attention is not a physical object at all. Sometimes you want to think about the future, about ideas and solutions, about a relationship, about Einstein's law of relativity. None of these things are tangible; they exist in thought only.

To concentrate on something you can't see, hear, touch, taste, or smell, put yourself into motion. I know a guy who races dirt bikes as a means of getting himself into deep concentration. The ride gets him into HCA mode quickly, which allows him to concentrate on whatever else he pleases while he rides. President Reagan said as president he would go horseback riding to concentrate on the difficult presidential decisions he had to make. By the time he'd finished his ride, he'd made his decisions.[2]

I often walk through the park or drive to nowhere in particular to get myself into HCA mode more quickly. Have you ever driven past your intended freeway exit and not realized it until much later? You went into HCA mode and didn't even know it, though it wasn't your driving you were concentrating on. At the office, I often walk back and forth or in circles. As my brain goes into HCA mode, I then sit down and perform the work.

---

[2] R. Reagan, *An American Life* (New York NY: Simon & Schuster, 1990).

HCA MODE IN AN ACH ENVIRONMENT

What if you don't have the luxury of finding some remote locale in which to do your HCA thinking? What if your job requires you to concentrate in a hectic, distraction-rich environment? For instance, say you were a doctor, nurse, air traffic controller, athlete, newspaper reporter, construction worker, or the like. Could you get into, and stay into, HCA mode in such a case?

You can achieve HCA mode in an ACH environment by executing these auxiliary steps in addition to the steps listed above:

- **Auxiliary Step 1: Keep your eyes focused on one small object.** Air traffic controllers, for example, sit in front of a radar screen for the duration of their shift. Surgeons wear magnifying glasses and focus on one specific object at a time.

  Jerry Rice, the record-setting wide receiver for the San Francisco 49ers, stares at the ball while it's sailing through the air toward him. He's not looking at anything else. With the crowd screaming, the other players running wild, the ball sailing through the air, and him racing down the field, Jerry looks at one thing only: the ball. In fact, he actually stares at an even smaller object than the ball, the *tip* of the ball. "I'm so intense I can't hear the crowd, I can't hear the footsteps," Jerry explains. "I concentrate on the tip of the ball."[3]

  Focus your eyes on the smallest section of whatever you want to concentrate on. If the desired subject isn't something you can actually see or hear, such as a problem you wish to solve, visualize one small aspect of the problem in your mind. Think of one small aspect of the problem, and see it or hear it in motion.

- **Auxiliary Step 2: Create a wall of sound.** Sounds will distract you if they're erratic, like when all is quiet and your better half sticks his or her head in your room and says "Hey!" Have you ever been so startled by someone simply calling your name that you jumped like you were scared? You were jolted out of HCA is what happened. But if sounds are steady rather than erratic, like the crowd at a baseball, basketball, or football game, you can tune them out. The steady drone of a particular sound can

---

[3]TNT Network, August 30, 1992.

become a "wall of sound" that transforms itself into nondistractive background sound.

Ironically, you can reduce the distractiveness of sound by adding to the sound instead of trying to eliminate it. Turning on the radio while working, for example, creates a steady wall of sound that negates sound distractions. I used to wonder how other students in college could study with the radio or television on. I used to seek a secluded spot, myself. Years later, I learned they were simply creating a wall of sound that actually enhanced their ability to concentrate.

- **Auxiliary Step 3: Become acclimated to your ACH environment.**
  At first, you'll find concentration very difficult in an ACH environment. But in time—many days or weeks, perhaps—you'll get used to the environment and be able to get into HCA mode easier.

  I used to believe that I couldn't write unless I was in some secluded, quiet environment. Then I became the copywriter at a radio station, and I was forced to write commercial copy in an environment where anything can and does happen. And I had to turn out halfway decent copy at that. There wasn't time to dillydally around and wait for distractions to subside—they never did. When I had no choice, I began to write under ACH conditions and I learned to concentrate. Eventually I was able to get into HCA mode quickly at will, despite the distractive environment.

  Recently, I met a guy who mentioned that he goes to a particular restaurant on Sunday afternoons, when the place is very crowded and noisy, to concentrate on things. He, like many people who have learned to concentrate in an ACH environment, actually finds the hectic, noisy environment stimulating. You can learn to concentrate in an ACH environment, and even have it stimulate your concentration above normal, if you allow yourself time to acclimate.

Chapter Nine

The Power of Micro-Macro Vision

M ost people are either detail oriented or concept oriented. The detail-oriented people, who mentally zero in and focus on the smallest elements of whatever they're involved in (the micro view), can be productive. The concept-oriented people, who constantly pull back and focus on the big picture (the macro view), can also be productive. But neither maximizes their productivity potential. In fact, both detail-oriented people and concept-oriented people usually operate at less than their full potential, regardless of how long and hard they work.

A small percentage of the population are both detailed oriented *and* concept oriented. They mentally zoom in and focus on the details part of the time, and they zoom out and focus on the big picture part of the time. And most important, they know when to do each.

People who can shift their viewpoints between the detailed and the big picture possess the quality called *micro-macro vision*, productivity thruster number three. They have levels of productivity far above those who are strictly detail or concept oriented. In fact, the simple zoom-in/zoom-out process of balancing one's focus, from detailed, or micro, and big picture, or macro, is a source of incredible, almost magical, productivity power. You'll see how this is so as you read further.

Micro-macro vision is somewhat rare and arcane. It's not because such vision is some inherited trait found in only few people's genes, which it isn't. It's because few people have ever heard of it or understand how it works. Micro-macro vision can be learned by anyone who takes the time to do so. If you put forth the effort to develop micro-macro vision, you will experience a rise in personal productivity far beyond what you ever imagined.

TRAITS OF DETAIL-ORIENTED PEOPLE

To develop into a micro-macro vision person, you must first learn how each opposing view, detail and concept, works. Let's look at detail-oriented people first.

A detail-oriented person will usually have four key character traits. Although there are exceptions, detail-oriented people tend to:

1. **Believe that both opportunities and solutions are based in the details.** The way to capitalize on opportunities and the way to solve problems is to focus on the details, they believe. To angle for promotions, for example, detail-oriented people will emphasize their handling of numerous details. This might include everything from keeping precise paperwork, demonstrating unwavering punctuality, keeping errors to a minimum, and maintaining a neat and clean workstation. To the detail-oriented people, details make the difference. Details are supreme.

   Whenever it comes to exploiting opportunities or solving problems, detail-oriented people will dissect the particular situation, zero in on one aspect (or one aspect at a time), and spend all their attention dealing with it in its minutest form. To them this makes total sense. It seems, without question, to be the way to go about taking advantage of opportunities and solving problems.

2. **Be just as concerned with the means as the end.** How they think, act, look, or communicate is very important to detail-oriented people. The process of accomplishing is just as crucial as the result.

   Bill, the owner of a restaurant, decided to participate in his city's annual downtown festival. His restaurant would be one of a dozen food suppliers at the three-day event. Bill began preparing three months in advance, by first listing every supply he would need and every logistical maneuver that would be required to set up, operate on-site, and clean up afterward. He calculated the amount of supplies needed and ordered them weeks in advance. He created teams of employees and assigned them specific duties. Bill devised specific procedures for transporting the money to and from the site, including duplicating sets of keys for the cash boxes. He created a special form to track sales and expenses. In short, Bill planned it all well in advance, so that everything would go as smoothly as possible to make it a successful venture. To a detail-oriented person like Bill, it's not only important to plan well but to execute in a very specific, methodical manner.

3. **Think in small time increments.** Detail-oriented people think about what is happening this month, this week, today, this hour, right now. They spend a lot of time thinking of the immediate present, not the distant past or the far future. All productivity eventually boils down to the here and now, what happens today, minute by minute. When you can focus on small increments of time, you can make every hour or minute pay off. Detail-oriented people can be very productive with specific tasks, and this is why.

4. **Be neat and well organized.** As you might expect, detail-oriented people tend to be neat and highly organized.

   At a small social gathering a few years ago, a debate ensued regarding whether or not the apartment management would allow more than one pet in an apartment. Ed, in whose apartment the gathering took place, said, "That's easy to resolve. Let's just check the lease." He got up, went into another room, and returned 20 seconds later with his lease in hand. Then an interesting thing happened. People forgot about the pet issue and the topic of conversation suddenly became Ed's "amazing" ability to produce his lease on demand. When Ed, looking somewhat surprised by the new discussion, explained that he simply went to his filing cabinet and pulled the file marked "Lease," people went wild. "He's got a filing cabinet!" one woman announced, as though she'd uncovered some rare, ancient artifact. "Look at this," declared another voice from the other room, "phone, electric, car, IRA, he's got everything filed—in alphabetical order!" People were amazed that Ed had his personal papers so well organized, and Ed was equally amazed that the others thought that was amazing. Each thought, "You mean other people actually live this way?"

The Advantages and Disadvantages of Detail Orientation

It's good to be detail oriented, though not exclusively so, as we will see later. Breaking down opportunities or problems into smaller chunks and concentrating on them is a great way to accomplish things. It's productive activity. After all, isn't that how anything is accomplished—one small piece at a time? Think about the construction of a building. It all boils down to each little brick squarely placed on top of others, each pipe fitted firmly into another, each wire solidly screwed onto a receptacle—it's nothing but a zillion details bunched together. And it takes a bunch of detail-oriented people, each doing his or her part, to produce one whole building.

Zeroing in on the details is a great way to deal with difficult or enormous tasks. It's an effective way of dealing with problems that might otherwise be unwieldy or overwhelming. Divide and conquer, the saying goes. When you view problems as nothing more than an amalgamation of smaller units and concentrate on one unit at a time, you can solve problems much easier. And you can't say enough about the benefits of organization. Laugh all you want about the guy who has all his personal and business papers meticulously filed and available in an instant. When others are drowning in disorganization, the detail-oriented people are enjoying the last laugh.

Now for the downside. When you spend an inordinate amount of thought or time on detail-oriented endeavor, you end up stunting your productivity beyond a certain point. In other words, your productivity hits a certain level and increases no more. You reach a point of diminishing returns. It's like installing a ceiling above which your productivity will not rise.

When you spend too much thought or time on the details, you suffer in three ways:

1. **You waste a lot of time doing things that simply don't need doing.** You may have just spent three days in the company library researching something, looking up every obscure article, and every book that even remotely deals with the topic. But was that what you should have been doing in the first place? Was that the best use of your time? Is all this information you've gathered going to make that much of a difference? That old management adage "doing the right things versus doing things right" comes

into play. Detail-oriented people are often so burrowed in the small stuff they fail to pop their head above it all and look at the whole landscape. They waste a lot of time with details that either don't need doing or make no difference once done.

2. **You disqualify yourself from promotion.** An overemphasis on details keeps you from rising in your organization; it keeps you from gaining responsibility and authority. As you rise in position or responsibility, you must delegate more of the detailed work and think with a wider viewpoint. It doesn't mean the detailed work becomes less important, it just means you yourself spend less time with it. You delegate it. You let go of it. To detail-oriented people, the thought of letting go of the detailed work is so uncomfortable, they just can't seem to do it. Hence, they stay in the position they're in.

Remember the Radar character in "M*A*S*H," played by Gary Burghoff? He had every "i" dotted and every "t" crossed on every piece of paper in the office. He was incredibly organized and productive. But he was only a lowly corporal. Henry Blake and Sherman Potter, played by McLean Stevenson and Harry Morgan respectively, weren't nearly as detail oriented, and they were colonels. A person like Radar would not be a likely candidate for advancement, due to his inability, or unwillingness, to focus on anything but the details.

3. **You tend to be more easily frustrated or flustered.** Your detail orientation often raises your sensitivity to small, insignificant occurrences. Your threshold of tolerance is smaller. You can easily overreact to things, which can cause frustration or discontent to appear quickly.

As you can see, being detailed oriented has its advantages, but it can spawn a whole set of disadvantages if you spend too much thought or time on the details.

TRAITS OF CONCEPT-ORIENTED PEOPLE

Concept-oriented people, who focus on the big picture, have their own set of character traits as well. They tend to:

1. **Believe all opportunities or problems are based in the whole.**
The way to capitalize on opportunities and the way to solve
problems is to concentrate their efforts on the whole, the big
picture, they believe. To gain promotions, for example,
concept-oriented people believe they must demonstrate leadership ability, decisiveness, direction, and other nonspecific qualities. They believe that the key to success in any endeavor is the
overall idea, the concept, or the strategy. They believe their
productivity lies in their ability to look at the big picture and
assess the whole thing.

2. **Be concerned with the end rather than the means.** Concept-
oriented people place importance on the end result but discount
the means of achieving the result. They just don't care much
about how something gets done, as long as it gets done. They're
the ones who take Nike's "Just Do It" slogan to heart.

   Remember Bill, the guy who planned every detail of his restaurant's festival participation? A fellow restaurateur named Chuck,
a concept-oriented person, thought Bill was making the project
much more complex than it actually was. "Why do all that extra
work, all that detailed planning and preparing?" he asked. "Just
cook some food beforehand, pile it all in the van, and sell it at
the festival. What's the big deal?" Concept-oriented people don't
really care how things get done. As long as the end result is acceptable, the process, whatever it might be like, is fine.

3. **Think in large, far-reaching time frames.** Concept-oriented
people spend a good deal of time looking into the future. They
see things months and years ahead. As you might expect, they
envision how the end results will be farther down the road.
Sometimes they're called dreamers, idealists, or visionaries.
They come up with a lot of ideas and a lot of philosophical
remedies. They can also be very persuasive and inspiring.

The Advantages and Disadvantages of Concept Orientation

It's good to be concept oriented, though not exclusively so, as we
will soon see. Taking a big-picture view and assessing things in the
aggregate keeps you going in the right direction; it keeps you from

straying off course. When you focus on the grand outcome, on what you're trying to achieve over the months and years, you avoid getting sidetracked, derailed, or bogged down.

Solutions to problems can often be found by stepping back and looking at the big picture. When you see how everything relates, how it will all play out over time, things can look quite different. When you concentrate on the whole, often you will get a new and different idea or solution you hadn't otherwise considered.

Alas, there's a downside to concept thinking too. As happens with detail-oriented thinkers, when concept-oriented thinkers spend an inordinate amount of time or thought on the big picture, they end up stunting their productivity beyond a certain point.

When you spend too much time or thought on the big picture, you hurt yourself in three distinct ways:

1. **You waste a lot of time thinking instead of acting.** Concept thinking is somewhat like daydreaming. You could spend your life doing it yet accomplish nothing. Eventually you've got to stop assessing the big picture, roll up your sleeves, and get to work. Quite often, however, concept-oriented people seem to remain content conceptualizing instead of acting.

2. **You sacrifice completion for start-up.** Concept-oriented people keep coming up with new ideas. Sometimes those ideas have nothing to do with the present direction of their lives or their current responsibilities. So they keep changing direction, starting new projects or endeavors. Consequently, they often abandon their present endeavors or responsibilities in favor of the next new concept they're cooking up. They can never reach completion on nor fully accomplish anything.

3. **You make bigger and more frequent mistakes.** Because concept-oriented people concentrate on the big picture, they let a lot of things fall through the cracks. Hence, a lot of mistakes can occur under their realm of responsibility. Do you know why 80 percent of new businesses fail in the first year and why 80 percent of the surviving ones fail within the next four years? One big reason is that they are started by concept-oriented people who lack the detail orientation to get the job done.

   Diane, a concept-oriented thinker, bought a small decorating business. She spent all her time visualizing her business growing. After six months, she started thinking of franchising; after a year, going public. Diane was a big thinker and a big talker. But after her second year, everything collapsed. Her preoccupation with the future and the empire she had created in her mind began to take its toll on the present. Low morale and high employee turnover affected the quality of her product and service. She left the details to others, but when others discovered the details weren't important to Diane, they too let things slide. The book-keeper Diane hired to ''take care of the details'' embezzled most of the funds and drove the firm into bankruptcy. Diane found out too late that she must focus on the details once in a while.

THE UNHAPPY MEDIUM

It's time to assess your own viewpoint orientation. Are you a detail-oriented person or a concept-oriented person? Most people are one or the other. Like being right- or left-handed, a detail or concept orientation is a natural tendency we exhibit from child-hood on. As you read the traits of each orientation, did one seem familiar to you? Did one describe you fairly accurately?

Perhaps you find neither orientation solely applicable. Perhaps you are a combination of both extremes, partially detail oriented and partially concept oriented. If so, you're entering a dangerous area. Let me give you a clear distinction that is crucial to your understanding of and your success with micro-macro vision.

If you feel you're neither detail oriented nor concept oriented, but somewhere in between, you're in the worst position possible. In-between people, with neither a strong detail nor a strong concept orientation, operate at the low ravine of their productivity potential. There is no happy medium when it comes to micro-macro vision.

Realization 43

To be highly productive, you must be extremely detail oriented *and* extremely concept oriented.

Remember, detail-oriented people can be very productive, at least to a point. So can concept-oriented people. But when you lack either a strong detail orientation or a strong concept orientation, your productivity will languish. When the power of each orientation averages out, you end up with very little productivity power.

On the other hand, if you're extremely detail oriented at times and extremely concept oriented at other times, you're in the strongest possible position. That's what the term *micro-macro vision* means. You zero in on the details at times, demonstrating supreme reverence for the minutest aspects of your endeavors. And you step back and assess the big picture at times, demonstrating supreme reverence for the whole and how everything relates over time. It is this combination of detail and concept thinking—both orientations strongly entrenched in one person—that contains the magical powers that cause your productivity to erupt.

I said earlier that it's natural for most of us to be either detail oriented or concept oriented, like being right- or left-handed. If that's so, can we learn to be both detail and concept oriented? Yes. Learning micro-macro vision is like learning anything else. You study it and put it into practice; over time, you get pretty good at it. And that's exactly what's going to happen to you. Regardless of whether you're strictly detail oriented or concept oriented, or an average of the two, you will become a micro-macro vision person. With practice, you'll master it. And you'll love what it does to your productivity.

THE DETAILS CONTAIN A TREASURE CHEST OF INTEREST

To develop micro-macro vision, you must first develop a strong appreciation for the orientation that you are not. You must learn what each orientation has to offer and see yourself tapping into its treasures. Let's start by discussing the real power of detail-oriented thinking.

Have you ever known people who don't seem to be interested in anything? They may spend their lives drifting aimlessly, moving slowly, taking little interest in their work, going from job to job, or not even having a job. They just never seem to develop more than a feeble, fleeting interest in doing or accomplishing anything. What is the problem? Chances are, they suffer from a distinct lack of detail-oriented thinking.

Realization 44

The farther you get into the details, the farther your interest rises.

Each of us is surrounded by an abundance of treasures. Whatever you value—your job, companionship, art, health, love, money, the ocean, stature and respect, whatever—is available to you here and now. But you have to open your eyes, turn on your microscope, and begin zeroing in on the details to find it. When you begin to zero in on the details, you begin to pique your interest. Get immersed in the details, and your interest in the endeavor will percolate.

By the time George hit 40, he'd been in and out of a dozen different careers. He did everything from selling cars to painting houses to farming. Nothing seemed to interest him. He drifted through life, aimlessly latching on to the next job he happened upon, and leaving each when he couldn't stand the boredom any longer.

Then one day, George sat down at a computer and soon found himself involved in a hardware glitch that needed fixing. The problem challenged him, and he was delighted with himself when he eventually solved it. Then he began flipping through computer magazines and learning what they're all about. With computers, George discovered a whole new world to step into. And step in he did. George became engrossed with computers, learning all he could and working with them day and night. Today, he's a free-lance systems designer/installer—he's very productive and very happy.

George's story is not exactly what it seems. This is not someone who finally found something that interested him. It's a fellow who first decided to get into something, then became interested as a result. Effort in, interest out.

What about people who claim nothing interests them enough to get into the details of it? Developing interest in something and reaping the rewards of detail-oriented endeavor is like love. You must give love to get love. You have to make the initial effort. You must actively zero in on the details of something—choose something at random if you like—show an interest in the details, and the details will begin to interest you back. In fact, the more detailed your focus becomes, the more interesting things will become.

Showing an interest in the details can also motivate others. If parents want to motivate a child to learn, all they have to do is show an interest in the child's schoolwork. (This needs to be done on a regular basis, for more than three minutes at a time.) Amazingly, when you take an interest in what someone else is doing, that person's interest in that area rises. In this case, it's you getting into the details that piques the interest of another.

The same technique can be used by managers to motivate the troops. I'll never forget my first radio station general manager's job. I learned a lot, mostly from my mistakes. Many times people would come to me with certain problems, all of which seemed trivial and not worth my time. A common and deadly mistake made by first-time managers is viewing subordinates' problems as too trivial in comparison to their own. If it's a significant enough problem for someone to come to you with, it's a significant problem for you too. One day it occurred to me that morale was rather low. People were shuffling in and out, doing their jobs in perfunctory fashion, and grumbling all the while.

Then it dawned on me. I had inadvertently been dousing their enthusiasm by ignoring their concerns. "If it's not important to the general manager, it must not be important to me either," they surmised. So no one cared much about anything. It was a situation that needed turning around quickly, I concluded.

I decided to demonstrate an intense interest in the details from that point forward. It didn't take long for an opportunity to present itself. The disc jockey on the air one day popped his head into my office and told me his headphones went dead. He couldn't find another pair and wanted to know what he should do. When a similar thing happened a few months earlier, I told the jock to just make do until the headphones could be repaired someday. This time I knew better. I immediately dropped what I was doing, went into the engineering room, and repaired the headphones myself in a matter of minutes. When the jock realized how important his headphone problem was to me, his morale shot up on the spot. When I showed that the details were extremely important to me, the details became extremely important to the people.

By the way, it's not enough for managers to say they are interested in the details. They must honestly demonstrate interest by their actions. The top executives of McDonald's hold an admirable reverence for the details, and they show it. They provide extensive training and reward for detail-oriented work. They rate all their managers on detailed criteria, making sure the reverence for details gets passed on down the line. And at least once a year, the top executives go to work in a McDonald's store, cooking the burgers, salting the fries, and waiting on customers. The entire McDonald's company has micro-macro vision, and that's one reason they remain at the top in productivity year after year.

THE CONCEPT CONTAINS THE EXCITEMENT

How do you get excited about something? How do you get excited about your company, your job, your office or workstation, and the people you work with? You step back and focus on the big picture.

Realization 45

The more you step back and look at the big picture, the more your excitement level rises.

When you take time to examine the big picture, when you see how everything relates to everything else, when you contemplate the concept, you become more excited. Excited about what? About everything! About your work, your relationships, your life. When you look at the whole, the aggregate, things come alive in ways you never saw before.

I take time every day to exercise my concept thinking. I start out with a really big picture—I see how perfect the world really is. I literally look at the sky, the trees, the ground, and the squirrels running around. I think about how the trees give off oxygen and how we humans use that oxygen and give carbon dioxide back to the trees. I think about how the clouds form and periodically provide rain, which in turns causes things to grow, and how the rain invisibly evaporates, somehow ending up back in the sky. I think about the sun burning away day after day, year after year, energizing everything on Earth, including people who enjoy basking in it. I could go on, but you get the idea.

Then I look at the whole of something in particular, my career, for example. I see everything unfolding just as it's supposed to over time. I can see how far I've come and how far along I'll be in the coming years. I see how all that relates to my health, age, and relationships. Everything fits together; it just takes a little thought to see it.

Stepping back and assessing the big picture is invigorating, inspiring, and stirring. When you look at the whole, life's smaller imperfections disappear. You only see goodness, perfection, in whatever area you're thinking of. Sometimes you see things you're not happy with, but along with that you also see the changes occurring to improve it all. Some of your best ideas can come to you when you're engaged in conceptual thinking.

Try it. It may take time and effort, but you've got enough of that to devote a little to something with such a high upside. See if you don't find your excitement level rising little by little as you think more and more about the whole. Some people say their excitement level suddenly explodes after a few short periods of conceptual thinking. It's your turn to give it a shot.

HOW DETAIL AND CONCEPT ORIENTATION FIT TOGETHER

As we've noted, both detail thinking and concept thinking have distinct advantages. And both have distinct disadvantages that surface when you spend too much time or thought with either viewpoint. Therefore, the optimum position for you is to be neither a detail-oriented person nor a concept-oriented person, but both.

Remember, you access the tremendous productivity power of micro-macro vision by being extremely detail oriented at times and extremely concept oriented at other times. You don't want to be a watered-down average of the two orientations. You want to be both orientations to their fullest.

There is another danger I must alert you to. Some people conclude that if one person can become so productive by applying both orientations, then two people of opposite orientations can accomplish much by working together. Say, for instance, that a detail-oriented person and a concept-oriented person work on a project together, go into business together, or get married.

Does that work? If the combination of detail and concept thinking is so powerful, then a team composed of each type of person could be dynamite, the thinking goes. Theoretically, yes. But problems quickly arise that usually cause a downfall for the pairing. Take Steve Jobs and Steve Wozniak, the founders of Apple Computer. Wozniak was the detail guy. He built the prototype computer and invented the disc drive. He literally spent his time hovering over a bunch of electronic parts, actually soldering this, wiring that. Wozniak says he never ever dreamed of the computers being mass produced and marketed to the world.

But Jobs, the concept person, did. He thought about computers by the thousands rolling off assembly lines and being mass-marketed. He envisioned people in all walks of life using Apple computers at work and at home. He thought about how Apple computers could change the world. He spent a lot of his time staring out the window. Together the two Steves, with their opposite orientations, were a dynamite combination that created one of America's great companies.

But they didn't stay together. For different reasons, Wozniak left the company, then Jobs left. Today, they're involved in separate endeavors and are not working partners.

They Drive Each Other Crazy

A recent "20/20" program profiled couples who were having marital problems. In one instance, the woman spent her every waking moment vigorously cleaning the house. Her big complaint was that her husband didn't do his share of the work. He was content to plop down in front of the TV while she slaved away from dawn to whenever day in and out. John Stossel, the ''20/20'' reporter, noticed something interesting. The woman would clean at breakneck speed, as though there was no tomorrow, while the man, when he did help with some of the cleaning, would move at a very leisurely pace.

You can see where the problem lies, can't you? She's a detail-oriented person who believes it's of supreme importance that every nook and cranny of the house be spotless. Consequently, she's irritated that her husband doesn't share her view and help with the ''monumental'' amount of cleaning. He, being concept oriented, feels that their nice house in a nice community, their great children, and their health are all that matters. He's disturbed that she keeps creating all this unnecessary cleaning work. And they're driving each other crazy.

No question about it. Detail-oriented people will drive concept-oriented people crazy by their seemingly unnecessary obsession with the details. And concept-oriented people will drive detail-oriented people crazy with their big-picture obsession. (Remember *The Odd Couple?* The play, movie, and entire television series were based on detail- and concept-oriented roomies driving one another nuts.)

In the early days of my consulting practice, I was hired by a radio station owner to help him turn around a station with dwindling listenership. I visited the market, listened to his station and his main competitors, gathered demographic data, analyzed, and concluded. I hadn't actually met the owner until the day I delivered my recommendations. After a few pleasantries over breakfast, we discussed the situation. The conversation went something like this:

Me:

Let's look at how your station is positioned in the market.

He:

I don't think the disc jockeys are giving the time enough, do you?

Me:

Perhaps not. But before we discuss that, let's look at your overall chances of success in the next few years with the present format.

He:

I listened between 7:00 and 7:22 this morning and counted only three time checks! The problem, as I see it, is that the jocks aren't giving the time enough!

Me:

Yes, three time mentions in 22 minutes is low. But before we get into the details, we need to look at the big picture. I believe we're going in the wrong direction with the present format.

He:

People expect to get the time when they tune in—they want to know what time it is! (pounds fist on table, hurling spoon across room). How do we expect people to listen if we don't give 'em the time? The jocks should do 33 time checks an hour. Thirty-three an hour! If these jocks have some kind of problem giving the time, I'll fire 'em all and get jocks who will!

I kept trying to pull this guy back and get him to focus on the big picture, which was necessary if we were to fix his problem. (Not that the time, or any other detail, wasn't important; but the details weren't relevant at that early point in the discussion.) And the more I kept trying to discuss the big picture, the more irritated he became at my lack of detail focus. Only when I opened my briefcase and pulled out a dozen monitor forms, listing every little detail I heard on his station the previous day, did he calm down.

Two or more people from opposite orientations working together is theoretically good but practically problematic. It's just too difficult getting people of opposite orientations to work closely together without each eventually accusing the other of being from another planet.

TRAITS OF MICRO-MACRO VISION PEOPLE

The real way to combine detail thinking and concept thinking is in the minds of individuals. In other words, one individual becomes both a detail-oriented and a concept-oriented person.

Here are the three main characteristics of people with micro-macro vision. They have the ability to:

1. **Zoom in and focus on the details.** At times, people with micro-macro vision concentrate their attention on one or more relevant

details. They even become obsessed with the details at times, demonstrating unwavering commitment to accomplishing some small, minute task, or the many different, detailed portions of tasks. They recognize the importance of details, and display a generous appreciation for them. People with micro-macro vision in management watch over the details, making sure their people have the time, money, or other resources necessary to conduct detailed work.

2. **Zoom out and focus on the big picture.** At times, people with micro-macro vision pull themselves back and concentrate their attention on the big picture. They look at how everything fits together, how each aspect affects the other aspects. They look at a longer time frame, years down the road. They appreciate the wisdom that concept thinking can provide. Micro-macro vision people in management focus on the big picture regularly and communicate what they see to subordinates so others can share the vision.

3. **Switch back and forth between detail and big-picture thinking when appropriate.** What makes the micro-macro vision people really effective is their ability to switch viewpoints at will. Even more admirable is their instinctive ability to know when each viewpoint is appropriate. It could be said people with micro-macro vision possess the wisdom to know when to adopt which viewpoint, but that implies such wisdom is innate and can't be learned, which is false. You can and will develop the ability to know when which viewpoint is appropriate.

Let's look at some examples of people with micro-macro vision. Ray Kroc, the late founder of McDonald's, was a classic micro-macro vision individual. He was obsessed with each and every detail that had to do with hamburger cooking and marketing. He created "Hamburger University" so that employees could be taught exactly how to prepare the food and run every aspect of the restaurant. No detail was overlooked: the exact way each food item was to be prepared, including the precise measure of ketchup and mustard, and onions that go on each burger; the exact way the french fries would be cooked; the exact wording the counterpeople would use; and the exact way the stores would look, down to the finest detail. Ray personally zeroed in on all the details with a burning obsession during the formative years of the company, understanding that the companywide detail orientation would rest on his shoulders.

But Ray spent just as much time assessing the big picture. He would step back, contemplate the world, and see how McDonald's restaurants could fit everywhere. In the early days, when there were only a few McDonald's stores, people thought old Ray had lost his mind when he'd talk of having thousands of McDonald's stores all over the country, all over the world. But to him, the big picture revealed all. It inspired and excited him enough to make it all happen.

Sam Walton, the late founder of Wal-Mart, was another micro-macro vision person. He did the same thing as Ray Kroc only in different ways. Spending the majority of his time on the road each year, he'd personally visit every Wal-Mart store, checking the folding and placement of the towels, the cleanliness of the shelves, and the price markers on various items. No detail escaped his eye. He even took it upon himself to personally mingle with the employees and listen to their suggestions, which was all detail-oriented talk. Sam Walton was obsessed with the details.

But Sam spent just as much time looking at the big picture. Without that concept orientation complementing his detail orientation, Wal-Mart might very well have remained a single store in Little Rock, Arkansas.

Bill Gates, the founder and chairman of Microsoft, is another example. He can zero in on such details as the intricacies of a computer program, for example. (Is there anything more detailed than the multitude of little ones and zeros that compose a computer program?) He can also zoom out and contemplate the future of his company, the computer industry, and the world years ahead. Zoom in, zoom out. Micro-macro vision.

I've used three examples of entrepreneurs who created monster-sized companies because I want you to see how powerful micro-macro vision is. But don't think micro-macro vision is limited to entrepreneurs or those in upper management. Anyone, at any level, can tap into the power of micro-macro vision at any time.

Fran increased her personal productivity substantially and garnered a promotion by developing micro-macro vision. She decided to really zero in on the details of her job, which was managing a real estate office. She became obsessed with the little things, making sure every small aspect was dealt with properly and handled with precision. Simultaneously, she spent some time in concept-oriented thought. She thought about the general mood and mindset of people in her city, the real estate market in the years to come, and her company's role in serving the community. As micro-macro vision became her habit, miraculous things began to take hold. Within six months, her office became the top producing office in the firm, and Fran became a vice president a year later.

If you want to shoot up the promotional ladder in record time, display a little micro-macro vision. Be so obsessed with the details of your job that no one knows it better than you, no one performs it better than you. Solve problems that have to do with small aspects of your job. Then step back and look at how your job relates to the company as a whole, and how the company relates to its industry and the world. Come up with broad ideas that can help the company take advantage of opportunities. In discussions with your superiors, talk from both orientations, detail and big picture. Watch how fast things happen for you.

Can you see the power? Your productivity intensifies and wondrous things happen when you balance your vision between the micro and the macro.

HOW TO DEVELOP MICRO-MACRO VISION

Unlike most of the other techniques in this book, micro-macro vision is not a function of your subconscious mind. It's a consciously controlled behavior that requires a simple, two-step technique to implement. The steps are simple but not necessarily easy. You will have to put forth effort.

- **Step 1: Develop a strong appreciation for the opposite orientation.** If you're detail oriented, you've got to adopt an equal appreciation for concept-oriented thinking, and vice versa. Realize that there's tremendous power in the opposite orientation. It harbors advantages you cannot afford to be without. Spend some time with people of the opposite orientation. Closely observe how they think, how they operate. Keep an open mind, reminding yourself that people of the opposite orientation are just as productive as people of your orientation. See how the other half functions. You will find a wealth of amazing tricks the others use that you can work into your own repertoire.

- **Step 2: Spend time in the opposite orientation.** If you're a detail-oriented person, you are now going to spend some time thinking conceptually. If you're a concept-oriented person, you're now going to spend some of your time thinking about the details. Most likely, you'll have to force yourself to think the opposite way. Until you get used to it, which you will in time, you may find yourself resisting the other orientation.

In fact, your resistance to the opposite orientation may be quite strong. We can, for instance, dunk a concept-oriented person's head in the details and she'll fight it all the way. And we can yank a detail-oriented person out of his funk and show him the big picture, and he'll kick and scream all the way. If it weren't natural to find the opposite orientation uncomfortable, we'd all naturally possess micro-macro vision, which very few of us do.

You must deliberately say to yourself, "I must now focus on the details" or "I must now look at the big picture." And force yourself to spend a good deal of time doing each. Dedicate the time. If you spend the time in the opposite orientation, your resistance to it will begin to diminish. You'll eventually become comfortable with the other orientation and actually develop an affinity for it.

WHEN TO SWITCH VIEWPOINTS

The key that makes micro-macro vision people so productive is the ability to know when to switch viewpoints. You must have a good sense for when each viewpoint is appropriate. In time, you'll develop the wisdom to know instinctively when to be in which orientation. Here are some hints to get you there in the early stages of your micro-macro vision development.

When to Zoom Out and Focus on the Big Picture

- **When initially considering or beginning a new task or endeavor.** It's always big picture first, details second. The brain is trained to sequentially receive the big picture, or conceptual information, first and the detailed information later. It's the way the brain best understands and processes information.

  Ever notice how movies and television shows convey scenes to you by showing the big picture first, then the detailed pictures second? Directors show shots of the city, landscape, or outside of buildings first, as a way of setting the scene. It's called a *master shot* in the trade. After the master shot has been established for a few seconds, a more detailed shot comes on the screen. This might be the inside of a room or a close-up of an individual's face.

The big picture establishes where you are and where you're going. Like looking at a map of the entire city before you look at the individual roads, it gives you a sense of place and relation.

- **When frustrated.** Frustration almost always occurs in detail orientation. You will not only put an end to your current frustration when you switch to concept-oriented thinking for a while, but you will bring about viable solutions sooner. You will also feel more calm and relaxed.

- **When in an argument.** Most arguments are about details—quite often, about inconsequential details. Unfortunately, people often focus so forcefully on the details of an argument they inadvertently damage their relationship with one another. Before that happens, switch to a big-picture viewpoint. Stepping back and looking at the big picture can help you realize that your relationship with a co-worker, supervisor, business partner, friend, or spouse is much more important than the relatively inconsequential details you're arguing about. The big picture viewpoint slaps you in the face and stops you from harming a relationship that you really don't want to harm.

- **When feeling tense or stressed.** When you zoom out and look at the big picture, you'll feel relief, a sense of calmness. A conceptual or big picture viewpoint has a way of making whatever is bothering you seem less severe.

- **When you seek increased excitement.** Remember, the concept contains the excitement. Think big picture and get excited. Begin by appreciating all the great things in the world and in your life. See the greatness in your company and your job. As you conceptually contemplate, you'll make new realizations and get new ideas that will excite you, I promise.

- **When productivity seems to ebb.** When your personal productivity ebbs, and it will from time to time, switch orientations. If you were mainly in detail orientation, switch to concept orientation. The new viewpoint can unstick your brain and rejuvenate you and your productivity.

- **When making career decisions.** Instead of listing all the pros and cons of a new job opportunity, for example, shift your focus to the big picture. Determine if the new venture would keep you on track, if it would take you closer to your ultimate career objective. When you think about the whole, your instincts take over and guide your decisions correctly. Always go with your gut feeling when making career moves.

When to Zoom In and Focus on the Details

- **When it's time to take action.** Remember what constitutes real action: talking to people, committing yourself, and physical movement. Those are usually detail-oriented things. Once you commit and begin moving, more and more details require your attention. If you fail to get out of concept orientation and into detail orientation eventually, however, you'll never really get any real, effective action going.

- **When you seek to boost your interest level.** If you're not interested in something you think you should be, it's time to delve further into the details. Remember, the details contain a treasure chest of interest just waiting to enthrall you.

- **When you want to get into highly concentrated attention (HCA).** Focusing your attention on some minute aspect of something can coax your brain into a deeper level of concentration.

- **When productivity seems to ebb.** If you're mainly in concept orientation when your productivity slows, switch to detail orientation for a while. That unsticks your brain and rejuvenates your thinking.

- **When you want to prevent or curtail mistakes.** There comes a time in every task or endeavor when it is ripe for mistakes to happen. To keep things from falling through the cracks, you've got to fill those cracks. You do that with a solid dose of detail-oriented thinking, detail-oriented planning, and detail-oriented follow-through.

Chapter Ten

Visualize Your Way to Success

I t seems a lot of books have an obligatory chapter on visualization these days. It's even spread beyond esoteric subjects. "Visualize your cake rising . . . see it popping out of the oven perfectly," says this cookbook someone handed me the other day. ("Pop psychology" in its truest form, I suppose.)

This visualization chapter is different. Instead of merely trumpeting the benefits of visualization and suggesting you do it, I'll explain why visualization *doesn't* work for most people. You'll get the real story here, including the shortcomings of visualization.

However, since *visualization* is productivity thruster number four, you must know I'm a proponent of it, shortcomings and all. There are, after all, certain conditions under which visualization can be very effective. You'll learn what those conditions are, and how you can get visualization to boost your productivity every day.

Let me caution you against concluding at the outset that visualization is only a metaphysical theory with no practical application or benefit. It may seem that way at first, as we discuss some of the more fun aspects of visualization. But rest assured, if it weren't of practical, down-to-earth value, with the potential to increase your personal productivity tremendously, it wouldn't be included in this book. You'll understand how it works and how you can get it to work for you right away as this chapter unfolds.

WHAT VISUALIZATION CAN DO FOR YOU

Visualization affects your productivity in many ways. It can give you direction and guidance that keeps you on course throughout your career and personal life. It can bolster your self-confidence and strengthen belief in yourself and your abilities. It can sharpen your skills and raise your level of experience. Visualization aids you in accomplishment by improving your performance.

As you visualize properly, it begins working for you immediately. The small things you want to accomplish each day at work and at home can happen with greater ease and frequency. The more grandiose things you want to accomplish, your dreams for example, can also happen with greater ease and frequency, though they may take a bit longer. In short, visualization provides you with immeasurable benefits with no real downside.

THE VISUALIZATION CONCEPT

In case you're not up to speed on the concept of visualization, and even if you are, let's take a minute to review it as a basis for our discussion.

By visualizing something in your mind, by thinking about it and seeing it in your imagination, you are able to bring whatever you're envisioning into reality, the concept goes. A popular example among visualization proponents is "creating a parking space" by visualizing an empty parking space in an otherwise crowded lot. Sure enough, just as you near the area, someone pulls out of a primo spot and you slide right in, as though it had been planned that way by a scriptwriter. That is the whole idea behind visualization. By visualizing, you are "writing the script"; you're imagining something in advance, only to have it play out in reality some time later.

Let's look at it from a different angle. Wasn't every man-made thing that presently exists in the world created by someone? Take your house, for example. Human beings physically constructed your house with saws, hammers, nails, and staple guns. They used materials, including wood, pipe, brick, and plastic, that were all made by other human beings. Your house was created by people making parts and people putting all those parts together.

But before the construction workers put all the parts together, someone else drew the plans, right? The actual construction didn't begin until the blueprints existed first. That means someone, most likely an architect, mentally created your house and preserved that creation in the form of a blueprint prior to the builder creating the house in reality.

Take anything else that exists in your life. Your car, television set, shirt, newspaper, or steak dinner. Before someone created it in reality, someone else thought of the idea. Someone created it mentally first. Intangible things work the same way. Before a philosophy, belief, or sentiment takes hold among people, someone had to dream it up. Someone, somewhere, had to create it in his or her mind first before it became reality later. Everything that presently exists in reality at one time existed only as a thought. Thus, you have the "everything is created twice" theory. Everything is created first in thought and later in reality.

That leads us back to visualization. When you visualize in your mind something not presently existing in your reality, you activate the forces necessary to make it a reality. Your thought, or vision, is the seed. And like the seed that grows into a real, living, breathing plant, so grows your vision into something real. Thought first, reality second.

Realization 46

Everything that exists in reality was once only a thought or vision in someone's mind.

Nothing comes to be, or is created in material form, without having first existed as a thought. Visualizing nonexistent things, material or intangible, is therefore crucial to making those things reality. In other words, visualization helps you accomplish; it boosts your productivity.

DOES VISUALIZATION REALLY WORK?

If visualization aids accomplishment, with no offsetting downside, why doesn't everyone visualize all the time? Alas, many people who have tried visualization say it doesn't work. They visualize an accomplishment—something new materializing in their lives—and it never materializes. Can that happen? Can you visualize something desirable like a smooth-running sales meeting tomorrow, a promotion to district manager or foreman, or a new, paid-for Lexus sitting in your driveway and never get it? Can visualization fail you?

Does visualization work or doesn't it? Here are two arguments put forth by people who believe visualization is nothing but a pop psychology gimmick with no real power to affect things. Let's hear their reasoning and determine how valid their points are.

Visualize 18 Hole-in-Ones

A few years ago, someone on some golf course somewhere told someone else about the latest secret to increasing one's productivity on the course: visualizing the ball going where you want it to go. Golfers, an otherwise semi-intellegent lot who hold down responsible jobs in society, often turn into highly irrational, giddy people when presented with the opportunity to adopt some new, score-lowering gimmick. Golfers have been known to try most anything, however cumbersome or impractical, they think might shave a stroke or two off their score. It didn't take long for visualization to become standard procedure, routine practice for anyone remotely serious about their game. Approach the ball; get into position; visualize; swing.

Has all this massive visualization produced a nation full of better golfers? Has the average golf score dropped any measurable degree in recent years? Have courses had to lower their pars in reaction to visualization's pervasiveness?

Visualization nonbelievers will tell you the only thing visualization has done, as far as anyone knows, is slow down the game. Now, instead of stepping up to the ball and swinging, everyone steps up and visualizes for however long, while everyone else stands around and waits.

If visualization worked, you'd play 18 holes and your score would be 18, they reason. Or 22, if you visualized the ball falling short of the pin once in a while. If visualization worked, what would explain a really lousy shot, assuming you didn't visualize that happening? Perhaps while you were visualizing it going straight down the fairway, the three others in your party were visualizing it going into the lake. Maybe opposing visions weigh out in favor of the many. Maybe visualization simply doesn't work, some conclude.

What about That Paid-for Lexus?

Betsy called me one day in a high state of excitement. "I'm going to come over and show you my new Lexus!" she exclaimed. "You bought a new car?" I asked. "That's great."

"Well," Betsy went on, "I don't have it yet. But I'll have it on November 1." "Oh, you special-ordered," I concluded. "Not exactly," she explained. "I haven't bought it yet. I'm not even sure if I am going to buy it, actually. But somehow I'm going to own a new Lexus by November 1, and best of all, it's going to be paid for!" (Hey, if you're going to visualize a new car, go ahead and visualize a *paid-for* new car!)

Betsy couldn't contain her excitement. She'd read one of those visualization chapters in someone's book, and she became an instant devotee. "By visualizing a new, paid-for Lexus in my driveway, I will bring it into form!" she explained. And visualize she did. For the next three and a half months (it was the middle of July when she first began), she visualized with vigor. Like the book suggested, she cut out pictures of the car and posted them on the bathroom mirror and the refrigerator. She looked at the pictures often, burning the vision into her mind. Betsy also set a definite deadline by which her vision would become reality: November 1. Three and a half months seemed like a reasonable amount of time for the magic of visualization to do its thing.

She also took action. Visualization, after all, is not simply dreaming, wishing, or hoping. Burning the image into your mind is only part of it. Another key part is taking action to make the vision a reality. Every day you must take some action to bring the vision into form, and that is exactly what Betsy did. She went to the car dealer more than once and "connected" with the model of her choice. She looked at it, touched it, listened to it, smelled it, sat in it, and drove it. She talked to current Lexus owners and referred to herself as a current owner in conversation.

Belief is also a key part of visualizing. Betsy learned that visualizing and taking action isn't enough. You must believe, truly believe with all your heart, that the vision is not only possible, not only probable, but unquestionably true. There can be no doubt in your mind. If the vision is to become reality, you must believe it is *already* reality, even though it hasn't materialized yet.

Betsy believed. In fact, she told everyone, including me, that she owned (as in already possessed) a brand new, paid-for Lexus. I'm convinced she did believe it, especially when I witnessed her walk out of a shopping mall one day and subconsciously, while engaged in conversation with me, mistakenly go up to a Lexus thinking it was her car.

Never mind *how* a vision is to become reality, the theory states. Betsy knew she couldn't afford even the down payment, yet alone any additional payments. But that didn't matter. The how is not important. If you do everything you're supposed to do—visualize with emotional intensity at least twice a day, take action every day, and truly believe in the vision's existence—the how will take care of itself. Something, or a series of somethings, will happen that will bring the vision into form. She might win a contest (she was entering them as part of the action she was taking) or the state lottery. A distant relative might pass on and will her the car. She might meet a handsome, debonair gentleman who gives her a Lexus as a let's-go-steady gift. She might simply wake up one day and find one in the driveway with no explanation as to how it got there. Don't laugh. How it gets there could be any one of a thousand ways, none of which matters anyway.

Eventually, November 1 arrived, followed by November 2, 3, and 4. Around the tenth of November, I called Betsy to get an update. "I haven't got the car yet, but I know it will arrive soon," Betsy said with conviction, albeit noticeably less intense than before.

Then came December 1, January 1, and eventually, November 1 a year later. And November 1 came a year after that, two and a half years after she first began visualizing her paid-for Lexus, and still no paid-for Lexus. Not even a payments-due Lexus.

Does visualization work? Betsy's conclusion is fairly clear. "Visualization is a crock, man! A stupid idea that someone made up to get gullible people like me to bite. I'm more likely to get a Lexus if I build one myself 'cause I sure ain't gettin' one by visualizing it!'' she declared.

WHY VISUALIZATION DOESN'T WORK FOR SOME

The reason some people cannot get visualization to work for them is because they're asking it to do things it cannot do. Visualization is not a genie ready to grant your every wish. It's not a magic wand that automatically produces something on demand. Visualization is just a simple mental technique that aids your productivity, which it can do with great impact when used properly.

There are many things visualization can't do. People who report poor results don't seem to be aware of the limitations. Here are four of visualization's limitations. Understanding these will prepare you for understanding what visualization can do, which is coming next.

- **Visualization will not alter the known laws of physics.** You're in a bumper-to-bumper traffic jam. You visualize your car floating up in the air above all the other cars and flying like George Jetson's. Will the vision become reality? Sorry.

  Of course, there is an argument that such a vision is valid. If, after all, the Wright brothers hadn't imagined themselves flying, and believed they could do it while everyone else in the world thought flying was impossible, they wouldn't have invented the airplane. If you see your car flying through the air and dedicate your life to making the vision a reality, you might very well invent a car that flies. But until you or someone else does exactly that, your present car isn't going to fly out of today's traffic jam, regardless of how strong your vision is.

  Nor will you be able to leap tall buildings in a single bound, stop a speeding locomotive in its tracks, or have machine gun bullets bounce off your face. Maybe someday someone will invent ways for those things to happen. Maybe that someone is you, maybe it isn't. But in the meantime, your vision won't make it so today.

- **Visualization doesn't change the mathematical odds.** Let's say there are 500 of us in the room—501 actually, since I'm there too, only I'm standing up in front of you and 499 others seated in the audience. I announce that there's a special tag taped underneath one of the chairs that means that chair's occupant wins a free book. (Yes, I do this in my seminars). What are your chances of winning the book?

  One in 500, obviously. But what if you're intensely visualizing yourself as the winner? What if you imagine the tag under your seat and see yourself coming to the front of the room to receive your book? Does your vision increase your odds of winning? No. No more than if someone else were visualizing themselves as the winner and such a vision somehow reduced your odds to nothing. Visions don't change the odds.

  Think of it this way. When the state lottery runs a particular contest, they know what the odds of winning are. They even print the odds right on the tickets so players will know as well. Do they take visualization into consideration when posting the odds? Does the ticket say ''odds of winning are one in seven million, unless you're visualizing, in which case you're certain to win and everyone else who bought a ticket is certain to lose''? No. Visualization doesn't change the odds.

  That's not the same thing as saying you can't increase your chances of succeeding with or without visualization. You could run out and buy two tickets, for example, thereby doubling your chances of winning. The odds are still the same, one in seven million, only you've increased your chances to two in seven million by buying two tickets.[1] This is why golfers don't suddenly start racking up hole-in-ones through visualization. The odds of getting a hole in one are slim. The odds of getting more than one in any round are astronomically small. Visualization doesn't change the odds.

---

[1] Or you could buy 5.5 million tickets, at $1 each, and increase your chances to 5.5 million in 7 million. In 1992, an ''Australian syndicate'' did just that in the Virginia lottery. And darn if one of their 5.5 million tickets didn't win the $27 million jackpot. Of course, the $27 million is paid out incrementally over 20 years, which means the winners won't actually break even until the tenth year. Considering the time value of money, their $27 million payoff on a $5.5 million investment, spread over 20 years, isn't that great. But it makes for a nice little story.

- **Visualization doesn't replace effort.** Some people think visualization and effort are inversely proportional. If they spend a good deal of time visualizing, they reason, they can spend less time taking action. They see visualization as a nifty shortcut to success. They're the type who visualize Ed McMahon ringing their doorbell with a $10 million check in hand and sit around day after day waiting for it to happen. And it never does. Is it any coincidence that every person who credits their success to visualization also gives equal credit to tremendous effort? I've talked to hundreds of highly successful people in all walks of life, from all over the world, who all have at least one thing in common. They all say the same three words: "It isn't easy."

  Visualization can grease the slide of success. It can help you attain success by giving you direction, belief, confidence, and enthusiasm. It can guide you tremendously and cut down on the amount of resistance you encounter. But it doesn't replace effort. Those people who dedicate their lives to evading effort of any kind, and the world is full of them, will not find visualization effective.

- **Visualization doesn't dictate when.** Visualization doesn't provide you with answers to any "when" questions. (If you've successfully cured your When Disease, you shouldn't be asking those questions anyway!) This is where Betsy went wrong. She attached a deadline to her Lexus vision. Some visualization proponents recommend you use deadlines to pressure your subconscious into faster action. They fail to understand Realization 29. The great forces of the universe dictate when something is going to happen; you can't control when.

  Some visions materialize quickly; others take longer. As a high school student, Emmitt Smith attended Super Bowl XXI in January of 1987. From that day on, he visualized playing in the Super Bowl and even told people he would someday. Six years later, there was Emmitt Smith playing in Super Bowl XXVII for the Dallas Cowboys. His vision became his reality, but it took six years. It's not as if two weeks after he began visualizing he was mysteriously plucked out of high school and plopped down onto the Super Bowl field. Some visions take time to materialize.

  If Betsy continued to visualize her paid-for Lexus in the driveway, it would be there someday, without a doubt. But setting a deadline, dictating when it will be there, is counterproductive.

HOW VISUALIZATION WORKS

Despite its drawbacks, visualization does work. How does it work, you ask? Let's find out what gives visualization its potency.

Visualization is a sound scientific principle that really can cause your performance to improve, your accomplishments to happen, and your expectations to materialize. It's really not as arcane or mysterious as it seems. Visualization is simply a method of programming a desirable scenario into your subconscious mind. And your subconscious mind acts on that scenario, directing your thoughts, words, and actions accordingly. Here's how visualization works:

- **Visualization sensitizes your subconscious.** Visualization sensitizes your subconscious mind to detect anything that might help bring your vision into reality. Remember, your subconscious is receiving an infinite amount of information from your five senses continuously, and it has to sort through all that to determine what is relevant and what isn't. When a strong vision is cemented in your mind, everything that might support that vision becomes relevant and is acted on. Without the vision in place, your subconscious wouldn't have been alerted to recognize something as relevant, and it wouldn't have directed your actions to take advantage of it.

  Here's an illustration. How many gray Tauruses did you see on the road in the past week? You probably have no idea. You didn't know I was going to ask that question, so you weren't paying attention to gray Tauruses. But if I told you that I was going to reward you with $100 cash simply for counting the number of gray Tauruses you happen to see in the next week, what would happen? You would consciously and deliberately scan the road for them as you drove. But more than likely, your mind would drift to other subjects. You'd spend most of your driving time thinking of other things besides gray Tauruses. Nevertheless, when one came into view, your subconscious mind would interpret such a sight as relevant and alert your conscious mind. "There's another one!" you'd say to yourself, adding it to the list.

Go ahead and try this at home. Buy a gray Taurus. Then see how many other gray Tauruses you notice on the road. You'll see a lot more of them after you purchase yours. Why is that? Either you're of such fame and stature in your community that hordes of others feel compelled to emulate you (possible), or your purchase has sensitized your subconscious mind to make note of gray Tauruses now (probably).

Why do radio stations overplay that song you happen to hate? Every time you turn on the radio, there's that awful song again! The truth is, they're not playing it any more than any other song. But because your strong dislike sensitized your subconscious mind to the song, it seems like you're hearing it a lot more often than other songs, to which your mind hasn't been so sensitized.

When your subconscious mind is programmed with a vision, it ferrets out any relevant bit of information from the millions of bits it receives every day and acts on it. Over time, your words and actions shape your future. The things that happen to you align with your vision.

To put a jigsaw puzzle together, you have to constantly look at the finished picture on the box to figure out where the pieces go, don't you? When you visualize, you are giving your subconscious mind the completed picture; you are telling it to find all the relevant pieces that, put together, match the visualized picture. The puzzle comes together one small piece at a time, eventually producing a picture exactly like the one you were looking at all along.

- **Visualization bolsters belief.** If you don't believe something is going to happen, you are greatly increasing the chances that it won't happen. To make visualization work, therefore, you must have a strong belief that your vision will become your reality— or the strongest belief possible: that your vision is *already* reality. So how do you go about establishing, building, and maintaining belief? You visualize.

It's a feeding circle. Belief feeds off the vision, and the vision feeds off belief. You don't have a problem believing in something that existed in your past, do you? Let's say you once had a special friend who is now out of your life—for instance, a person you worked with years ago in another job. You believe that person existed because he or she was once with you and is now a solid memory.

Now imagine another friend existing in your life, someone equally special, but someone you haven't met yet. Since you haven't actually met this person, he or she is only a thought, an image, created by your mind. Now compare the level of belief you have in each person's existence—the person in your memory versus the person in your imagination. Which is easier to believe in? Which source, your memory or your imagination, produces the stronger level of belief? If you're like most people, you will find quite readily that the memory is far more believable. The belief in a memory will almost always be stronger than the belief in something imagined.

You can, however, make a vision just as strong as a memory. Something happens in your life and you remember it. That's how a memory is created. Occurrence first, a memory second. With visualization, you are reversing the order. A vision, strongly implanted in your brain's storage, is a *reverse memory*. You create the memory first by visualizing, and the event happens later. The vision becomes lodged in the same part of your brain as a memory and can take on the same level of belief as a memory.

- **Visualization builds confidence.** You will perform better if you feel confident in your ability to succeed. Confidence fuels success. And the way you gain confidence is through experience. The two ways of gaining experience are taking action and visualizing yourself taking action. In other words, your visions are pseudoexperiences.

  Airline pilots train in flight simulators. The idea is to give them experience under varying conditions. They could get the same experience in actual flight, but that could be dangerous. They're likely to make less mistakes in real flight if they gain experience ahead of time in simulated flight. Visualization works the same way. When you visualize yourself doing something, you're simulating reality in your brain. You're gaining experience the same way a pilot gains experience in the simulator. And experience builds your confidence, which causes you to perform better.

With "virtual reality" computers, you can now strap on a helmet and enter a completely different world. Virtual reality is being used to rehabilitate people who have some brain damage. By gaining experience and confidence through virtual reality, people are better able to do the same in real reality. You can use your brain just like a virtual reality computer program. You can program your subconscious mind any way you like by visualizing experiences in your mind. When you do, you're gaining valuable experience and confidence and improving your actual, real-life performance.

How exactly does visualization improve your performance? Building your confidence is part of it, but there's more. Visualization gives you a script to follow. It's just like actors on a stage. They're acting out a play according to a script. What if there were no script? They'd all be standing around not knowing what to say or do. When you visualize something transpiring ahead of time, you're writing the script. Then when it's time to perform, you speak and move purposefully, confidently, and without hesitation. You will find it quite amazing once you try it.

- **Visualization completes your being.** Is it true that you are the sum total of all your past experiences? Many people think so because it sounds logical. It is, however, false. Your past experiences are only half of your being.

Realization 47

You are the sum total of your past experiences plus your visions of the future.

The truth is, you are the sum total of your past experiences *plus your visions of the future.* In fact, your visions may even be the dominant factor in the equation.

When you drive a car, you look forward through the windshield, observing the road and traffic. You are expecting certain things to happen as you cruise along. You expect to be farther down the road five minutes from now, or five seconds from now, or five tenths of a second from now. You expect other cars to stay on their side of the road, stop when they should, and travel at reasonable speeds. You expect red lights to turn green and green lights to turn yellow. Your actions at every moment— accelerating, braking, turning, and so on—are based largely on your vision of the road ahead as you drive.

Would you consider driving your car looking out the back window instead of out the windshield? Dumb question, I know. Yet many people go through life each day looking backward. They have *backward visions,* imagining a future that matches their past. In other words, there is no difference in their mind between their future and their past. No wonder they lead the exact same lives day in and day out, year in and year out. Nothing much changes in their lives because their visions don't cause things to change.

On the other hand, people who visualize successfully choose visions quite different than their pasts. That's how they make progress. That's how they accomplish and become increasingly productive. Who they are today and every day, and who they slowly metamorphose into, is the sum total of their past experiences plus their future visions.

Larry has been broke most of his life. He holds a responsible job and makes a decent living, but somehow he never seems to have any money. Because he's always been that way, Larry doesn't expect to be anything but broke. His future visions mirror his past. One day, Larry inherited $220,000, a respectable sum that could be parlayed into much more if invested wisely. But Larry's moneyless vision, imbedded in his subconscious, directed his behavior differently. Within one year, he'd blown all the money. Larry remained true to his vision, broke.

Melissa was just as broke as Larry. In fact, she had less than no money. She was $48,000 in debt. But Melissa expected to be wealthy someday. She visualized herself living in wealth every day. Her vision of the future was far different than her past or present. Sure enough, as the years went on, Melissa dug out of debt, saved, and invested. It didn't happen overnight, but it did happen. Three years ago, she sold her interest in a chain of children's clothing stores for $1.2 million.

If you're not visualizing a different future, you're not supplying that part of the equation with what it needs to create you in the present or the future. In that event, your brain will choose default visions to fill that part of the equation. And those default visions will be based solely on your past, since you've fed your brain nothing to the contrary. Give your brain the number of good, solid, strong, different, and exciting visions it needs to create your being. You will become, over time, the person in your vision.

THE CAREER VISION

Let's begin applying what we know about visualization to your performance. First, we'll see how you can use visualization to accomplish some major career expectations.

Are you in the ultimate career position you aspire to be in? If not, you can use visualization to help advance your career in the direction you desire. Most people feel that entertainment and professional sports are two of the most difficult businesses to succeed in, with the odds of making it astronomically low. Here are some examples of people who through strong career visions turned themselves into extraordinary performers with good careers in entertainment and sports.

Richard Marx saw himself as a successful musician and singer since he was a child. It's the only thing he ever saw himself doing. And there was no doubt in his mind he'd do it. When you have no doubt about your fate, doing whatever it takes to make it happen doesn't seem so monumental an undertaking. So at the age of 18, Richard left home in Chicago and moved to Los Angeles, where he landed a job as a studio musician, backing up Lionel Ritchie, among others. Then he landed a record deal of his own and made a hit single, followed by a hit album, then more hit albums. All this was according to his vision. I'm not implying all this came quickly or easily. It took a lot of hard, relentless work. But that's part of visualization.

Bill Cosby did the same. As a young man he began to visualize himself as a successful comedian. At that time, there were no successful black comedians for him to use as role models. His was a trailblazing vision. A number of people, including his parents, tried to discourage Bill from pursuing what they saw as a high-risk, miniscule-chance-of-success endeavor. But when the vision is strong and not in doubt, it doesn't seem like a risk at all to the visionary.

As a kid growing up in Minnesota, Jack Morris watched the Minnesota Twins on television. But what he saw was a little different than what most other kids saw. Jack saw himself pitching for the Twins. In his mind, he was on the team. He was the starting pitcher. He was on television. Over the years, he took action to back up his vision. In the first game of the 1991 World Series, guess who was the starting pitcher for the Minnesota Twins and on television around the world? It was no big deal, really. Jack Morris envisioned it for years before it actually happened.

Can any of us do the same? Visualizing doesn't guarantee success, of course, but it sure does help. The idea is to see yourself in the career and position to which you aspire. At a seminar I attended years ago, I went up onto the stage during the lunch break when everyone was gone from the room. Standing where the speaker had been, I looked out over the auditorium. I visualized hundreds of people in their seats listening to me speak. I visualized myself speaking to all these people who came to my seminar. Within a year, I was speaking before groups of 50 or so people. Within three years, I was speaking before hundreds, just as I had visualized.

Now it's your turn. Think of what you'd like to be doing and what position you'd like to occupy. Create a career vision, and replay that vision every day in your mind. Remember, you must also take plenty of action to make your career vision pan out. But visualizing sensitizes your subconscious, bolsters your belief, builds your confidence, and completes your being, all of which makes taking action a lot easier.

THE DAILY PERFORMANCE VISION

Visualization has the power to improve your performance each and every day, on the job and at home. You can improve your performance and your productivity with regard to any given task or event by visualizing it ahead of time. Daily performance visions are time sensitive, that is, they are about some specific task or event that will take place at a known, specified time, as opposed to career visions, which materialize sometime in the future.

I make liberal use of daily performance visions. For example, before I meet with a client, I visualize the meeting in some detail.

I see myself standing at the end of the table, talking, and writing on a blackboard. I see the others seated at the table, staring at me. I see happy clients who accept my recommendations. I've been doing this for years now as standard procedure before each meeting I walk into, and with few exceptions, the real meetings turn out exactly like the visualized meetings.

Take some event that you know is going to occur within the next week, and visualize how it will transpire. Visualize yourself performing; see yourself in fine form, doing everything with precision and finesse. You can even visualize ordinary, routine events. What are you going to do at work tomorrow? The night before, visualize yourself doing it. See yourself performing in detail. Visualize how you will stand or sit, how you'll move, what you might say, and the expressions on your face. Visualize others agreeing, cooperating, and assisting.

Some visions may take 10 or 15 minutes or longer if you're deciding on what actions to visualize. But most ordinary, routine events can be visualized in as little as 30 seconds to a minute. Before you walk into that next meeting, place that important phone call, meet with that new client, or sit down at your workstation to begin another project, take a minute and visualize it transpiring as you would like it to. By doing so, you're writing the script for your subconscious mind to follow as it directs your actions later during the actual event.

You will be amazed how quickly and dramatically daily performance visions can affect your performance and overall productivity. Rather than me continuing to tell you how great it is, I'd like you to find out for yourself. After completing this chapter, go ahead and visualize something that will happen tomorrow. If it's a nonroutine event, visualize it once the night before and again the morning before. By tomorrow night, you'll be telling me how well visualization has worked for you!

VISUALIZATION WORKS ON AVERAGE

There are some additional angles of visualization we must discuss before you put it into practice. The first deals with the obvious question of reliability. Can you rely on visualization to make things turn out the way you visualize them?

Let's answer that question by way of example. You're a salesperson about to walk into a meeting with a prospective client. Before the meeting you take a minute to close your eyes and visualize how it will go. You see the client in a great mood, yourself operating in top form, and the client signing the contract. Your vision puts a smile on your face and confidence in your walk. Will your vision make the sale happen?

Yes and no. Visualizing a great meeting will give you all the advantages visualization provides: a script for your subconscious to follow as it guides your actions through the actual meeting, a strong belief in the outcome, and a high level of confidence. Therefore, your visions are effectively doing what they're supposed to do. But unless you're selling a genuine vaccine for cancer or a surefire antiaging device, your client might not sign the contract. For any one of a thousand reasons, she might say "no." Maybe even "no way ever." She could stand you up and the meeting might not even take place at all. Those things do happen. Do they only happen to nonvisualizers?

There is no way your visions can guarantee how other people will act. They can't make things happen precisely the way you want them to. Sometimes, despite having a great vision of the client excitedly lapping up your product, he might throw you out of his office. But your vision can make you perform better regardless and therefore increase your success average. In other words, visualization works on average.

The key to making visualization effective, however, is not to abandon it whenever a situation doesn't play out according to your vision. Not all of them will. You'll be thrown a curveball once in a while. In some cases, it may take numerous tries to produce the visualized result. Things will happen that you wouldn't have ever thought possible, things exactly opposite of your visions. But that's okay. Keep your visions alive, and they'll work for you on average.

THE PLAN-B VISION

Let's go back to our sales example. You envisioned the client in a good mood, salivating over your proposal, and signing the contract. But the actual meeting turns out nothing like the vision. The client just returned from court, having lost a major settlement to her ex, whom she can't stand, and she's in a rotten mood. She only gives you 8 minutes instead of 30, isn't paying much attention, and eventually says ''no.'' There is no way is she going to buy. Ask yourself three questions:

1. What were your facial expressions, demeanor, and words like after it became apparent the meeting wasn't going according to your vision? Did you exhibit any disappointment, dejection, frustration, or anger?

2. Were you performing well, or did the curve throw you so far off your game plan you performed below your ability?

3. Was the meeting a success or not?

If you had only one vision, only one positive scenario for the meeting, and it didn't happen, you might very well become disappointed or angry. You could have been jolted so strongly that you didn't know what to say or do and therefore performed poorly. You might have left the building believing the meeting was the farthest thing from a success.

Or, you could have had a *plan B vision* implanted in your brain that took care of you in such a circumstance. For instance, you could have visualized yourself reacting in a certain way if something derailed the plan A vision. You could have visualized yourself remaining cool and collected and handling yourself with style and grace. You could have envisioned yourself actually smiling and exuding even more warmth when facing a moody client.

A plan B vision simply recognizes that plan A visions don't work out every time. The plan B vision gives you the power to make an adverse situation work out for you too. In other words, you're prepared to turn in a top-notch performance regardless of what happens.

Say you go in to see your supervisor about a raise, and your plan A vision of him nodding in total agreement and approving it doesn't happen. What are you going to do? Without a plan B vision, you're leaving it up to the installed commands that have randomly entered your subconscious over the years to guide your behavior. You might even react in a way that surprises you. Without thinking about it, you might suddenly feel dejected or angry. You might say things you regret later.

But with a plan B vision in place, you might very well strengthen your position in the wake of a negative response from your supervisor. Remember, you can control what happens in your life to a large degree, but you can't control when. You might not get the raise today, but if you handle yourself consummately after an initial rejection, you'll strengthen your position and have a much better chance of getting a raise down the road.

I know a golfer who visualizes a plan B scenario. He sees his ball in a tough position, in the sand or behind a tree, and sees himself brimming with coolness and confidence as he expertly hits out of the trap. Even though he spends most of his time visualizing plan A (a great shot), the plan B vision is implanted in his brain, ready to guide his behavior whenever it's needed. Sure enough, when he finds himself in a difficult situation, his plan B takes over and guides him out. Unlike other golfers who throw their clubs, mutter obscenities, and perform even worse after a bad shot, he recovers from a bad shot beautifully and plays a great game overall.

It's Not Negative Thinking

A plan B vision is not negative thinking, if you do it correctly. With a good plan B, you see yourself in a difficult situation, but you don't see yourself failing. You see yourself handling the difficulty with style and grace. Like James Bond, you face particular challenges as you go through your mission of accomplishment, but you handle each one consummately.

A negative vision would depict a situation turning out bad no matter what you did. A plan B vision is a vision of you achieving success, albeit a different type of success than what the plan A vision might depict. A good plan B vision can strengthen your position and actually make it more likely your plan A vision will happen in the future.

THE PROCESS VISION

When we visualize some desirable occurrence, we typically visualize the end result. For example, you might visualize yourself standing at the podium and making a great presentation in front of your work group at the upcoming company retreat. But what about visualizing yourself doing all the preparatory grunt work necessary to make a great presentation? Why not visualize yourself not only standing at the podium making a great presentation but sitting at your dining room table preparing the talk?

Visualizing the end result is fine. But it may not be as strong a force as it could be with a little help. You may want to create another vision, a *process vision*, that bolsters the primary vision. The process vision is like a booster rocket that gets your payload into orbit. It depicts you in the process of bringing the end-result vision into existence.

At one time this book was nothing but a vision in my mind. To make it a reality, I began by visualizing the end result, the completed book. I saw it in my imagination. I saw what the jacket design looked like and saw it on bookstore shelves. I saw people reading it with extreme interest and excitement—for all we know, I may have been visualizing *you* reading this book. I felt the emotional exhilaration and pleasure I got from reaching people and helping them in written form. I visualized the finished product as a way of inspiring me to create the material and write the book.

But that vision wasn't enough. After all, I have an endless number of other things I could do rather than spend hours and days writing. So I created a process vision to supplement my primary vision. I visualized myself at my computer, creating the manuscript. I added a positive emotion to the scene—fun. I made it fun in my mind. With the process vision, I was much more willing and able to spend hours at a time, day upon day, writing at my computer. It was, after all, what I was supposed to be doing— doing the work was in harmony with my vision.

When you create a primary, or end vision, ask yourself if a process vision might also be beneficial. There may be times when you don't know what processes should be involved in making the primary vision a reality, but that's okay. Eventually, what you must do to make your primary vision a reality will become clear. When that happens, visualize the productive process to expedite things.

HOW TO VISUALIZE SUCCESS AND MAKE IT HAPPEN

- **Step 1: Create a career vision in your mind.** You are the scriptwriter; you can make things happen any way you like in your imagination. Create a scene that includes you doing what you want to be doing, in the position you want to be in. Add emotional expressions to your face as things happen. See yourself reacting with positive emotions as things happen. See the other people showing certain emotions also. Life transpires with motion, so you want your vision to be a motion picture, not a few still snapshots. Let the scene play in your imagination like a movie. (Although we think of visions as mental pictures, it isn't necessarily so. Sometimes simply thinking about something, without actually picturing it in your mind, can be just as effective a vision.)

- **Step 2: Repeat the career vision twice a day.** Allocate special time for visualizing. If you don't dedicate the time, anywhere from 30 seconds to 10 minutes, you'll end up forgetting to do it. When you wake up and just before you go to bed are good times. Repeat it at least twice a day until the vision becomes reality.

- **Step 3: Know that your career vision will really happen someday.** You know it will definitely happen, so you have a great deal of belief in the vision. You do not know, however, exactly when it will happen. That does not concern you in the least. You know fate runs its own agenda, and the great forces of the universe will be working for you when you leave ''when'' up to nature. You do not set any kind of deadline for when a career vision is to become reality.

- **Step 4: Create daily performance visions.** Choose a particular task or event that you know will happen in the near future, and visualize yourself performing at your best. See yourself producing the results you desire. Rerun the vision within the hour preceding commencement of the task or event or the morning of the event.

- **Step 4: Create a plan B vision.** Envision things happening differently than your preferred performance vision (plan A). See yourself reacting with composure and confidence. Don't try to create a reason why this adjusted scenario happens. Simply see it happening and yourself performing exquisitely, regardless. Put a smile on your face. Decide on a positive emotion or two that you will feel if and when this scene plays out.

- **Step 5: Create a process vision.** See yourself taking the action necessary to bring your other (plan A) visions into existence. Add a positive emotion to the process vision, and feel the emotion in your mind as you see yourself perform.

Chapter Eleven

Rise to the Top with Creative Thinking

C reative thinking, productivity thruster number five, is the lifeblood of productivity. Think about this: If human beings were a noncreative species, like animals, we'd still be living the same way the first humans on Earth lived. New people would be born and old people would die, but other than that, nothing would change. No new inventions, no new companies, no new fashions, no new foods, no new forms of entertainment (imagine the same songs on the charts forever! Then again, no one would have created any songs or charts to begin with, I suppose). Without creative thinking, there'd never be anything new.

Human creativity is such a pervasive force we take it for granted. Take the production of goods and services, for example. As consumers in a free enterprise system, we simply expect new things to pop up on the shelves, without giving thought to how that happens. New companies form, new products and services show up, marketing and distribution methods improve, even new episodes of your favorite television shows appear every week. How does that happen? It all starts in the brains of individual people. People like you.

Realization 48

You are a creative person. You are much more creative than you think you are.

We tend to think of creativity as a special talent reserved for the few who make it big in the arts or sciences. While certain talents are helpful in expressing creativity, talent is not creativity. Creativity, or creative thinking, is a natural, instinctive trait of all human beings, regardless of what talents they may or may not possess.

You are just as capable of thinking creatively as anyone. You are as much a creative person as anyone who displays some flashy talent, even if you have no flashy talent. One particular woman I know doesn't have any flashy talent. She doesn't sing, dance, write, paint, sculpt, crochet, design, or excel in any sport. She doesn't create anything. Or does she? She's a great conversationalist and a great reader of people. She has the talent to assess people and circumstances quickly, instinctively knowing how to handle herself in any type of social situation. In fact, she creates desirable situations by turning even the most mundane affair into something interesting and pleasurable. I've seen her create fun and excitement in situations where none existed before. I've seen her get people excited about themselves and their jobs. This woman influences and inspires people! And that takes a whole lot of creativity to accomplish.

You're just as creative as anyone who purports to be so. Not many people think of accountants as "creative types," yet I can assure you they are just as creative as the advertising professionals who actually have the title Creative Head or the like on their door. A CPA friend of mine says he turns mundane numbers into "dreamy, delectable, desirous digits" that excite and motivate people. Entire companies, products, and relationships—which probably affect you every day—are based on those little numbers accountants create.

You're creating new things every day and not realizing it. Can you recall a time when you were faced with a task that didn't seem possible, yet you thought of a way to pull it off? Or a problem you solved by thinking of a new solution? Or a time when you convinced someone of something he opposed earlier? Do you spend time playing with your children? Thinking of what to do and say as you play requires a great deal of creativity. When you stop to think about it, everyday life requires you to create the ways and means of dealing with it. If you're alive and functioning, you're creative.

CREATIVE CONCENTRATION

Although you are a creative person, creating things every day, you may wish to enhance your creative abilities above their present, natural level. One of the best productivity-propelling abilities you can have is to create ideas or solutions when you need them. There are two different methods for doing so, *creative concentration* and *programmed cogitation*. One uses your conscious mind, the other your subconscious mind, to do the creative thinking. We'll start with the one that uses your conscious mind, creative concentration. Creative concentration is a short burst of concentration, lasting anywhere from 15 seconds to a few minutes. It can produce an idea or solution with amazing speed.

Martin Snead likes to use the creative concentration method. In fact, he thought of this book's title that way. (We first used *Unleashing Productivity!* as the title of a seminar we created; it then became a book.) One day when we were discussing some of the material, I asked Martin to think of a title. "The word *productivity* should be one of the words," I said. "But we need something more to convey the concept of people turning their natural productive ability into something far greater than it is."

Martin sat down on the edge of his chair, put his head down into his hands, and sat perfectly still and quiet for about 30 seconds. Then he looked up and said, "Unleashing . . . unleashing productivity." "Perfect!" I said, knowing immediately he had hit the bull's-eye.

The procedures for getting into deep concentration and creating an idea or solution upon demand are similar to those described in Chapter 8 for achieving highly concentrated attention. The idea is to stop whatever else you're doing and concentrate on the subject at hand, thereby inducing an idea or solution within mere seconds or minutes. The step-by-step procedure for doing this appears near the end of this chapter.

PROGRAMMED COGITATION

While the creative concentration technique utilizes mainly your conscious mind, the programmed cogitation technique uses mainly your subconscious. The results can be the same, but the procedures and time required are quite different.

With programmed cogitation, you enter the relevant information regarding an opportunity or problem into your subconscious and let it create an idea or solution on its own. With this method, you don't have to concentrate at all. In fact, once you enter the information into your subconscious, you don't have to think about the situation to create the answer you seek. Your subconscious works on the information you've entered and comes up with an answer some time later, perhaps hours or days.

You've been using the programmed cogitation technique without even knowing it. When was the last time an idea or solution suddenly popped into your head, when the old lightbulb went off? How did that happen? At some time previously, perhaps hours or days before, you thought about the situation and set your subconscious to work on the answer. And later, perhaps when you least expected it, the idea or solution presented itself.

I prefer the programmed cogitation method. That's why I keep paper and pen with me at all times. When I least expect it, when I'm driving, sitting at the airport, eating dinner, or asleep, ideas often surface.

I use both creative concentration and programmed cogitation when writing or creating a seminar or speech. Days or weeks before I sit down and actually compose the material, I think about the topic. Then I collect all my ideas on paper as my subconscious randomly creates them over the ensuing days. I've got an array of good ideas to incorporate into my piece when I finally sit down to string the words together, which I do in creative concentration mode.

The one drawback to the programmed cogitation method is that it takes longer. If you've got the time, you'll probably come up with more and better answers using programmed cogitation, with less mental energy expended. But if you're hanging on to a cracking limb above a pool of hungry gators, you should opt for the faster creative concentration method.

To implement the programmed cogitation method, you ponder the situation for which you seek an answer. You ask yourself a few relevant questions, then you forget it all. You allow your subconscious to work on the problem while you consciously think of other things. Your subconscious will then produce an answer at some time in the future, hours or days later. The step-by-step procedure for this also appears near the end of this chapter.

SUCCESS IS IN THE EXECUTION

Creating ideas and solutions, using creative concentration or programmed cogitation or both methods, is essential if you want to improve your personal productivity. But creating ideas and solutions may not be enough to make you highly productive. You need to implement those ideas and solutions to move the productivity needle appreciably. As football players are fond of saying, "we gotta execute." That's what you gotta do. Execute. And executing can take even more creative thinking than coming up with the original idea or solution.

The truth is, ideas and solutions are bountiful. Everyone's got an idea about what ought to be done. Just look around you at work. How many people think they could do your job better than you? How many times have you thought of ways someone else might better perform her job? I'll bet you have a never-ending supply of ideas about the way things "ought to be." There really is no shortage of ideas in the world.

Ross Perot, a man with impressive accomplishments to his credit, said "Ideas are worthless unless you can implement them . . . execute them." He also pointed out that there's no shortage of ideas or plans in existence. But there is a great shortage of people willing or able to implement them.

A lot of people take credit, jokingly, in most cases, for inventing the overnight package delivery industry. After all, the idea of getting a package from one destination to another overnight must have occurred to a lot of people over the years, just like the wristwatch communicators we all hope to have someday.

But one man, Fred Smith, decided to actually execute the overnight package delivery idea. Imagine that—someone bold enough to step up to the plate and turn an idea into reality. Fred named his company Federal Express, and you know how that turned out. Fred Smith is the guy who really invented the overnight package delivery business because he committed himself to the project, even though he didn't have the money, contacts, or know-how at the time he began.

Realization 49

You achieve a much higher level of success when you create the execution rather than when you create the idea.

Raw ideas and solutions are great. But if you want to achieve much more, and get the major rewards, execution is the key.

One of the few commonalities among the nation's most successful entrepreneurs is that most of them didn't think of the original idea behind their particular business. In other words, it was someone else's idea. But the entrepreneurs took the idea and executed it. They created not the idea, but the ways in which it could be executed.

Have you ever noticed someone else achieving great success executing an idea you had? Ideas are great, but if you fail to implement your idea, it's fair game for anyone else to come along and turn it into something substantial. Don't blame anyone else for plucking the ball out of your hands and running with it if you elected to stand still.

Wally "Famous" Amos did not invent the chocolate chip cookie. But he started baking them with more chocolate chips than anyone else and sold them himself on the streets of Los Angeles. He simply executed creatively, becoming rich in the process.

If anyone told you you could become enormously successful,

and enormously wealthy, making pizzas back in the 60s, would you have believed him? "Pizzas? You've got to be kidding," I hear you saying. "The space race is in full gear, computers are blossoming, and color television and stereo audio are happening. High-tech is the wave of the future, not pizzas." But remember, it's not so much the idea as it is the execution. Tom Monaghan built Domino's into a worldwide, billion-dollar enterprise, not on a new or revolutionary idea but with superior execution of simple home delivery. And Michael Ilitch built his own pizza business, Little Caesars, into a huge enterprise by executing just as well but a little differently. No dine in, no delivery—customer picks up the pizza. It's not exactly a sizzling, high-tech idea. But once again, superior execution of the idea led to success.

Michael Dell founded Dell Computer in 1984, just about the time IBM clones were becoming a commodity. So how did he compete with not only IBM but all the other clones out there? Execution of one simple idea: telephone sales directly to customers rather than retail distribution. It wasn't that direct phone sales was such a great idea; it was that Dell turned it into a great idea through superior execution.

Charles Schwab didn't invent the brokerage business, nor was he the first to come up with the idea for a discount brokerage. But seeing an opportunity to build a discount brokerage, he committed himself to executing the idea. The early days of Charles Schwab & Co. were rough going, and a few of his partners quit along the way. But as others quit, Charles kept executing. Over the years, he built his company into a huge firm, one that prospers, incidentally, on first-rate execution.

Small, Simple Things

I used examples of successful entrepreneurs to emphasize the importance of execution and what can be accomplished with it. But don't think you have to be an entrepreneur to execute an idea. Nor do you have to dedicate your life to some major undertaking. You can accomplish more and gain greater rewards by executing small, simple things.

Take any one of your own ideas and think about how you can execute it at work. Perhaps you've thought of a better way to organize your files. Great idea. Now execute it. Or perhaps you know how someone else's idea can be implemented successfully. Make a proposal to your supervisor. Propose not only how it will be done but how you will lead the team that will do it. Remember, the really big rewards come to those who execute, even if they're executing small ideas.

CREATE THE EXECUTION

You may have noticed I've not only talked about execution but of *creating the execution*. Have you ever felt motivated to execute an idea or solution but felt stymied because you simply didn't know how to go about it? That happens to all of us most of the time. We're ready to execute but we haven't the faintest idea how.

Before you can execute, you've got to create the execution. You've got to determine what to do, how to go about it. Creating the execution means exactly that. It means thinking of the methods, the actual procedures, that will be required to put an idea or solution into practice. It means creating a plan of action, with specific steps, to implement and execute. Note that the actual execution may be done by you or by a host of others under your direction. When you create the execution, you put yourself in a leadership position; you're the architect of the plan and the field general.

So how do you create the execution? How do you create the things you must do to put an idea or solution into practice? You don't have to have an entrepreneurial mind-set as do the people I've just mentioned. You don't need a long list of credentials or degrees. You don't even need any experience. Michael Dell, for one, founded his company when he was 19 and started selling and manufacturing computers with no degree and no experience.

Why We Don't Create the Execution

Unfortunately, few people create the execution of an idea or solution. That is bad in the aggregate, but good for you. Since so few others are willing to do it, you have a golden opportunity to do so. Remember, life's greatest accomplishments and rewards are not reserved for the people who merely think of an idea or solution but for those who put an idea or solution into effect, even if it isn't their own.

Here are the primary reasons most people choose not to create the execution. As you read, determine which reasons have been hampering you from creating the execution of an idea or solution.

- **We're reluctant to commit ourselves.** Execution—creating it or actually doing it—requires an unwavering, solid commitment that may need to be maintained through rough seas over a sustained period of time. Few people seem to be willing to commit to that. When we remain uncommitted, our brain fails to create the ways and means of executing.

- **We're preoccupied with other things.** We spend all our hours, both on the job and at home, putting out fires, evaluating and debating alternatives, and maintaining relationships. The various tasks that fall under these headings may indeed need doing, but they end up consuming virtually all of our time and brainpower, or so it seems.

- **We lack an appreciation for logistics.** Logistics, a major part of execution, is a lost art. Other than in the military, fast-food, and package delivery industries, no one seems to be practicing and teaching the art and science of logistics.

Creating the execution takes commitment, time, brainpower, and an understanding of logistics. All of that sounds like hard work, which it can be at times. But the payoff can be so great, it's worth it. As you create the execution and oversee its implementation, your productivity rises exponentially. You may indeed realize a phenomenal return on your time and energy investment.

HOW TO CREATE IDEAS OR SOLUTIONS
USING CREATIVE CONCENTRATION

- **Step 1: Reduce distractions.** You may have to turn the television off or leave a hectic setting momentarily. If anything jolts you while you're trying to concentrate, you will have a difficult time of it.

- **Step 2: Allocate special time for creative concentration.** Devote one or two minutes strictly to creative concentration. Making a time commitment establishes a priority your brain recognizes and respects. Your brain understands that it's not supposed to be doing anything else during this allotted time, so it tends to de-emphasize other thoughts in favor of the one you're trying to concentrate on.

- **Step 3: Think strictly about the subject at hand.** Block out all other thoughts. It's not that difficult to focus your thoughts on only one thing for short durations of 15 seconds to a few minutes.

- **Step 4: Create visual or auditory motion.** Even though Martin wasn't riding in a car or running when he thought of the *Unleashing Productivity!* title, he did create motion in his mind. "I imagined the word *productivity* moving from left to right, and I imagined hearing people saying it. I played this over and over with various other words in my mind, and suddenly the word *unleashing* came to mind," he reports. Motion, even if it's only in your mind, stimulates your concentration and creativity. Use your imagination to see or hear things in motion, and you'll find it much easier to concentrate and create.

HOW TO CREATE IDEAS OR SOLUTIONS USING PROGRAMMED COGITATION

- **Step 1: Think about the opportunity or problem for which you seek an idea or solution.** Review it. Contemplate it. Ponder it. As you go over it in your mind, it will automatically seep into your subconscious. This doesn't take deep concentration, only casual thought.

- **Step 2: Ask yourself for the answer.** "What can I do to . . . ?" "How will I . . . ?" "What would work to . . . ?" Ask the pertinent questions over a few times in your mind. Caution: Avoid "when" questions. Remember, you are not concerned with when. Double caution: Avoid using rhetorical questions that incite negative emotions; for example "Why oh why did he do that to me? Why oh why?"

- **Step 3: Divert your attention to other things.** Whereas the creative concentration method requires you to focus strictly on the subject at hand, the programmed cogitation method requires you do exactly the opposite.

You may need to repeat steps 1 and 2 a few times, over a few days, perhaps. But in between repeats, forget it all. Your subconscious works best when you're not concentrating on the relevant topic. It works in the background, by itself.

- **Step 4: Write down your ideas or solutions as soon as they come to you.** Because your subconscious is doing the creative work with the programmed cogitation method, remembering what it creates is often difficult. Like remembering dreams after you've awoken, it's difficult to do.

    I've learned the hard way. Many times a great idea has suddenly popped into my head, and I failed to jot it down right then and there. How could I not remember such a great idea? Sure enough, hours or days later when it came time to utilize the idea, I couldn't for the life of me remember what it was. After losing a number of such ideas over the years, I finally decided to write them down on the spot no matter how inconvenient it might be at the time. For my neighbors who sometimes see the light in my bedroom window going on and off throughout the night, now you know what it is I'm doing.

HOW TO CREATE THE EXECUTION OF AN IDEA OR SOLUTION

- **Step 1: Commit yourself to executing the idea or implementing the solution.** Why is it always someone else who is supposed to make an idea into something substantial? Why not you? Go ahead and pick your answer to that one from the standard list: "I don't have the money." "I don't have the time." "I don't have the contacts." "I don't know how." "I'm too busy making a living." "It's not my area of responsibility." "It's too monumental a task." All of these things may be true when you start, but after you commit yourself and begin creating the execution, they all begin to dwindle in veracity. As your plan, methods, and procedures take shape, you gradually emerge as the person with the foremost know-how to execute the idea.

Think about an idea or solution that's sitting idle on a shelf in your mind. Think about all the benefits you would produce by executing it yourself. I'm not asking you to create the next Federal Express—that really *was* a major undertaking. Just create a simple, little thing. Decide that you are going to create a plan to implement the idea or solution. Once you make the commitment to do it, your brain gets ready to engage in the creative process.

- **Step 2. Allocate extracurricular time for creating the execution.** Creating the execution takes time. Most likely, it will take extra time. Of course, you haven't got any extra time; attending to your present duties is time consuming enough.

  I used to think the same way. I used to believe there was no way I could undertake any new project, however small, because I simply didn't have the time. Then one day I had a radical thought. What if I were to alter my lifestyle? What if I were to, say, watch less television in the evenings after work and actually work on a new project instead? Such thinking boggles the mind at times.

  There are times now when I go for weeks, even months, without turning on the television, not even to watch the news. It's amazing how much more I accomplish when I'm not sitting in front of the tube. And even more amazing, I have a heightened appreciation for television when I eventually do turn it back on. (If you think television is really a "vast wasteland," you're watching too much of it.)

  Alter your lifestyle a little. It doesn't have to be a drastic alteration, although at first any change may seem drastic. Shuffle things around, prepare a new agenda. Can you alter your schedule at work? You may think not, but if you have management's blessing to execute an idea or solution, perhaps a change could be arranged.

  You will be amazed how refreshing it can be to change your lifestyle a bit, even if that means eliminating something you enjoy for a while. Altering your lifestyle can be like going on a retreat or sabbatical. And guess what? You will find the time to create the execution of whatever idea or solution you commit to.

- **Step 3: Think of the execution pipeline.** Think about what needs to happen each step of the way to go from where you are now, the idea or solution, to where you want to be, the idea or solution in operation. See things happening in domino fashion, each occurrence tripping the next in line.

Everything happens through a pipeline. Before such and such can happen, what has to happen before that? Think about it. Imagine it all happening in your mind. Mentally run through different sets of occurrences until you create one that seems plausible. Write down the key processes or occurrences. Keep imagining it all happening in different ways and finally in one way. This is the creative process in action.

Don't expect to think of a perfect, bug-free system immediately. Things really won't smooth out until you're actively executing, it turns out. But thinking of the pipeline ahead of time prepares you and gets you going. This, by the way, is how you develop an appreciation for logistics. Think of what has to happen, how it's going to happen, and who is going to be involved. Then think of how much time it will take for each maneuver or task. Logistics is really nothing more than commonsense thinking applied to an execution pipeline.

- **Step 4: Think of systems and procedures.** The term *systems and procedures* sounds like we're getting into a complicated area, but that isn't really true. Systems and procedures are simply standard ways of doing things—ways that can be communicated and taught to others if necessary; ways that can save valuable time for you and others by eliminating the need to keep creating ideas and solutions for recurring tasks.

  Here's an example of a procedure that made the execution of an idea workable. Back in my radio days in the early 70s, it was customary for DJs to pick the records they would play on the air from a stack the program director put in the studio. As a song was playing, the DJ would take anywhere from 20 seconds to three minutes to shuffle through all the records and decide which one to play next. Then someone came up with the brilliant idea of arranging the songs, which were actually on individual tape cartridges, in two separate stacks, in a particular order. The jocks were then instructed to simply pull the bottommost song from stack A, play it, and replace it on top of the stack. Then pull the bottom-most song from stack B and do the same with it. Thus, the songs rotated in precise manner, without the jocks having to expend redundant brainpower deciding which to play all the time.

- **Step 5: Develop new relationships.** Chances are, for the actual execution to happen the way you're mentally creating it, you'll require the assistance and cooperation of others. These may be people you don't know at present. Understand that meeting and inspiring others is part of the execution process. This doesn't mean you do it full time. It just means you must be aware of the need to develop relationships and allocate some time and effort to it. Remember, if you want to conquer new ground, you must deal with new people.

Chapter Twelve

Program Your Subconscious for Super Productivity

M any of the productivity-propelling techniques we've discussed work by subconscious directive. Put another way, your subconscious mind makes them work. Even though the steps I've given you to vaporize worry, stop energy and enthusiasm from eroding, reduce your negative emotions, cure When Disease, become more patient and relaxed, and so on are consciously implemented, they're really designed to program your subconscious mind. It's your subconscious that really makes the techniques effective.

This chapter will help you program your subconscious mind. You'll have a better understanding of how new information gets into your subconscious and how your subconscious acts on it.

YOUR SUBCONSCIOUS IS YOUR AUTOPILOT

In Chapter 4, we talked about your subconscious mind controlling 80 to 90 percent of all your brain work. I used driving as an example. You can drive from work to home and not even consciously think about accelerating, braking, and turning. Your mind is on something else entirely, yet you drive. It's your subconscious mind that's aware of what's happening on the road and making your driving decisions.

Your subconscious mind also controls your emotions, your actions, and your personality to a large extent, which means you're not consciously aware of most of your words, actions, and facial expressions, for example. As you talk, words rapidly pour out of your mouth without your having to consciously choose each one. When you walk, each leg quickly moves in front of the other, and your body weight shifts back and forth, without you having to consciously think about directing that to happen. And smiles, frowns, and dozens of other facial expressions just pop up on your face without you deliberately putting them there. It's your subconscious mind pulling all the strings.

It's as though your subconscious mind is your automatic pilot. Give it some flight data and a destination, then sit back and leave the flying to it. The key to arriving safely and soundly with your subconscious doing the flying is the information you program into it. Program lousy or erroneous information, and your subconscious will have you flying in circles or headed straight for a mountain.

You've got to program good, empowering information into your subconscious. When you do that, you live a healthier, happier, and more productive life. But if you program faulty, weakening information into your subconscious, even if unintentionally, you end up leading a subpar life in practically every area.

You can program the good, empowering information into your subconscious by following the step-by-step procedures I listed in each chapter. To install that new information, you may have to replace older, conflicting information. For example, you may presently have information in your subconscious that directs you to keep focusing on when something is going to happen. It may make you a When Monster. To stop such behavior, you'll have to replace certain information in your subconscious. The new information, which directs your behavior differently, needs to be firmly installed, and it must wipe out or overpower the old information.

HOW INFORMATION GETS INTO YOUR SUBCONSCIOUS MIND

There are four different ways in which your subconscious accepts new information. Let's look at each and see which might be the best to use.

The Impressionable Years

Children, who come into the world with nothing but human instincts programmed into their subconscious minds, are information sponges. They soak it up rapidly. By the time a child is only six, 80 percent of his or her personality is formed.

New installed commands fly into the subconscious minds of children without opposition. A child spills her bowl of cereal, for example, and then sees her mother displaying anger toward her. It only takes a few such occurrences for the child to adopt an installed command that directs her to feel inferior. She may very well carry that installed command with her into adulthood. It can affect her for the rest of her life.

If I played a hit song for you that was first popular when you were 17 years old, I'll bet you could instantly tell me the name of it and the recording artist. In fact, you'd probably have no trouble singing along with the lyrics. But unless you're under the age of 30, I could play a currently popular song for you and you'd probably have no idea of the name it or the artist. And you could hear it 20 times and still have difficulty remembering the words. The songs you heard during your impressionable years left indelible marks.

The impressionable years seem to go from birth to about the mid-20s. The music you heard then will be your favorite for the remainder of your life. Since musical awareness seems to disintegrate when a person turns 30, the songs you heard before that age made a major impact on you. The songs you hear after age 30 just don't seem to "have it." That's why each generation thinks the music of its era is the best.

During your impressionable years, all kinds of new information gets implanted in your subconscious. Most of it gets there without you realizing it. You just experience life day after day, and information randomly ends up in your subconscious.

The Traumatic Experience

A new piece of information can enter your subconscious instantly when you experience something traumatic. Remember what it was like when you were jilted by someone you were in love with? Or when you were laid off? Or when someone close to you died? You're not likely to ever forget the feelings such an event triggered in you.

When we experience something traumatic, it can change our behavior quickly and dramatically. The jilted lover can become very guarded and leery of other potential love interests. The fired employee can become bitter and contemptuous toward the former employer or toward employers in general. The person who lost someone close can become cold and detached toward others, or conversely, cling to others for fear of losing them.

A traumatic experience can oftentimes leave an indelible mark on the subconscious. It may take years of effort, which might include professional help, to alter the programming installed in your subconscious through trauma.

Hypnotic or Subliminal Suggestion

Sometimes the conscious mind can block new information from entering the subconscious. That's why hypnotism and subliminal messages can be effective when regular, conscious messages fail to get through.

You may be familiar with those subliminal self-improvement tapes you can buy in bookstores and through the mail. You hear ocean waves or light music, and the actual voice messages are inaudible—only your subconscious mind can detect the behavior-influencing information. Do these tapes work? They can have a profound effect if you use them repeatedly and regularly. Most people who report poor results simply have not used them enough. Sometimes you have to listen to the tape regularly for months or years before results kick in.

Conscious Repetition

Through repetition, new information eventually lodges in your subconscious. Let's say you're learning to play the piano. At first, you must consciously think about which keys to push in which order. And you practice this day after day. Eventually, the information seeps into your subconscious. After that happens, you find yourself able to push the right keys in rapid succession without consciously having to think about them.

You can learn anything if you take the time and effort to repeat or practice it over and over. Let's say you constantly vaporize worry whenever it pops up by executing the six-step procedure discussed in Chapter 2. Not only are you vaporizing worry when you execute the steps, you're programming your subconscious mind at the same time. You're training your subconscious to stop producing worry. Eventually, when your subconscious accepts the new information, you'll find yourself experiencing a lot less worry to begin with. You won't even have to consciously vaporize worry in many instances because your subconscious has learned to stop producing it in the first place. Your subconscious mind can be programmed very effectively through conscious repetition of new information.

BREAK YOUR SUBCONSCIOUS

Which of the four programming methods should you use to install new, empowering commands into your subconscious?

If you're reading this book at an age younger than 25, you're in good shape. The empowering information will make a greater impact on you than it would for someone older.

As effective as traumatic experiences are in impacting the subconscious, they're not really under your control. But you wouldn't want to create trauma even if you could; it's not a practical method.

Hypnotic or subliminal suggestions can be effective and somewhat practical. Go ahead and get yourself some subliminal tapes. But don't listen to them only three times and never again. Listen to them repeatedly, for weeks, months, or years. Eventually, when you least expect it, you'll notice yourself adopting the new behavior.

Conscious repetition is actually the best and most practical method you can use to program your subconscious. New information will make an impact if it keeps hitting your subconscious over and over and over. It usually takes numerous such impressions, over time, to supplant the existing, contrary information. But once it does, results show up in great measure.

When a cowboy first climbs aboard an unbroken horse, the horse bucks like crazy, trying to free itself of the foreign object on its back. But in time, the horse suddenly stops bucking, having suddenly accepted the rider. The horse has been broken and is now programmed to accept humans riding it. Your subconscious is like an unbroken horse. It will reject new information that conflicts with its present information, bucking all the way. But eventually, if you keep repeating the new information, the subconscious accepts it and acts on it.

GO THROUGH THE AWKWARD STAGE

Did you ever take karate, typing, or golf lessons? What happens when you first start learning? You make a bunch of awkward moves. None of it seems natural. You've got to learn the moves by consciously repeating them over and over—practicing—until eventually they become imbedded in your subconscious. Once the moves are installed into your subconscious, they seem natural. You do them without thinking. You spar with a karate partner and execute the moves at lightning speed without thinking. You sit down at the keyboard and rapidly push the right keys in the right sequence without conscious thought. You step up to the golf ball, automatically assume the swing position, and away you go.

Realization 50

Your personal productivity will rise in direct proportion to the number of times you repeat or practice the implementation steps presented in this book.

Through conscious repetition, new information gets imbedded into your subconscious. But for that to happen, you must be willing to repeat the new information, practice it, while it still seems awkward. You must be willing to keep practicing during the awkward stage. Only by repeating it does the information lose its awkwardness and become a natural part of your being.

For example, many people have trouble with affirmations. Affirmations are those positive-oriented statements that you repeat over and over in hopes of convincing your subconscious that they're true. For example, you may keep saying to yourself "I weigh 120 pounds" when the scale says you really weigh 150 pounds.

What happens when you first start saying some "untrue" affirmation? Consciously, you feel silly saying things about yourself that aren't true. Subconsciously, the affirmation gets rejected completely. Your subconscious finds the affirmation, such as you weighing 120 pounds, in conflict with the information it already accepts, namely that you weigh 150 pounds. So the new information gets rejected. Your affirmation is ineffective.

You must repeat it and repeat it and repeat it over a long period of time, despite how awkward it seems. Eventually and suddenly, after getting bombarded endlessly with the new, conflicting information, your subconscious reverses its beliefs, accepts the new information, and rejects the old. It now believes you really weigh 120 pounds. Then the magic begins. Once it believes the new information, it guides your actions accordingly. You will find yourself eating less and exercising more. You will become 120 pounds.

Have you ever known anyone who repeated a lie so often he actually came to believe it? Repeat an untruth often enough over time, and your brain really does get confused and thinks the lie is the truth.

Eventually, the Subconscious Accepts

In the 50s, scientists conducted an unusual experiment to ascertain how the subconscious mind accepts new, conflicting information. As you may recall from high school science class, the human eyeball actually sends an upside-down picture to the brain—the lens of the eye flips everything we see. Then, the subconscious mind flips the images again, and we see things right-side up. The scientists wanted to find out if the subconscious would not flip the images if they were already right-side up when they reached it. So they rigged a special pair of goggles that a volunteer wore all day long. The goggles, which looked like small binoculars, reversed the images reaching the subconscious, resulting in right-side-up pictures instead of the normal upside-down pictures. Of course, since the subconscious was programmed to flip the images it received, it did so with these new, goggle-altered images as well, making the person see everything upside down.

Imagine everything you saw looking upside down. The goggled man saw everything this way for days (he took off the goggles only when he slept, and then he wore a blindfold). Think of how his subconscious mind dealt with the flipped pictures it received. The new, upside-down pictures were in conflict with what his brain expected to receive. Yet his subconscious ignored the fact that the new pictures were already flipped, and it flipped them as it had always done in the past. The double flip resulted in the man seeing everything upside down.

Then an interesting thing happened. As the goggled man was walking down the street one day, assisted by someone who could see right-side up, suddenly he saw right-side-up. His subconscious suddenly stopped flipping the pictures. After receiving a constant flow of new information (flipped pictures), it eventually accepted the new information and acted on it differently, stopping its life-long flipping activity.

Your subconscious will eventually and suddenly accept new information and act on it. But for that to happen, you've got to feed it constant or regular doses of the new information. You must consciously repeat the new information to program it into your subconscious. This will mean repeating the implementation steps we discussed in each chapter over and over, day after day, until they become imbedded in your subconscious. It may also mean reinforcing the new information through repetition after it's been installed into your subconscious.

Once Installed, Magic Happens

Once you have successfully installed the powerful information into your subconscious, things become a lot easier from that point forward. What once seemed difficult, like lowering your usage of negative emotions, for example, will come easily and naturally. Once your subconscious mind has accepted the new, empowering information, you will not only be highly productive, you'll be highly productive with ease! Repeat the step-by-step procedures often, install them into your subconscious mind, and watch the magic happen!

HERE'S TO THE NEW, HIGHLY PRODUCTIVE YOU

You've completed this book, which tells me you're serious about increasing your personal productivity. You really want to accomplish new and greater things, and you really want to receive the great rewards to which you are so entitled.

The difference between you and others who only say they'd like to be more productive is that you're putting forth the effort. You're devoting the time to not only learn how to be more productive, but to implement what you learn and put it into daily practice. I tip my hat to you. You are well on your way to a highly productive, highly enriched life!

I wrote this book for you, so I have vested interest in your success. Martin Snead and I would like to know how you're progressing, how you're using the material in your own life. Feel free to drop us a line with any comments or suggestions. We can be reached at:

Ott & Associates
9225 Chatham Grove Lane, Suite D
Richmond, VA 23236

Appendix

Here's a summary list of the 50 Realizations contained throughout the book. The number in parentheses indicates the page on which the Realization originally appears.

1. Your brain is the engine that drives your productivity. The ways in which you think and act determine your level of productivity. (vii)
2. The quickest way to solve a problem is to first stop worrying about it. (16)
3. Responsibility does not entail worry. (17)
4. Worry does not equal caring. (17)
5. Worry generates artificial, short-lived feelings of emotional pleasure, solution, love, and protection. Only with an absence of worry can you attain genuine, lasting emotional pleasure, solutions, love, and protection. (18)
6. Nine out of 10 problems you worry about are phantom problems that will never affect you. (19)
7. Ninety-nine percent of the time, good things happen. (21)
8. Action turns destructive worry into harmless concern. (23)
9. When you help others, help comes to you. (25)
10. You will become immune to the thrill of whatever you spend a lot of time with. (31)
11. Difficulty and adversity are the parents of energy and enthusiasm. (39)
12. Your energy and enthusiasm rises and falls in direct proportion to your expectations. (47)
13. Life naturally appreciates; it really does get better with age. (49)
14. You control your emotions. Nothing outside of your brain controls your emotions. (56)

15. The amount of happiness you experience is directly related to the number of positive emotions you experience. (60)

16. Most of the things you think are bad for you really aren't. Seemingly bad occurrences are often much better for you than they initially appear. (64)

17. The bad aspect of an occurrence tends to show itself immediately, whereas the good, and most often dominating, aspect tends to appear later. (74)

18. By interpreting occurrences as good for you, you cause the good aspects to surface sooner, and thereby turn seemingly bad occurrences into good experiences. (75)

19. A seemingly bad occurrence may actually be a better alternative than what you had in mind. (75)

20. To be highly productive, you need the cooperation, assistance, and recognition of other people. (85)

21. All action takes place after a decision. To take more action, make more frequent decisions. (93)

22. Other people aren't concerned with how you look, they're too consumed with how they themselves look. (96)

23. Most mistakes are quickly forgotten. (97)

24. You are judged on your average performance, not on any one failure or any one triumph. (99)

25. Your failures don't count. Only your successes count. (99)

26. If you're not feeling tinges of embarrassment or humiliation from time to time, you're not taking enough action. (101)

27. People in positions of authority who deny you don't know what they're talking about. (102)

28. Even when people in authority are "correct" in denying you, they are wrong. They are basing their assessments on what is today, not on what can be tomorrow. (104)

29. There are an infinite number of forces at work in the universe that affect when you accomplish a particular endeavor and when the rewards arrive. You can't control when. (113)

30. If something doesn't feel right, you're out of alignment with the universal forces; you're forcing it to happen. If it does feel right, you've got the forces with you; you're making it happen. (114)

31. There exists an inherent time lag between productivity and reward. Sometimes it can be a very unfair time lag. (118)

32. In time, you always get your just reward. (120)
33. Deadlines are beneficial only when they're attached to simple tasks under one person's control. (127)
34. You are accomplishing faster than you think you are. (132)
35. If you accomplish 30 percent of what you set out to accomplish, you're doing great. (134)
36. You are having more fun than you think you are. These are great days! (135)
37. Life is supposed to contain a great deal of uncertainty. (145)
38. You make uncertainty latent by making plans. (146)
39. Change as a whole is good for you. Even negative changes are always balanced out by positive changes that render the negative harmless. (153)
40. Time really isn't running out as fast as it seems. You have more time than you think to accomplish what you desire. (155)
41. You're supposed to be relaxed while you work or perfom. (159)
42. Your brain likes operating in highly-concentrated-attention mode, even though it fights going into HCA mode. (171)
43. To be highly productive, you must be extremely detail oriented *and* extremely concept oriented. (183)
44. The farther you get into the details, the farther your interest rises. (185)
45. The more you step back and look at the big picture, the more your excitement level rises. (187)
46. Everything that exists in reality was once only a thought or vision in someone's mind. (200)
47. You are the sum total of your past experiences plus your visions of the future. (210)
48. You are a creative person. You are much more creative than you think you are. (220)
49. You achieve a much higher level of success when you create the execution rather than when you create the idea. (225)
50. Your personal productivity will rise in direct proportion to the number of times you repeat or practice the implementation steps presented in this book. (239)

Index